Psychic Medium

Unlock the Secrets of Psychic Development, Mediumship, Divination and Pendulums

Your Free Gift (only available for a limited time)

Thanks for getting this book! If you want to learn more about various spirituality topics, then join Mari Silva's community and get a free guided meditation MP3 for awakening your third eye. This guided meditation mp3 is designed to open and strengthen ones third eye so you can experience a higher state of consciousness. Simply visit the link below the image to get started.

https://spiritualityspot.com/meditation

Contents

Part 1: Psychic Development

An Essential Guide to Telepathy, Divination, Astral Projection, Mediumship, Clairvoyance, Healing, and Psychic Witchcraft

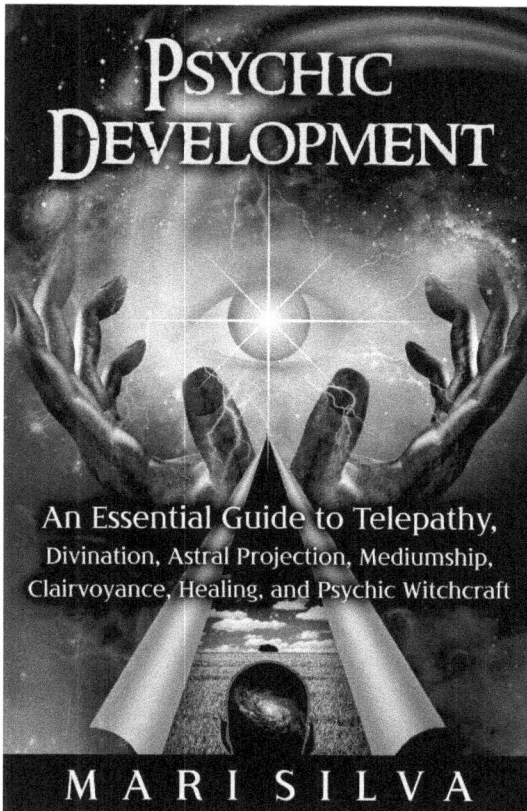

Introduction

If you were told right now that you have special psychic abilities that border on the supernatural, you'd likely laugh hysterically. Well, that is, if you are not yet familiar with psychic development. Do you just presume that you are a regular Joe with nothing special going on? Well, you are far from being ordinary. You have a lot of things going on for you, but you have yet to realize it. No, this does not mean you are unusual or different from others. If you were to call everyone "special" based on psychic powers, everyone would be exceptional in one way or another. Why? Because everyone, including you, has psychic abilities.

Since you are new to psychic abilities and powers, your perception of psychic gifts might be based on what you have seen on the TV over the years. As a result, you may have grown up believing that psychic abilities are only accessible to a handful of people who you presume to be unusual or extraordinary. Well, whatever you learned about psychics and mediums from the TV is a fluke, or at least most of it is. Everyone has psychic abilities. Some people may be more predisposed to these abilities than others. That means that certain people may be better than others with their psychic powers, but in the end, everyone has psychic abilities.

The problem lies in recognizing your psychic ability and learning how to use that ability to improve every aspect of your life; I aim to help you understand that. The process needed to discover your psychic power and awaken your psychic senses is called *psychic development.* Psychic development is a journey of awakening that involves realizing your true capabilities as a human. The purpose of this book is simple: It serves as your guide through your psychic development journey, taking you step-by-step through your psychic awakening process.

Written in clear and concise language, this book caters to anybody from beginners to those with basic knowledge of the psychic development process. So, it does not matter whether you are just learning about psychic abilities or know the basics this book is for you. From the first chapter to the last, I give an in-depth breakdown of different psychic abilities and how you can hone them. There are simple and straightforward exercises, techniques, and examples to aid your understanding of the topic to make it easier for you. What makes this book different from similar books on the market is that it has up-to-date and easy-to-understand information. More importantly, the exercises, techniques, and instructions are hands-on, meaning you can put them to practice at any time.

If you want a book with a healthy mix of theory and practical instructions to help you unlock your psychic gifts, this is the book for you. Without further delay, let's start your journey!

Chapter One: Are You Ready to Become a Psychic?

Regardless of how you feel about psychics and psychic abilities, you also have psychic powers – to a certain extent. As I said in the introduction, everyone possesses psychic abilities. Many have learned to hone and use their abilities, while others leave their abilities dormant, waiting for them to be awakened. If you have ever used your intuition or "gut feelings" to make a decision that turned out to be right, you are undoubtedly psychic. This begs the question, "Is having intuition the same as being psychic?"

To some degree, yes. Being intuitive is the same as being psychic, but psychic abilities can be honed to go beyond just intuition. This means you can train yourself to improve your psychic powers beyond the power of your intuition alone. Rather than relying on your gut feeling to make a decision, you can hone your psychic senses to where you just know what to do or what not to do. It can be that easy. But the process of learning is not an easy one.

Many people begin their psychic awakening journey, believing it will be a simple and straightforward one, but they often become disappointed. The disappointment stems from their going on the journey, thinking they can achieve a lot within a couple of months.

In fact, I met someone who called psychic abilities a fad because they couldn't achieve astral projection a week after they began learning. I was dismayed to know that a supposed psychic made them believe that they could learn astral projection in five days if they practiced consistently. Consistency may be vital in developing psychic abilities. Still, it won't help you understand any of the skills in a few days.

When one begins their psychic learning, the best thing is to think of it as learning a new skill. You probably would not know everything about a skill such as graphic designing in five days. So, why would you expect to learn clairvoyance or telepathy in five days? Just as you would need to advance in any skill you learn by continually learning new techniques and methods, you need to do the same with psychic development. This means you must be patient, enduring, and open to advances in learning. Before you answer the question, "Am I ready to become a psychic?" you must make sure that you will be patient throughout the journey. Patience is single-handedly the most critical element in developing psychic abilities. Unless you are patient, you likely won't last more than a few weeks before you give up on honing your psychic skills.

You must understand that people learn at different paces. Some learn faster than others. If you begin your psychic learning with a friend today, you won't both learn at the same rate. Your friend may have become good at seeing auras with colors before you even start seeing just a faint light. If this happens, it does not mean you also won't get to that point. It merely means they are a faster learner than you, which is fine. You need to work at your own pace, not theirs. So, it shouldn't matter what someone else is achieving. You only need to focus on your progress because that is all that matters. Once you understand these simple facts, it is safe to say that you are ready to become a psychic. But really, *what is a psychic?*

The simplest way to define a psychic is to think of a person with extrasensory perception. The key phrase here is "extrasensory perception," which can acquire information without using the recognized sensory channels. To put it simply, someone with extrasensory perception can obtain information without using their normal senses of sight, hearing, touch, smell, or taste. If you have extrasensory perception, you can see things that your ordinary eyes cannot see. Extrasensory perception is the basis of any psychic abilities, including clairvoyance, telepathy, mediumship, etc. As a psychic, you can see, hear, sense, feel, or taste beyond the limitations of the material world.

Throughout history, there have been documented and undocumented reports of "special" people who could solve different problems in multifarious aspects of life, from business to relationships. There are examples and instances of people using clairvoyance, mediumship, precognition, and other psychic abilities in cultures worldwide.

In Ancient India, sages were masters in the art of clairvoyance. One such example of an Ancient Indian philosopher using clairvoyance is the story of Sanjay, an assistant to Dhritrashtra, the father of Kauravas. During Mahabharata's war between Pandavas and Kauravas, Sanjay relayed everything happening on the battlefield to Dhritrashtra, who was blind. He did this even though he was thousands of miles away from the venue of the battle. Everyone believed that Sanjay had the gift of the psychic eye. In other words, he had the gift of clairvoyance.

Even in Europe, there are stories of known psychics such as Edgar Cayce, an American psychic famous for his clairvoyant abilities. Cayce was regarded as a seer, mystic, clairvoyant, and psychic diagnostician. He was able to heal many people of their illnesses by going into a trance meditation to determine their disease's roots and discover a cure.

Also famous is the story of Victor Race, who was regarded as a "slow-witted" person. Race was a peasant, yet he could diagnose and cure himself of his disease. But he didn't stop at that. He also helped countless other people with their illnesses by inducing a trance to find solutions to these diseases.

Besides these, there are many other reports of people with psychic abilities around the world. Many of these people come from different cultures. Still, they all had psychic powers. This establishes there are no exceptions to becoming a psychic. Anyone can become a psychic if they are willing to look within themselves.

Suppose you are unfamiliar with the true meaning of psychic. In that case, the first thing that comes to your mind when you hear the word "psychic" may be a person in a dimly lit room with crystal balls, contraptions, fog machines, and other things used to manipulate supernatural events or happenstances. I refer to this as "smoke and mirrors."

You have likely learned that psychics are dubious and fraudulent people from childhood – basically, scammers out to exploit you. So, even if you have experienced an otherworldly occurrence at an early age, you have probably discredited it based on your perception of psychics. Thanks to the media, we neglect psychic occurrences because they aren't as glamorous and dramatic as portrayed in the movies and TV shows we are familiar with.

Most people don't know it, but mediums and psychics are different. I often meet people who think that being a medium and being a psychic is the same thing. A few even use both terms interchangeably. They may seem like the same thing to a person with little to no knowledge of both terms, but there is a distinctive difference.

Unlike psychics, mediums obtain information through channeling or temporary possession. In other words, they are usually possessed by otherworldly beings who pass information through them, but there are psychics with the ability to be mediums.

These are often referred to as psychic mediums. Psychic mediums obtain information through extrasensory perception, but the critical factor is that they can communicate with otherworldly beings. Communication often takes place through their psychic senses. This means that a medium may also be a psychic, but a psychic isn't necessarily a medium. As someone inclined toward psychic practices, it is best to learn the difference between both terms and not misuse them.

There are usually three ways that mediums can help a person. The first is to help you channel recently deceased spirits for communication. Suppose you have a dead relative you would like to communicate with for valuable information. A medium or a psychic medium can help you obtain the information by inducing a trance through which they channel your deceased relative's spirit.

The second way that mediums may use their abilities is to provide medical (physical) relief to a person whose illness seems incurable by science. To do this, a medium would have to channel benevolent spirits willing to help. The spirits will help ascertain the root of the illness and find the cure, which may be as simple as using a crystal.

The third is that mediums can use their powers to solve crimes, especially those that seem unsolvable.

Any psychic with the ability to induce trances and channel spirits may also do the same things as a medium. But this does not mean that psychics and mediums are the same.

As a psychic, you learn of your abilities in two ways. The first is that you naturally become conscious of the fact that you were born with psychic powers. Growing up, you may realize that you usually know things that other people don't know. For instance, you may see things that others claim they can't see. If this is the case with you, it means you are more predisposed to the powers than others. The second way psychic powers materialize is through traumatic or life-threatening experiences. This means if you are not already seeing signs of being psychic, a near-fatal accident, or any other event that causes physical or emotional trauma may trigger your psychic senses.

Psychic development is easily achieved with consistent training and practice. But know that opening up your psychic pathways leaves you vulnerable to the aftereffects and consequences of the psychic practice. This means you must be ready to overcome any fears you may have about becoming a psychic. That way, dealing with the consequences becomes easier for you.

The origin of the word "psychic" is from the Greek word "psyche," which means spirit, soul, mind, etc. By extension, the meaning also refers to thoughts, emotions, and sentiments. Perhaps being a psychic is the same as being a psychologist. The only difference here is that psychics take the mind's study to a higher spiritual level. Instead of just focusing on the mind as psychologists do, psychics extend their study to the soul or spirit. Although your spirit is a divine entity, it dramatically affects your feelings, thoughts, moods, etc.

You can see people's thoughts, feelings, or intentions by reading their auras. Aura reading is also part of psychic development.

To understand who a psychic is, there are few things you must learn by heart. Knowing these things will help you correct any misconceptions you may have about psychics and psychic development. More importantly, they will change your perception and attitude toward extrasensory perception.

One of the vital pieces of information to have about psychics is that they cannot tell you the future in full precision. Yes, this is contrary to what most people believe. You may have heard or read that psychics can accurately predict the future, but this isn't exactly right as a psychic. Training and honing your psychic skills may give you insight into events yet to occur. It does not mean you will predict the event exactly as it is about to happen.

The future is a dynamic thing, so it is impossible to tell it in full precision. An authentic and genuine psychic would never tell you they can see your future precisely as it is. Instead, they help you understand that the future is undefined. You create the future as you make individual decisions and progress in life. What psychic development can do for you is to help you decide to achieve your desired future.

Being a psychic means being extremely sensitive, making you sense energy and other things you cannot see with your psychic pathway locked. A point I should reiterate is that we are all intuitive and sensitive to an extent. Everyone is born with their intuition and psychic senses intact. The difference between a psychic and a non-psychic is that the non-psychic is yet to awaken their psychic senses. If you have never engaged in psychic activities before, it is safe to say that you are a non-psychic. The psychics you know or hear about are not unique or different from you. Suppose you choose to hone and refine your psychic abilities. In that case, that is all you need to identify as an authentic psychic.

Finally, I should note that even though we may all have different abilities, psychics are the same around the world. The difference in abilities stems from the most active psychic sense (s) in everyone. For instance, if your dominant psychic sense is clairsentience, you are most likely to fare well as a psychic medium. On the other hand, an individual with clairvoyance as their primary psychic sense is more likely to perform well as an energy reader. Never forget that everyone has diverse views, experiences, and backgrounds.

Naturally, these factors influence how they interpret readings through psychic channels.

The first step to understanding your psychic senses' power is to divorce this misleading perception of psychics. You need to dissociate "psychic" from deception or fraud. Of course, I'm not neglecting the fact that there are charlatans who exaggerate their abilities ridiculously or even ultimately make them up. People like this often rely on tricks to do psychic readings. They are certainly not real psychics. It is much better to describe them as con artists who exploit the gullibility and vulnerability of others. Once you understand this, you become more open to understanding who a genuine psychic is.

An authentic psychic is an individual with the ability to perceive beyond the physical world. Such individuals can use their extrasensory gifts to obtain the information they ordinarily can't acquire with their normal senses. It is difficult to define what to deem as "normal" senses. We have all been conditioned to believe that perception is limited to the physical. Hence, we have a reasonably concrete view of reality.

Due to this conditioning, you might assume that the sky is blue to everyone or that everyone can detect mood changes. But when you expand your knowledge of the sensory spectrum, you will find that not everyone knows the existence of other senses beyond the ones we are all familiar with. This is how you become conscious of your innate psychic abilities.

One fundamental knowledge to have about psychic abilities is that they exist on a spectrum. Sure, it is easy to say that someone is "psychic," but if you were asked *what* their psychic ability *is*, you probably wouldn't have an idea. "Psychic" is a rather broad term for a range of abilities and skills that all concern an inherent ability to obtain sensory data on a profoundly spiritual level. Psychic skills vary in intensity and application, which is why it is best to think of them on a spectrum. Just as psychologists describe traits like narcissism on a spectrum based on the degree of intensity, psychic skills should also be imagined on a spectrum. To bring this imagination alive for you, let's use an example of three friends.

The three friends agreed to walk their dogs together at the park on a Saturday. On D-day, the first friend arrives at the park. She finds a spot to sit and keeps her dog nearby. She barely notices that the park is teeming with people and dogs. After a while, the second friend also arrives with her dog. She approaches her friend and notices that she's absorbed in a game she's playing on her phone. Delicately, she calls out to her friend with a gentle greeting. They exchange pleasantries, and she sits down and adjusts the leash on her dog.

Soon, their third friend arrives, and he is immediately overwhelmed by the teeming population at the park. The different sounds, movements, smells, lights, etc., all come at him at once. He instantly knows the complicated relationship between a couple walking their dog nearby. He quickly moves toward his friends to relay his observations. The first friend says that they weren't even aware there were more people than usual.

From the example above, the first and second friends exhibit a relatively normal range of sensitivity. In contrast, the third friend demonstrates more sensitivity. This means that the third friend likely has more powerful extrasensory abilities. He is likely an empath or a highly sensitive person. Relate this example to your own daily experiences. To what degree do you absorb stimuli every day? Which stimuli resonate with you the most? How do the stimuli impact you physically, emotionally, and spiritually? By answering these questions, you are opening yourself up to understanding your psychic gifts on the spectrum. This is the foundation for tapping into your innate psychic senses.

In the next chapter, I will be focusing more on how you can tap into your inherent psychic powers. Remember that the power is already there, but how do you awaken your psychic senses? There are so many processes involved in self-induces psychic awakening. Let's find out what they are.

Chapter Two: How to Tap into Your Inherent Psychic Abilities

Over the years, you might have lost access to your inherent psychic abilities. But one never loses their gifts. Regardless of what happens in your life, your psychic senses are lying dormant inside you. To awaken them, you need to look within and find them. Now, the problem is, how do you find and tap into your psychic abilities?

The first step is to identify your dominant psychic sense. Different people have different psychic senses. Although clairvoyance is the most known psychic ability or sense, there are tons of other psychic abilities. Knowing this is crucial to your psychic development journey. Start your psychic awakening process without discovering your prevalent psychic sense. You may find yourself trying and trying without achieving a tangible result.

This is because every psychic sense has specific exercises that are tailored to make awakening easier and faster. For example, if clairvoyance is your dominant ability, visualization-based exercises are the best ways to awakening your clairvoyant sense. But what if you are not clairvoyant? If you keep doing clairvoyance exercises, your journey may take you nowhere, but the first step is to identify your psychic sense. Your psychic sense is directly tied to the psychic ability lying dormant inside you.

Suppose you have ever been to a professional psychic. There, you may wonder how the psychics can gather information during a psychic reading. Well, their key is to tap into their psychic sense (s) to communicate with the spirit world. These psychic senses are called the "claims" of intuition. When you get that gut feeling about something you didn't know before, it is one of your psychic senses at work.

A common misconception about the psychic senses is that one cannot have more than one ability. This is not true. One thing about the Clair senses is that you may be more inclined towards one, but you still have all of these senses. This means that even if clairvoyance is your most vital psychic sense, you can still access any other Clair senses.

Ultimately, there are six Clair senses, but only four are generally found in most people. So, I will only be talking about these four.

The first psychic sense is clairvoyance, which you already know. Although many people use "clairvoyant" synonymously with "psychic," it is one of the four Clair senses available to a psychic. Clairvoyance translates to "clear seeing." Clairvoyant people typically receive psychic messages in the form of images. Simply put, they see images that give them information beyond the physical realm.

As a clairvoyant, psychic messages often appear to be in the form of a scene, playing like a movie. Sometimes, I just receive images. Whether it is images or scenes, the peculiar thing is that the messages are metaphorical. For example, suppose I do a reading on a client who is emotionally overwhelmed. There, I might see them carrying a heavy burden on their back. The messages are not always straightforward, so it is up to you to analyze what appears to you to arrive at the literal meaning.

As a clairvoyant psychic, the images you receive when you do a reading for your clients will always be different depending on each client's situation and other factors, such as their background and physical and emotional states.

To tap into your clairvoyance sense, the most essential thing you can do is to always pay attention to images that pop randomly into your head out of nowhere. Chances are that these images are psychic messages you need to analyze.

Clairaudience is the second Clair sense. It is the psychic ability to hear voices without using your physical ears. If you are clairaudient, psychic messages may come as if someone were speaking out loud in your head. Often, the voice will sound to you like your own, but you can tell it is not your voice. It will never be harsh, cruel, or tormenting. Clairaudient messages come in an even and calm voice.

Usually, clairaudient messages are direct and straightforward. You don't have to analyze anything. Suppose you want to make a big decision, and you use your psychic ability to discover whether to make that decision or not. A clairaudient message may tell you to "wait until the summer is over." Being clairaudient means you will receive short and brief messages.

The message may be a single number or word. When this happens, you naturally need analysis to make sense of the message. If you receive a single word, you may need to tie it back to something in your life to get the actual message or meaning. For example, let's say you are doing a reading for another person, and you hear "15." It can mean different things.

A typical meaning might be that something traumatic happened to the client at 15, causing blocks and obstructing their life's progress. To get the true meaning of the number, you have to work with your subject. Clairaudient messages are sometimes poetic, so you will have fun if your dominant psychic ability is clairaudience.

The most basic way to tap into your clairaudience sense is to pay attention to voices that pop in your head. You also need to become more in tune with your intuition to unlock your clairaudient potentials. Clairaudience is sometimes the dominant psychic ability in mediums and psychic mediums.

The third Clair sense is clairsentience, which means "clear feeling." It is the dominant psychic ability in empaths and highly sensitive people. As a clairsentient, you receive psychic messages in the form of feelings. If you can tell the particular emotion an individual is feeling, you may be a clairsentient psychic. Clairsentience makes you read other people's emotions, receive gut instincts, or get information about the energy moving through your environment.

When I read a client, I always get a feel for their energy. I can tell if they are feeling serious, bubbly, sad, or nurturing. When I get a chill after meeting a client, I know that they have come for something vital. If a client is physically ill and they don't even know it yet, I can tell by getting a feel of their energy. In other cases, I feel the physical symptoms as soon as I come in contact with the client.

If your dominant psychic ability is clairsentience, you can also do all these. That is the point of a clear feeling. It means you can tell the emotion and energy of people you meet exactly as they experience them.

One tactic I used to strengthen my clairsentience ability was to write down in a journal whenever I get a powerful feeling I can't seem to shake. If you do this, you will be surprised at the number of messages you can pick up intuitively. Most people receive clairsentient messages without even realizing it. Keeping a journal of your intuitive feelings is a sure way to tap into your clairsentience ability. The more you recognize the messages, the better you will become at picking upon them.

The fourth and final Clair sense, which you should know about, is claircognizance. This means "clear knowing." It is the psychic ability to know without previous information about a situation, event, person, or object. When a client comes for reading, I know certain things about them before reading them. This is due to my claircognizant ability.

As a claircognizant psychic, you know things without understanding how you even know them. For instance, you can meet a person, and you will be able to tell the exact kind of person they are before you even get introduced. Claircognizance is like receiving a download of information into your brain's hard drive. This happens within seconds, making you feel like the information has been there all along.

To tap into your claircognizance sense, just look within yourself whenever you need answers to anything. Intimately ask your intuition for the solution or answer to any problem you want to solve. If your prevalent psychic ability is claircognizance, you will find the answer somewhere within yourself. Your intuition is there to listen and give you answers whenever you want them.

These are the four Clair senses, which you should be familiar with. Knowing your Clair senses is one step to awakening your psychic abilities. The more important thing is to do things geared toward helping you achieve the psychic awakening you seek.

There are several exercises you can practice while you develop your inherent psychic abilities. These exercises can be combined or practiced individually. It all depends on you and your schedule. The good thing is that you don't have to practice all the techniques every day. Only doing one technique per day can go a long way in helping you access your dormant psychic abilities. It is best to start with whichever of the techniques is the easiest for you to do. The more you practice, the better you will become at all the exercises, even the seemingly difficult ones. In just a few months, you may be amazed at the level of accomplishments you have amassed in your journey.

Meditation

Meditation is the key to connecting with the deepest levels of your soul. Without meditation, you simply cannot unlock your psychic abilities because there is no other way to connect with that part of you. It allows you to raise your vibration on the same wavelength as the spiritual and otherworldly beings that will bring your psychic messages.

Raising your vibration is a critical part of psychic awakening. Unless you reach a high level of vibrational energy, psychic awakening may be practically impossible for you. Spirit operates at a very high frequency, and you must, as well, if you want to connect.

Daily meditation puts you in a relaxed, calm, and aware state, making it easier to increase your energetic vibration. The more you meditate, the more connected to Spirit, universal energy, and your higher self you become. Fortunately, meditation takes little of your time. All you need is 10 to 15 minutes of daily meditative exercise to keep your vibration on a high frequency.

Naturally, you can meditate anytime you choose, but it always helps you find a good time. The time you choose should be when you feel alert and aware the most. More important, it should be a time when you may practice without distractions and interruptions.

You can meditate early in the morning when you are fresh out of bed and confident you won't fall asleep. You can also choose right before bedtime when you are done with all the hassles of your daily activities. If it works for you, midday is also an excellent time to meditate. The point is to make sure that the time you choose for meditation is right for you.

When you first start meditating, you may think you have to complete 10 to 15 minutes of practice. How long you meditate should depend on the time that is right for you. There is no definite amount of time for meditation. Everything depends on the person involved; in other words, you. Even if you can manage only five minutes every day, that works. You have the liberty to gradually increase the length of your meditation time the more you practice and become better at it.

I like meditation because it is so relaxing and calming that sometimes I forget myself in the process. This helps me spend more time meditating, and it will probably happen to you. The key is to choose a timeframe that does not cause discomfort. Start slowly and build yourself up from there.

A suitable venue is vital in meditation. The place you meditate should be somewhere you are comfortable, but not to the point of sleepiness. It should also be where you are less likely to be distracted, disturbed, or interrupted. Your meditation should be quiet and peaceful, making it easier for you to focus your mind. When you meditate, you can sit in a chair or on the floor. What matters is that you sit comfortably.

Sitting comfortably is essential, but don't be too comfortable. Sit in an upright position, so you don't slouch. This makes it harder to lose focus or fall asleep. The best way to sit when meditating is to keep your spine straight, and your shoulders relaxed. Don't allow yourself to feel stiff.

Once you get the sitting position correctly, the next thing is to breathe. Simply breathe. Let go of any attempt to regulate your breath. Just focus on your breathing. There is no pattern of breathing during meditation. If you pay attention to yourself, you may notice you start breathing quickly, but your breathing will become slow and relaxed as you focus your mind.

The key to meditation is to be mindful of your breathing. You take attention from everything else and focus on your breath. Pay attention as you breathe in and out. Focus on the sensation of your breath as you inhale and exhale.

Naturally, your mind will drift away from your breathing. This is normal, and you don't have to fret when it happens to you during meditation. So many thoughts will pop randomly into your head. Don't try to suppress or shun them. Acknowledge the thoughts as they wander into your mind. Any attempt to stop yourself from thinking will only result in more thinking.

What you can do is to notice every thought, feeling, and sensation that comes up while you are sitting in meditative practice. After that, bring your focus back to your breath. Do this every time you notice your mind wandering.

The most important thing in meditation is the focus. Unless you focus, you cannot induce that state of calm and relaxation you seek. Besides breathing, another way you can focus your mind is by chanting mantras. Many psychics prefer mantra meditation. A popular mantra you can use when meditating is:

"Breathing in, I know I am breathing in.

Breathing out, I know I am breathing out."

This mantra is by Thich Nhat, a famous Buddhist monk and spiritual leader.

Meditation need not be difficult, as long as you follow everything we've just discussed. Finally, make sure you have fun as you practice. Don't be hard on yourself. Don't judge yourself when you get distracted. Just focus and breathe.

Spirit Guides

Your spirit guides are a part of your Divine spiritual teams. They are souls that have agreed to dedicate themselves toward your spiritual and personal growth. They have existed in several lifetimes, meaning they have more experience than you can imagine. They are there to help you notice and pay attention to things you ordinarily wouldn't. They bring valuable things and people into your life. Most importantly, they help you establish a life of serendipity. They can help you with anything.

Spirit guides are there to help you in your psychic and spiritual development journey. Communicating with them is one way you can tap into your psychic abilities. Spirit guides include spiritual teachers, masters, angels, and other spiritual beings. They can help you with anything you ask them. To meet your spirit guide, you have to channel them through meditation. During meditation, you can ask your spirit guides to reveal themselves to you. Then you can seek knowledge and gather information from them. When they appear, you must not filter your thoughts, feelings, and questions. Go with the flow.

Before you start your meditation, you must set the intention to meet your spirit guide. It's viable your guide won't appear to you on the first try. Don't relent. It just means you need more practice. More important, it means you have to establish trust with your guide.

Visualization will help you in meeting your spirit guide. It is a very effective way of opening up your psychic portals to tap into your abilities. Combining meditation with visualization is a useful technique for psychic development. Using your imagination, visualize what your spirit guides look like.

What do your guides look like? How do they dress? What are their names? What about their personalities?

Answer these questions and write them down in a journal. Whenever you are ready to meet your guides, use your answers to visualize. Your guides will appear to you precisely as you have imagined them to be. Let your imagination flow so you can establish a stronger connection with your spiritual team.

Communicating with your spirit guides requires that you have a sacred space dedicated to establishing that connection. The first time you try to connect with your spirit guide, choose a place where you can comfortably interact with them. You can connect with the guides anywhere you want, but choosing a specific space where you can always hang out comfortably can help you. I recommend your meditation spot because you need to raise your vibrations before they can connect with you.

Spirit guides are invisible, but, like I said, visualizing them can make communication easier for you. It may be hard for you to trust them on your first few tries, mostly due to being a beginner. But know that you can ask them for signs and answers. Asking for signs is a way to build trust between both parties. When you sleep, you become more open to the spirit world. This means that seeing your guides is easier when you are in the dream world. Before you go to bed, try asking your guides to connect with you. Do this with a strong belief they will. Then, you can seek guidance on any issue where you seem lost.

The most important thing is to open your mind and heart to your spirit guides. Look for signs and embrace that there are vast possibilities with your guides.

Psychometry

Psychometry is the practice of reading an object's energy through touch. It is one of the most effective and fun-filled ways to hone your psychic abilities. You will undoubtedly have a lot of fun practicing psychometry. I always tell beginners to psychic development to make psychometry a vital part of their daily exercises. That feeling of holding a physical object to read its energy boosts confidence and provides a sense of security. It can help you develop all of your psychic senses from clairvoyance to clairsentience. Practicing psychometry is also helpful if you have plans to become a medium.

Using psychometry, you can read the energy of an item to get information about it. You sense the energy, see images, smell things, and hear sounds, which give you insight into the history of the object and its owner. If you are already good at the art of psychometry, you only have to be near an object to read it. But as a beginner, you have to hold the object.

You are likely wondering how psychometry can give you information about an object. It's relatively straightforward. When you touch an object in your home, you leave your physical imprint on the object. But what you may not know is that you also leave your energetic imprint. You are made of energy, like everything else in the universe. You leave your imprint on everything you come in contact with. This means that every object you touch has a vibration of your energy impressed on them. Psychometry allows you to read the energy impressions left on objects. The more the energetic imprints on an object, the more information you can gather from the object.

To practice psychometry:

- First, get rid of any residual energy by washing and drying your hands.

- Get the energy flowing through your hands by rubbing them together for several seconds.

- Next, let your palms face each other with a little distance between them. Pull and draw your palms apart without letting them touch each other. Feel a heavy sensation between the palms. This is the feel of energy flowing. If you don't feel it, rub your hands together for a few more seconds.

- Find a physical object like a ring or bracelet and hold it gently in your hands. You can use any item, but make sure it is worn or used frequently. Use an object that does not belong to you or someone you know. Consider asking a friend for a family heirloom you can use for practice.

- Gently close your eyes and let yourself relax. Do a quick meditation if you have to.

- Pay attention to the sound, smells, and images that come to your mind as you hold the item in your hands. What do you see, smell, hear, and feel?

As you focus, the information will come to you about the owner of the item you are holding. I should note that emotional energy is the strongest you will get from any item you practice psychometry on. The most powerful emotions that emanate are love, fear, and hate.

Note you can use psychometry to practice mediumship and channel the spirit of a departed loved one. To do this, you need the photo of the departed person or an item dear to them while they were alive.

Other ways you can tap into your psychic abilities include:

- Taking a walk in nature
- Visiting antique store to practice energy reading
- Honing your intuition with third eye meditation
- Joining a psychic development group
- Taking courses on psychic development
- Keep a journal to record and track your progress as you practice daily

The bottom line is that you need to practice consistently to unlock your inherent psychic abilities. So, be willing to put the work in!

Chapter Three: Psychic Tools

Whether you are a beginner or an experienced psychic, you can use lots of tools to enhance your abilities. The point of using psychic tools is to help you consult metaphysical and spiritual beings with a little help. You don't need these tools. But having them can help you master your abilities much faster. Note that not all psychics need tools to get a reading done. Many have mastered the art of using just their intuition and psychic senses for reading. This is especially easy when they have more than one dominant psychic sense.

When you have more than one extrasensory ability, they are bound to overlap during readings. This gives you access to different facets of information during a psychic reading. To do readings without psychic tools, you have to be relaxed and calm. Unless you put yourself in a tranquil state, you may find it hard to connect with your innate information source. Relaxing makes your energy and spiritual field easy to read. As you have learned, the best way to do this is to meditate before you get started. This helps you stay connected to your psychic senses and the spiritual world.

Psychic tools include a range of items you can easily get or create by yourself. To make your learning easier, I have included instructions on how you can make homemade psychic tools without having to spend a lot of money. Suppose you would rather buy the items instead of DIY-making them. There, you can easily find them in online stores where they sell esoteric items. Below are tools that can be combined with your inherent psychic abilities to make you powerful.

Pendulum

A pendulum is an effective tool for diving deep into the collective consciousness of the universe. Naturally, this also means you can use it to tap into your subconscious and higher consciousness. It does not matter what you are looking for – whether it is a straightforward answer or something a little more in-depth, a pendulum can help you gain more insight into any situation. Throughout history, pendulums have been used effectively for finding lost objects.

People don't believe it, but pendulums can also access spirits. You can use this tool to gain spiritual guidance from the Divine. The good thing about using pendulums for your psychic readings is that they help you get fast and accurate answers to whatever problem. Suppose you want to know about your relationships, career, destiny, or life path. There, a pendulum reading can help you gain knowledge.

To use a pendulum for reading, you have to hold on to the attached chain, allowing it to move and swing freely. A swinging pendulum merely is guiding itself to the answers you seek. As it swings, it is moving through your deepest thoughts, feelings, and energy. The pendulum movements are what you have to interpret to get your answers. Coupled with your extrasensory gift, you should have no trouble with interpretations. If you are claircognizant, the answers may just come to you as you watch the pendulum move and swing.

You can easily buy a pendulum at any physical or online store that sells psychic-related items. If you would rather make your own, below are the instructions to guide you. Note you can make one from wood, plastic, cork, crystal, or even metal. There are different items in your home that can be used to make one quickly. To make your pendulum, you will need a long chain, preferably 15 to 18 inches, to attach the pendulum to. Make sure that the necklace's clasp is still functional. You will also need an adult ring, which could be gold or silver.

- Open the necklace clasp and insert your gold or silver ring through the hole. Close the necklace clasp. Do this so the ring moves freely without falling off.

- Gently place the elbow of your right (or dominant) hand on a flat surface, like a table. Extend your forearm vertically from the table. Then, hold your pendulum so the ring is about 2 inches from your fingers.

- The pendulum will start swinging. As it swings, label the swing motions. Suppose it moves left to right first. You can decide that it a "yes." A right to left motion may be labeled "No." An up and down motion could be "Unknown." This will help you understand what the spirits are saying when you conduct a pendulum reading.

- To test your new pendulum, hold it between your forefinger and thumb. Then, ask a question you know the answer to. For example, you may ask, "Did it rain yesterday?" Check if the pendulum's swing motion answers the predetermined question accurately.

- Repeat the above with at least ten different questions that have predetermined answers. Doing this will help achieve certainty about the movements of the pendulum. Depending on how it goes, you may be required to switch up the previously predetermined labels for the swing motions.

Make sure that the pendulum you make swings as freely as possible. The best way to make sure of this is to see that the holding chain is neither too short nor thick. If it doesn't move as freely and easily as it should, you may need to change the attached chain or ring. Switch it up until you find one just the right size and gives the desired results.

I recommend that you experiment by making multiple types of pendulums with different materials and chains. Make one with plastic, copper, crystal, or wood. Check whichever works best. Remember that all psychics are different, meaning that what works for you may not work for another person and vice versa.

Before using the pendulum, put yourself in a relaxed and calm state. Otherwise, you may get a lot of answers with which you are not comfortable. Being relaxed reduces your chances of getting negative and conflicting answers.

Tarot Cards

Tarot cards are one of the most popular tools for psychic readings. Many people are comfortable with them because they are easy to read and understand. You will find many psychics that use them to seek answers to their deepest questions, even on the internet. If you are curious and inquisitive, tarot cards can help you unravel yourself. Learning to read and interpret tarot is a lengthy process. You are bound to start with more questions than answers. It takes time to learn the meaning of the cards. A lot of practice is also required.

When you first get started with tarot, you may find yourself overwhelmed and confused by the sheer amounts of cards. The cards are plenty, and you need to master them all to a reasonable extent. Initially, tarot cards were used for games. They did not become a part of the divination practice until the 18th century. Tarot deals in universal symbols, meaning that the cards and the stories behind their meanings expand beyond culture, time, and continents.

When you buy your pack of tarot cards, you may notice that the cards have distinctive titles. They are also numbered from 0 to 21. On some cards, these are numbered from 1 to 22. Other cards are numbered in the usual way you find on your traditional card deck. They come with kings, queens, and aces divided into two: the major arcana and the minor arcana. The major arcana comprises all cards without suits. But the minor arcana has cards labeled as wands, cups, swords, and pentacles. A standard tarot deck has 78 cards, 22 in the major arcana and the remaining 56 in the minor arcana.

The cards of the major arcana represent archetypes. They suggest major patterns, themes, and lessons for you or the querent (the subject of your reading) to pay attention to. Different cards stand for the impending change. For instance, if you get the Tower, which is one of the major arcana cards, it means you will experience a huge change to be life-altering.

Note that all the cards of the major arcana are not created equally. Card names may be altered, depending on the deck. Thankfully, the cards always come with extensive information you would do well to read up on before practicing. This will make things easier for you.

The tarot deck's minor arcana comprises cards representing the challenges, triumphs, joys, fears, annoyances, and hopes you experience every day. Remember that just because we call it the minor arcana does not mean that the issues represented are unimportant. "Minor" means they are transient and less far-reaching than issues that appear in the major arcana cards. Also, minor arcana issues are easier to attend to.

The minor arcana is segmented into four suits, as I said. These are the wands, cups, swords, and pentacles. Each is linked to one aspect of the human experience. Swords are connected to cognitive processes and decision-making, wands are related to motivation and action, cups represent emotions and feeling, and pentacles are linked to material things, such as finances and works.

Depending on the kind of deck you buy, they may be mixed up. But these are the general meanings for the suits in any minor arcana.

If you don't want to buy tarot cards, you can, of course, make your deck at home. I suggest that beginning psychics do this because it makes tarot much easier to master. The decks will have a much more specific meaning to your life, meaning that the spirits' answers become more accessible.

Below are the steps involved to make your deck of tarot cards for psychic readings:

- Find a large piece of thick paper where you can cut out 78 pieces of card. The cards can be any size but be sure to put shuffling into consideration when cutting. Note how they feel in your hand and how shuffling will be. I suggest using card stock to guarantee durability.

- As you have learned, a deck of tarot has a single set of 22 cards and another four sets of 14 cards. So, remember this when cutting the 78 cards.

- When you have finished, you will need to design the card and name the minor arcana's suits. The most common design used by beginners is the Rider-Waite-Smith deck. Most resources for learning the meaning of cards follow this design. Know that personal design and deviation can help you achieve more profound meanings.

- Next, you need to sketch the card designs and add labels to them. Consider trying your best imitation of the symbols on the Rider-Waite-Smith deck for your cards.

- Finally, draw or paint the back design on your deck. You can make it simple or complex. It depends on what you like.

That's it. You have your homemade tarot deck to use for psychic readings. You can shuffle and learn the meanings. While drawing and creating your deck, you will have developed a sense of familiarity with each card. You will find this helpful as you master the art of using tarot cards for psychic development.

Unwavering concentration is vital to tarot reading. How you shuffle cards does not matter. What matters is how invested you are in the process. If you are not as invested as you should be, you may end up missing a lot of subtle details.

You shouldn't fret or worry if you didn't learn all the cards' meanings at once. Take your time. One of the critical parts of the whole process is that you end up developing and enhancing your intuition.

Crystals

Crystals are beneficial gemstones proven to contain spiritual energy. A crystal reading involves mastering these natural resources' many properties and how they can be used for the highest, divine purpose. Just like you, crystals also have energetic and vibrational powers. This means you can use them to increase or enhance your vibrational state. More importantly, you can use them to strengthen your connection to Spirit.

These gemstones' powerful healing properties are functional on both physical and nonphysical planes. Each has an intense and unique concentration of vital energy, thanks to the earth's mix of minerals. As a psychic, you need to know which stones are the most spiritually resonant. Highly resonant stones interact with your energy field so it uplifts and focuses it. Your energy field comprises physical, mental, emotional, and spiritual bodies, which all vibrate at varying frequencies. All these bodies can be positively affected by crystals.

Knowing how to use crystals and gemstones for psychic readings is a fundamental part of esoterism. Crystal reading involves using them to generate and interpret psychic messages. You can also tune into your energy field to discover which stones will significantly benefit your life at a specific moment in life.

The best thing about crystals is that they can also be incorporated into tarot and oracle readings. This greatly increases your chances of getting the answers and solutions you seek. Stones you can use for psychic readings include:

- Sodalite
- Amazonite
- Chrysocolla
- Blue Lace Agate
- Black Tourmaline
- Herkimer Diamond
- Clear Quartz
- Fluorite
- Amethyst
- Azurite

These stones can be used for a range of purposes. Sodalite and Amazonite are great for triggering and maintaining a state of calm during psychic readings. Meditating with these crystals will induce a sense of peace and calm should you receive information you do not particularly like. Clear Quartz is excellent for improving clarification and understanding during reading. It is associated with the crown and third eye chakra, meaning it can help you make sense of your reading and the messages you receive.

Blue Lace Agate and Chrysocolla are effective for ensuring good communication with Spirit when doing a reading. Suppose you are doing the reading for someone else. There, they help you relay received messages articulately to your client or subject. Both stones are tied to the throat chakra. Blue Lace Agate is called the "Stone of Articulation."

You can store your energy crystals and tarot deck together in the same place. Note you don't necessarily need all the stones listed above. They are simply recommendations on the kinds of crystals you should consider getting for psychic practice and development.

The most crucial thing is to go along with your intuition when choosing crystals and stones that can be used in psychic readings.

Runes

The literal meaning of the word "Rune" is "something secret" or "something hidden." Runes didn't become widely known until the 1980s. Only the most regarded mystics knew and understood the divinatory power of runes. In case you are unfamiliar with runes, they are ancient symbols that serve as esoteric and divinatory tools. Most people assume that runes symbols come from the Latin language, but they are from ancient Germanic languages that predate Latin.

Over the years, they have evolved to express a more symbolic nature. They are now utilized for specialty use. They often come in the form of wooden tiles and beads or glass. Each symbol on each has a specific meaning and message attached. Of course, the messages are from Spirit. To translate the meanings, you must learn the art of rune reading. Psychics who use runes for readings are called runes psychics.

As a rune psychic, you have the knowledge and expertise to consult rune stones for spiritual and divinatory purposes. Even if you don't want to become a master rune psychic, you can learn the basics of rune reading to help your psychic journey. Using runes in psychic readings can help you gain insight into any situation. You may also use runes as an intermediary for clarifying the messages you receive from your spirit guides. You may also use runes as a medium for conversing with the universe to make predictions.

Incorporating runes into your readings can help you establish a strong connection to the Source. This allows you to intuitively interpret psychic messages in tandem with your prevalent psychic ability. To put it simply, the presence of runes during a reading can heighten your dominant psychic sense to where messages become intuitively clear and meaningful to you.

As the querent, you have to start the reading with a specific question or intention. Or you can do a general reading to see if Spirit has anything to tell you. Like in a tarot reading, you have to spread out the rune beads or tiles, after which you do the reading and interpretation.

You may consult Spirit through Runes whenever you need clarity on something. Suppose you have a major or even minor decision to make. In that case, rune reading can help decide which direction to go. A rune spread is a means of getting an explicit picture of what lies ahead of you.

Astrology

Many people believe that astrology and psychic practices are detached from one another, but this is not true. For hundreds of years, different cultures worldwide have studied the planets and star movements to access divinity. Although astrology is a whole subject in esoterism in its own right, it can be used for a psychic reading. If you study astrology, it will directly affect your psychic growth.

Astrology is all about the alignment and placement of the stars and planets. It is based on the idea that the position of the planets and alignment of the stars during the exact moment of a person's birth influence every facet of their human life, including personality, karma, purpose, and overall mood. If you have any inclination towards the practice of astrology, you have likely observed that you share similarities with people of the same sun sign.

An astrology reading involves combining and incorporating the influences of your Sun sign, Moon, and Ascendant. Suppose you would like to gain insight into why events in your life unfold how they do or the level of compatibility between you and another person. In that case, an astrology reading can help with that. Add astrology to your natural intuitive abilities, and your psychic gifts will be as powerful as you envision.

Astrology isn't something you can fully understand or used just from reading a few sentences. To use astrology as a psychic tool, you need a resource focused on teaching you just that. Natal charts are complicated, so you might need a mentor to make the learning process easier.

These are essentially the best psychic tools you might need in your journey. Having these tools can make practice more manageable for you, but that doesn't make them compulsory. Use them only if you want to. If you would rather be a no-tool psychic, working on your third eye is the best way to go. Doing that will sharpen your intuition and psychic senses to where third-party tools don't matter. It will be just you and your psychic senses.

Chapter Four: Understand the Astral Body

Have you ever had an OBE? An OBE is an out-of-body experience. It involves your astral body separating from your physical body. It usually occurs when you are in a dream state. Right now, you are probably wondering what an astral body is. To help you understand this concept, I will break it down.

When you look at yourself in the mirror, you can see your physical body. You can see it because it is visible. Contrary to what you may think, the physical body isn't your only body. It is only a small subset of what makes up your whole human system.

You comprise two parts; your physical body you can see and another one you cannot see unless you train yourself to use your third eye. The second part is your energy body. You may also call it your energy field. Remember that I have mentioned the human energy field sometimes in the previous chapter. Well, your energy body is what I have been referring to.

The energy field is widely known as the aura. It is a mix of lights and colors that hand around your physical body. The aura is invisible to the human eye, which means you need to open your third eye if you want to see it. Psychics see the invisible body as a bright energy field that interpenetrates the body and extends about 6 inches from the body. Your energy field is interconnected with your physical body. Whatever affects your energy body will usually reflect in your physical body, and vice versa.

Remember that the energy field cannot exist as a separate entity, meaning it depends on your visible physical body's existence. Just like the body you can see, your energy field has things like a head and body, including arms and legs. The energy field exists because it is vital to the proper functioning of your material body. The body's primary function is to absorb vital energy from the universe and share it around your material form. In doing this, it is energizing your physical form.

The aura or energy body is also a kind of blueprint or mold for the physical body. Without its blueprint, your physical body would have continually changing features due to never-ending metabolism. Essentially, this suggests that the existence of the energy body is crucial to your physical health. As I have likely mentioned, anything that affects the energy field automatically affects the physical body.

Now, your energy field contains different layers and bodies, one of which is the astral body. You may also call it the spiritual body. The astral body is connected to your physical body. It is your one link between the physical plane and the higher (nonphysical) planes. This means that your astral body can function in both the physical world and the metaphysical world.

Suppose you want to travel into the astral plane to interact with higher-dimensional beings and do other things. In that case, you need your astral form to do this. The astral body is the form you use when you are in the dream state. When you dream about yourself doing something while sleeping, that is your astral form in your dream. In lucid dreaming, the astral body is also the one in charge.

The astral form cannot operate while the physical body is active, which is why it takes over when you are asleep, but if you learn how to astral project and astral travel, you can discover how to induce the astral state intentionally.

Your energy field has different energy channels through which it distributes energy to your material form. These channels are known as Nadis. It also has energy centers referred to as chakras. The energy centers and channels are essential for ensuring a clean energy system to flow freely to the physical body.

A clear and free flow of energy is key to the functioning of the physical body. Without it, the body cannot function at its peak. You need a clean energy system to maintain wellbeing and essential body functions. Briefly, let's talk about the energy centers and channels.

The chakras are the energy centers. Seven major chakras pump energy through to your physical form. They vitalize your whole body. You can find the chakras in the body's midline, and they go from down to up. When these energy channels are blocked, it can cause pain or illness in certain parts of your body.

Each of your chakras is associated with one part of the physical body. This makes diagnosis easier for energy healers who help with blockages in the energy field. Understanding how the chakras work and how you can keep open to energy is critical. If the chakras are blocked or nonfunctional, you simply cannot access your psychic portal.

What are the Seven Chakras?

- **Root Chakra:** This is the first chakra, located at the base of your spine. When the first chakra becomes blocked, it often results in physical symptoms such as sciatica, lower back pain, varicose veins, and several immune-related conditions. The root chakra is in charge of the functioning of your spine, legs, feet, kidney, rectum, and immune system. So, any blockage in this chakra will affect these specific parts of your body.

• **Sacral Chakra:** Located between your navel and lower abdomen, this is the next chakra after the root chakra. When the sacral chakra becomes blocked, it causes physical symptoms such as pelvic pain, sciatica, urinary problems, libido problems, and lower back pain. The second chakra controls your sexual function. It also governs your stomach, liver, kidney, upper intestines, pancreas, spleen, and the area around the middle of your spinal column.

• **Solar Plexus Chakra:** Chakra number three is the solar plexus, which you can probably tell from the name, is located in the solar plexus. This chakra is in charge of your upper abdomen, middle spine, liver, gall bladder, spleen, adrenals, small intestines, rib cage, umbilicus, and stomach. Any blockage in the solar plexus chakra may cause physical conditions such as diabetes, pancreatitis, stomach ulcers, indigestion, cirrhosis, bulimia, and many others.

• **Heart Chakra:** Your fourth chakra is the heart chakra, located at the center of the heart. But the heart chakra doesn't just govern the heart; it also controls other parts of the body such as blood, lung, breasts, arms and hands, diaphragm, and the circulatory system. Blockage in this chakra can cause asthma, pneumonia, upper back problems, and general heart conditions.

• **Throat Chakra:** This is the fifth energy center located at the throat, as made clear by the name. The throat chakra regulates functions in your throat, thyroid, mouth, teeth, esophagus, and hypothalamus. A blocked throat chakra may show physical symptoms such as throat ulcer, scoliosis, thyroid dysfunctions, and speech or voice problems.

- **Third Eye Chakra:** Chakra number six is the third eye chakra, possibly the most popular chakra. Even people who aren't invested in esoterism know about the third eye chakra. The third eye is popular across different cultures globally, but all agree that it is the seat of intuition. The third eye controls your brain, pituitary gland, neurological functions, and pineal gland. When blocked, the third eye chakra results in symptoms such as brain tumors, seizures, strokes, spinal dysfunction, blindness, and learning disabilities.

- **Crown Chakra:** This is the final and highest chakra. The crown chakra can be found atop your head, on the crown. It governs the midline above your ears and the top of your head. The crown chakra is the link to forming a connection with the Higher Consciousness, and when blocked, it will cause physical conditions relating to the skeletal system, muscular system, skin diseases, and chronic exhaustion.

The Nadis are the energy channels. They are much more plentiful than the chakras. As the energy channels, the nadis or meridians transport energy through the chakras. They affect your physical health just as much as the chakras. Any disturbance in the transportation of energy from the nadis to the chakras will cause physical disease and illness.

There are 12 major nadis and thousands of other minor ones across different locations in the body. The major nadis are named after their functions. You have the lung, spleen, stomach, large intestine, small intestine, heart, kidney, liver, bladder, heart constrictor, triple heater, and gall bladder nadis. These cover your whole physical system, helping your body maintain a balance. Blockage in the nadis upset the body's balance.

Right now, you are probably wondering what all of these have to do with the astral body and psychic development. Well, energy blockage is generally not good for psychic business. If you suffer from an energy blockage, it will affect your ability to access your psychic portals. It will also obstruct your ability to channel your astral body. Note that astral traveling is a crucial part of psychic practices.

I am saying that your energy system has to be clear and balanced if you want to use your powers. The third eye, as I said, is the seat of intuition. This means you can't access your intuition when the third eye chakra is blocked. Your energy body has to be free of blockages at all times.

The first step to ensuring your system stays free of blockages is to understand what causes energy blockages in the first place.

Your physical body is quite fragile, affected by both internal and external triggers. These often result in energy stagnation or concentration. Most of the time, the triggers result from mental and emotional imbalance. But they can also be caused by poor environmental conditions, unhealthy nutrition, and illness.

When any trigger sets off in the physical body, your energy flow starts diluting. This leads to pain and organ damage. Although blockage directly affects the specific area where it happens, it ultimately has a ripple effect. This means it disrupts the flow of energy to other parts of the body. Naturally, it causes a downward spiral in your energy system's overall functioning and the quality of your health. When this happens, energy healing is the key to getting rid of the blockage and providing relief across your energy system.

The best energy healing techniques used by expert energy healers include Reiki, Ayurveda, Acupuncture, etc. Besides Reiki, you can't do some of these techniques on your own. Below are simple energy clearing and cleansing techniques you can do in the comfort of your own home to make things easier on you.

I should note that your energy field has to be clear at all times to read other people's energy. As you can see, learning these techniques is important.

Technique 1: Run Energy Through the Chakras

This here is one of my personal favorites for clearing energy. It is an exercise targeted at attuning your mind, body, and emotions with your soul. Doing this restores the balance within your energy system. Getting rid of dense energy improves your connection with the source of energy. This, in turn, enhances your clarity and intuition, allowing you to use your inner guidance to make important decisions and answer vital questions.

Running energy through the chakras is something I recommend you integrate into your daily spiritual activities. Daily practice is how you can get the full benefits of this technique. You can start small - five to ten minutes of your time every day will make a tremendous difference for your whole system.

The process is straightforward. You ground, run, and then clear the energy in your system every morning and evening. As you practice more, your vitality, clarity, and sense of focus increase. Then, you can increase the time you use for your daily dose. I like this technique because you don't need a quiet or tranquil location to do it. You can run energy wherever you are when you feel the need for it. You can even do it when having a heated conversation with another person.

At first, you may not be able to feel anything. This is quite normal. You just need to keep going until you can. Ask the energy to fill you up, and trust it will. As the saying goes, practice makes progress. The more you do it, the better you will become at it, and the more you will gain the benefits.

How do you go about this technique?

Get Grounded

First, you have to get grounded. We are rarely ever-present at the moment. Stressors and distractions from the activities of our daily lives abound. They often keep our minds fixated on the past or the future. Getting grounded is a way of immersing yourself in the present moment rather than the past or the future. Mindfulness and presence at the moment is the first step to attuning your mind, body, and emotions with your spirit.

Step 1: Create a Grounding Cord from Your First Chakra

Sit in an upright position with your arms and legs uncrossed. Place your feet firmly flat on the ground. Imagine at the base of your spine, traveling to the center of the earth, a beam of light originating from your root chakra.

Step 2: Open Up Your Crown Chakra

Visualize another cord of light traveling from your crown chakra directly up into the heavens to connect with the cosmic energy.

Step 3: Call Out Your Spirit Home

Call out your full name loudly. Repeat it three times. Your full name is unique to you. By repeating your full name, you call your consciousness into the present moment.

Step 4: Create Grounding Cords from Your Feet

Awaken the chakras on the base of your feet. With your feet firmly on the floor, envision beams of light traveling your feet to the core of the earth.

Step 5: Run Energy from the Earth

Once you have successfully created cords running from your feet and first chakra, and a cosmic cord from your crown chakra, it is time to run earth energy up. Call the energy from the earth's core and visualize it traveling into your feet, upwards through your legs, as far up as the crown of your head. Visualize the energy filling up the outer layers of your energy field. Let your aura and body be filled up with this energy. Once filled up, let the energy flush down the cord attached to your first chakra into the core of the earth.

Now, you have successfully grounded yourself through earth energy. The next step is to run your energy.

Run Your Energy

After successful grounding, you can channel energy through your chakras, clearing blockages and cleaning them one by one. Better than anyone, you know exactly what you want. Allow the healing energy to wash through your body, mind, emotions, and spirit. By doing this, you will have the vitality needed to project the high-vibrational energy that attracts higher-dimensional beings towards you.

Step 6: Run Divine energy

In contrast to grounding energy, which travels from the earth's core up to wash down the cosmic grounding cord, the divine energy travels downward from the crown chakra through the rest of the chakras until it reaches the center of the earth. Run the energy at least four times and visualize the colors of energy pumping through your body as you run it. There are four colors, and they all represent four types of energy you have to run.

The first is a royal deep-blue color for deprogramming energy. This is targeted towards washing out dense energies from your system. The second is a neon-electric-blue color for clarity energy. It is targeted toward improving clarity and enhancing knowingness. Third, you have a green color for healing energy. You run this energy to heal wounds in the physical and nonphysical systems. Finally, the fourth is a golden color for love and truth energy. Run this to revitalize yourself with light and love. It will remind you of who you are and the extent of your psychic capabilities.

Step 7: Switch the Grounding Cord

This is the final and most crucial step in this energy-healing technique. Before you round up, you have to replace your grounding cord with a new one. This will help realign and anchor you into the present moment. Allow all residual energies to run down and be released through the old cord. Then, get rid of the cord by visualizing a rose grounded to the earth through the stems. In this context, the rose is a symbol of forgiveness and a way of transmuting toxic energy into light.

Visualize your old grounding cord in the center of the rose and let it explode over a vast body of water, immersing the rose to be rinsed and restored to new.

Anytime you feel like there is a blockage in your energy system, use this technique to clear it out and revitalize yourself.

Technique 2: Visualize to Release Negative Energy

Visualization is a simple practice that can be done anywhere and anytime. You can do it at work or even while you are in a crowded space. It is normal not to get visualization on your first try. Even if you feel like it is not something you are good at, keep trying. Like the first technique, this also gets better the more you practice.

And this technique is not just about imagination. It involves creating an actual energy shift you can feel in real-time. The process is shown below.

Step 1: Set an Intention

The first thing you must do is set an intention to release all negative and toxic energy from your system and whatever you may have picked up from other people's aura. You can set your intention by saying, "I release all energy that no longer serves me from my system, whether it is from myself or others. I do this to achieve my highest purpose." Or you can form your intention. Just make sure that it goes along with the theme of what you are about to do – releasing toxic and residual energy and energy blockages.

Step 2: Establish a Body of Light

Envision a brilliant ball of golden light in the core of your chest. Imagine the light expanding and getting bigger as you exhale. Then, imagine the light expanding as you breathe in and out of your chest. It should get bigger with each exhalation.

Step 3: Spread the Light

Imagine the ball of light spreading from one part of your body to the next until it is across your entire body. Visualize it in your head, arms, torso, toes, and other parts of your body.

Step 4: Expand the Light

Envision the light to expand until it is beyond your skin. Let it expand until it is just about an arm's length outwards in all directions.

Step 5: Wrap Up with Shielding

Shielding is a way of forming a protective shell around yourself to avoid soaking up toxic energy from your environment. It dramatically reduces your chances of suffering energy blockage. It's relatively easy. Just imagine a big bubble of light around you. Picture the bubble as a solid filter covering your whole body completely. Ask the bubble to act as your shield from negative energy while allowing positive energy and love to filter inside. Visualize the bubble filling up with golden light.

That is all. As you can see, this technique is short and straightforward. But more important, it is highly effective for energy cleansing and healing. Incorporating this into your daily activities will make you much calmer, more peaceful, and more balanced. It will also make you less reactive.

Another thing you can do is to use minerals to eliminate all toxicity from your energy body. Get a cup of sea salt and another cup of baking soda. Dissolve both in a warm tub and soak yourself inside to banish toxicity and negativity. To avoid taking a full bath, give yourself a simple foot soak. But don't use a whole cup for a foot soak. Reduce it to a quarter of a cup. This is also helpful with grounding.

In the next chapter, we will be looking at how you can consciously use your astral body to project and travel the astral plane without needing to be in the dream state.

Chapter Five: Astral Travel

Whether you want to call it the astral body, energy body, or dream body, the fact is that you have a nonphysical body that can be used to travel the nonphysical realms. Everyone has an astral body. The experience of astral projection or traveling is universal. Different people across different cultures have talked about having an out-of-body experience. There is a widely known story about twins who used astral traveling to see each other after separation at birth.

The subtle body of the energy field is the one that projects into a spirit during lucid or unconscious dreaming. Astral traveling and dreaming are intertwined, and they are both regarded as out-of-body experiences. When cultivated, your astral body can exist separately from the physical body, acting as a matrix for your consciousness. Astral projection is one of the spiritual training mediums for cultivating your subtle energy body.

An out-of-body experience is typically involuntary in many people. You may have even had an OBE without realizing it. There have been reports of near-death experiences where people suddenly found themselves floating or hovering in a nonphysical form near their hospital rooms. At the same time, their medical doctors worked on saving their lives. OBEs are typically triggered by trauma, illness and water, food, and sleep deprivation.

Unlike science-recognized OBEs, astral projection is an intentional esoteric practice. By this, I mean it is something you do with the awareness of your consciousness. So, you can simply call astral projection an intentional out-of-body experience. When you astral project, your astral body transcends your physical body. You are basically in a dreamlike state while being fully conscious of your actions and decisions. This is achievable through self-hypnosis and meditation. In your astral state, you can travel through time, space, and dimensions. This might sound like something out of a superhero movie. It happens with people working on connecting deeper with the Divine. Worldwide, astral projection is recognized as a way of deepening your spiritual practices.

Astral traveling is one way you can explore different realms across the universe to strengthen your connection with the source of cosmic energy. The more you travel the astral plane, the more you will probably meet higher-dimensional beings to help you achieve your spiritual and personal goals. Note that the astral dimension is home to many otherworldly beings that could be high-vibrational or low-vibrational.

Learning astral projection and travel is not always as easy as you see in the movies. There is no definitive guide to astral travel. There is no one-size-fits-all guide that everyone can use to learn astral travel. What works for one person may not work for you. Even when it works, it may not work as quickly as it did for the other person. Everyone is unique, and so are their experiences with astral travel.

This does not negate that there are basics that anyone can use to travel the astral plane in their astral body. Before you get the spiritual passport and begin your journey, you have to master these basics. As you should know already, consistent practice is the key to mastering anything in esoterism.

Being a beginner, first master the art of meditating without snoozing or falling to sleep. Before you even project your astral body, start the daily practice of meditating for at least 5 minutes. By doing this, you will learn to calm and focus your mind. Projecting for the first time can be alarming for most people. But being in a state of calm and focus makes it less alarming for everybody. If you can't seem to find your Zen on your own, use crystals discussed in an earlier chapter to meditate.

After mastering the art of entering a calm state with meditation, you might want to learn self-hypnosis. The purpose of this is to help you learn how to enter an even deeper trance-like state. The more it feels like you are in a trance, the better your chances of projecting your astral body and possibly exploring the nonphysical dimensions. Self-hypnosis is similar to meditation, but it makes the astral plane more accessible so you can connect with others. The main difference between meditation and self-hypnosis for astral projection is that self-hypnosis requires you to set an intention and a specific goal. For instance, your intention for channeling your astral body might be to talk to your spirit guide on the astral plane.

Lucid dreaming is another technique you can use for astral projection. Since it is a way of tuning in with your consciousness in a controlled and intentional way, it helps astral traveling. Once you have learned how to put yourself in the trance-like state required for projection, the next thing to do is to tune in with your astral body and transcend beyond the physical.

Before attempting to travel, it helps to master projection first. During meditation or self-hypnosis, try to see your spirit emerging out of the material form. Once you master this, progress to turning around and looking at your physical body. Remember that this is not something that will happen overnight. To be successful, you have to keep practicing. It might take you many meditative sessions before you can even lift your astral form from your material form. Do not let this discourage you.

Once you feel comfortable being in your astral body, you can access and explore the astral realm. You can begin your astral travels if you don't want to travel on the astral plane, no problem. Your astral form allows you to do much more than that. In your astral form, you can explore the limitless space beyond the material world.

If you are wondering what you stand to gain from learning astral projection, there are many benefits. First, your astral form can be used to travel to the Akashic Records location. This is where you can find all the information about your past lives and selves. You may also find information about your future. The Akashic Records is home to infinite knowledge. By accessing the records, you can use whatever information you retrieve to improve your life and accelerate your personal development.

Another benefit of astral projection is that it helps with physical and spiritual healing. Remember I said that the energy body is the blueprint of your material form. I also said that whatever happens in the physical body starts in the energy field first. When you are in your astral form, you have direct access to your aura or energy field. In this form, you can examine your auric field for any blockages or building illnesses. If a disease forms in one of your auric layers, you can tell from examination in your spirit form. You cannot only examine and discover any developing illness or disease, but you can also treat and heal your auric layers before the disease manifests in your material body.

That is not all. Suppose an illness or disease manifests in your physical body before you even realize it. There, you can enter your astral form to heal it with energy. Astral projection can help you explore your past lives, accelerate your personal and spiritual development journey, and heal yourself of disease and illnesses.

Perhaps, the most important benefit of astral projection is that it allows you to connect and communicate with your spirit guides in astral forms. This means you can see and speak with your guides. That is a rare opportunity for you to seek guidance and direction on anything bothering you.

On the astral plane, you don't just find spirit guides. You can also find the spirits of your deceased loved ones. So, if you have loved ones you would like to meet and possibly ask questions, visiting the astral plane is a way to do that. I could go on and on about the benefits of astral projection, but I am sure you understand the drift now.

Now that you know what astral projection and traveling are and what they involve, how do you practice both to reap the benefits we have just discussed?

There are many techniques you can learn to start astral projection. We have as many as dozens. But know that not all of these works as effectively as they should. Yet, two approaches are peculiar to all of these techniques.

The first is to seduce your body into sleep while your mind is wide awake. This approach is tricky because your mind always wants to do what your body is doing. This approach aims to gradually seduce your body into deeper and deeper relaxation levels without the mind slipping into unconsciousness. The second approach involves allowing your body to enter the sleep state and then rolling your dream body out of your material form.

Ancient yogis used to tie two frogs together right before entering the sleep state. The tied frogs would relentlessly cloak as the yogi sleeps. The yogis used the sound to help their awareness/mind stay alert even as the body drifts into sleep. Eventually, they would enter a lucid dream state, or the astral form leaves the body.

Most of the astral projection techniques follow these approaches. Below, I will be explaining the most effective exercises for astral projection and how you can use them.

The Monroe Institute Technique

This technique was developed by Bob Monroe, a leading researcher in the field of human consciousness. It is recorded in his body of work, "Journeys Out of the Body." Monroe provides a detailed and step-by-step outline of how one can astral project. The technique is one that Monroe personally used for astral travels. In just seven steps, you can use this to project yourself astrally.

Step 1: Meditation State

Do a quick meditation exercise to induce a relaxed state physically and mentally. Relaxing your body and mind is the foundation of astral projection. You may also do a quick breathing exercise to put yourself in a relaxed state.

Step 2: Hypnagogic State

Put yourself in a hypnagogic state. In other words, allow yourself to enter a half-sleep state where you are neither asleep nor awake. You can do this by holding a forearm up while the upper arm rests on the ground or bed. As sleep is induced, your arm will fall, awakening you again and again. With consistent practice, you will eventually learn to enter the hypnagogic state without using your arm.

Another way you can enter this state is by choosing an object on which to focus. When other images start entering your head besides the one you are focused on, you have successfully induced the half-sleep state. Passively observe the images to help you maintain the near-sleep state.

Step 3: Near Sleep

Deepen the near-sleep state. Do this by clearing your mind and watching your field of vision via closed eyes. Don't do anything else for a while. Then, look through the blackness in front of your closed eyelids. You should start noticing light patterns. These have nothing to do with the process because they are merely neural discharges from your eyes. So, ignore them until they disappear from your vision.

When this happens, it means you have entered a deeper state of relaxation. From that point, you will enter a state where you have no awareness of physical sensations in your body. You may feel like you are in a void where your thoughts are the only source of stimulation. The point of this step is to prioritize mental sensations over physical sensations. If you can still feel physical stimulation, it means you haven't entered the desired state yet.

Step 4: State of Vibration

Induce a state of vibration where you become alert to vibrations around you. When you are in a state of deep alertness, vibrations become more heightened. This is considered the most critical step in this technique, and it can make or mar your attempt at astral projection. Vibrations may feel like mild tingling around your body. They also are more intense, making you feel like jolts of electricity are being shot through your body. In essence, this is your astral body trying to unroll from the material one.

Before you enter the vibrational state, make sure you don't have any jewelry on. Take off any item that has direct contact with your skin. Make sure that the room is dark to where you can't see the light through your eyelids. But don't shut out every source of light. Lie on the floor with your head pointed toward the north. Get rid of all clothing but leave yourself covered, so you feel warmer than usual. The warmth should feel a little uncomfortable for you. Make sure you are in a room where no one will disturb or interrupt you. If possible, lock the door from intruders.

Step 5: Regulate the Vibrational State

Control your vibrational state by mentally pushing the vibrations into your head. From there, allow them to travel down to your toes. Feel the surge as they pass through your whole body, and you produce vibrational waves from top to bottom. You should produce a wave effect.

To do this, focus on the vibrations in your body. Envision a wave of vibrations coming out of your head and direct it down the rest of your body. Repeat this step until you have mastered the art of producing the waves on command. Once you master this, it means you have reached the point where you can exit your body.

Step 6: Partial Separation

At this stage, what you need is thought control. You must focus your mind on the idea that you are exiting your body. Do not allow your mind to stray to anything else. Wandering thoughts might end with losing control of your current state. When you are in the vibrational state, you can begin partial separation by first attempting to release one part of your astral form. This could be one of your feet or hands.

You may lift a limb until you feel it touch a familiar surface or object. Then, you may push your limb through the surface or object. After this, return the limb into the physical form. If you do this successfully, reduce the vibrations across your body until you are no longer in that state. End the session and lie down quietly until you are sure you are back to your usual self.

Doing a partial separation first prepares you for the full separation.

Step 7: A Full Separation from the Physical Body

Detach completely from your material form. You can do this in two ways. One way is to ease out of the physical body gently. Doing this requires you to mentally visualize yourself getting lighter and lighter once you have entered the vibrational state. Imagine how you would feel were you floating upward. Let this thought remain in your mind as you remain in a vibrational state. Allow no other extraneous thoughts to chase it away from your mind. At that moment, you will naturally have an out-of-body experience.

The second way is to roll out of your body. This is called the rotation or rollout technique. When you are in the vibrational state, mentally visualize yourself rolling out of your material body in the same way you turn over in bed. Be sure not to do this physically—virtually rollover out of your physical form into the astral form. You will find yourself next to the physical body, which is now lying motionless. Visualize yourself floating upward, and you should feel as you begin to float.

Congratulations, you have successfully experienced astral projection. Now that you are in your astral form, you can do whatever you want. Explore the astral plane or go see your favorite celebrity in your astral form. There are no limits to where you can explore in your astral state.

Lucid Dreams

As I mentioned, inducing a lucid dreaming state is another way to enter your astral form and travel the astral plane. Lucid dreaming itself has many techniques that can be used for this purpose. Some are engineered to train you to awaken while having a lucid dream. Others help the mind lucid while the body enters the sleep state.

The moment you enter the dream state, you attain lucidity. You can train yourself to lucid dream with repetition. One method of doing this is to ask yourself multiple times a day for weeks, "Am I in a dream?" or "Is this a dream?" This question becomes repetitive, causing it to become stuck in the part of your mind where you store songs and jingles. It becomes a habit that starts repeating itself. Eventually, the mind will ask you this during an actual dream. If you answer, "Yes, this is a dream," you will automatically attain lucidity.

REM (rapid eye movement) sleep is your best chance to become lucid while already in a dream state. The REM stage occurs in the first two hours after you fall asleep. It also happens in the last two hours before you wake up. Waking up and returning to sleep during the night is one way you can increase your REM sleep timeframe. Using this sleep/wake technique, you can set the alarm to help you wake at intervals during nighttime. Then, you return to sleep, intending to keep your mind awake. If you wake up during a dream, go back to sleep instantly – try to go back to the dream with a lucid mind.

Once you become confident in your ability to astral project, you can start moving through the astral plane. With each successful attempt, the astral state becomes more accessible for you.

Whenever you visit the astral plane, you will meet different energy beings. Not all of these beings are good. Some may be there to suck energy from you. To avoid them, it is best to set an intention before you enter the astral plane. Have a specific goal in mind. For example, you can set an intention to see a loved one that passed on recently. Other intentions you can set include seeing your spirit guides, visiting a memory from the past, seeing into the future, or finding answers to questions about your spiritual development. Intention can be set before or after your astral project. Once you have connected with your astral self, you can consciously send yourself to a specific place on the astral dimension.

After every successful projection and travel, use the previous chapter's energy cleansing techniques to get rid of any unwanted energy you might have picked up while on the astral plane.

As someone new to astral traveling, you may find you can't enter the astral realm as easily as described. This is normal. You may also not reach your set destination on the first few tries. But don't fret – the more practice you put in, the stronger your astral traveling skills will become.

Apart from astral traveling, what is another psychic ability you can work on developing? Find out in the next chapter.

Chapter Six: Begin Your Mediumship

Mediumship is the psychic practice that involves bringing information from the spirit world to the physical world. A medium is anybody with the ability to do this. This psychic ability is called mediumship because the psychic or medium essentially acts as a middleman, a vessel through which spirits can get messages across to people here on earth. Although you may have seen in the movies that mediums are people who use powerful magic, this is not right.

Everyone, including you, is born with the ability to be a medium. As long as you have a soul with psychic senses, you have the inherent gift. What matters is whether you let it keep lying dormant or you work on honing the ability so it can benefit you and the people around you. Any psychic ability can be made stronger with practice.

Think of your psychic abilities as your body's muscles. When you go to the gym to work on your muscles, the biceps will bulge and come out. This makes you stronger. This is the same with the psychic sense associated with your psychic abilities. You may not realize it, but they are inside you. If you work on them, they too will start to show.

From an early age, you might have had one or more experiences with spirits. I remember seeing my first spirit when I was still at the tender age of 6. Sometimes, your ability to see, hear, and interact with spirit may manifest itself. At other times, a traumatic experience such as losing a loved one might be the key to opening the pathway to that ability. This usually happens because the passed loved one has an important message to get across to you or someone else they knew during their life. If your primary psychic sense is clairsentience, mediumship comes more easily.

If you feel like you are getting signs from someone on the other side, acknowledge and let them know that you are receiving their signs. Acknowledging them means you are more likely to receive more signs. Then, you can keep conversing with them. Sometimes, the spirits may visit instead of sending signs.

Beginning your mediumship is one of the most remarkable things you can experience as a psychic. The first time you connect with the spirit world will feel surreal and magical. You will find yourself filled with a feeling of peace and calm you have possibly never felt before. This goes beyond inner peace. It reflects physically as a sensation of pure love, peace, and acceptance.

Based on movies we watched while growing up, we have been conditioned to believe that ghosts (spirits) are generally malevolent spirits looking to hurt us. In reality, they are the spirits of people we knew while alive, so how could they possibly want to hurt us? You have absolutely no reason to fear spirits. They cannot physically do anything to you. The only thing they can do is inspire weird vibes and feelings in you. Other than that, they are harmless, which is a good thing.

How are you able to communicate with spirits?

Spirits are beings that haven't been able to move on to the other side after their death. Therefore, they are still operating in the same element as you, the Earth element. Due to this, you can communicate with them. Even after death, our spirits or souls live on. The body may die, but the soul doesn't, which is why many people have past lives. When some people die, their spirits remain tethered to the earth due to something meaningful. This leaves them stuck on the astral plane, where they can easily come down to earth. Some require mediums to deal with whatever is keeping them in the earth element.

If you wonder why you would ever need to communicate with spirits, know there are various reasons. One of the basic things you must understand as a medium is that the spirit world is full of guides that can benefit you immensely if you pay attention to their signs. Ghosts are not the only spirits. Mediumship goes beyond communicating with ghosts. Being a medium means you can communicate with just about any spirit, including the highest vibrational ones. You can learn a lot from your connection to spirits and the spirit world. That special connection can assist you in different stages of your life.

The good thing about mediumship is that you can learn it all on your own. However, there are a few things I always advise people just beginning their mediumship.

First, don't start your mediumship by using tools such as a pendulum or Ouija board. If you don't train yourself to connect without tools first, your abilities may depend on the tools. Setting that precedence is dangerous for your development in practice. But what makes it dangerous is these tools are used to open up a portal to spirits. This means that any spirit, not just the one you want to communicate with, can come through that portal.

Yes, the spirits cannot physically harm or hurt you. The problem is that you will have a lot of ghosts hanging around you with stuck energy.

Second, be careful not to lose your focus. Staying focused is an essential tool for any psychic medium. You have to be specific and focused when channeling any spirit. The process requires a lot of concentration because opening up a portal to the spirit world drains you of energy. It is a whole lot of work. If you don't focus on the spirit you want to connect with, you may end up channeling another spirit that will be of no help to you. After using a lot of energy, you may find it hard to refocus and invoke the spirit you want.

Third, listen to your guts. Listening to intuition rarely fails mediums. Sometimes, the spirits communicate with you through your guts. If your spirit guide wants you to know something urgent, you may feel a strong sensation in your gut. It's like when you meet a new person, and you feel a strong compulsion to exchange your contact details with them even though you usually wouldn't do that. That is your spirit guide prompting you through your gut feelings.

To hear what your guts have to say, you, of course, need to quiet your mind. Therefore, my fourth piece of advice is that you quiet your mind at all times. You can't hear spirits when there is a lot of noise and chatter in your mind. There are different ways you can quiet your mind. Discover whichever works best for you. Some things you can do this effect include walking in nature, practicing deep breathing, turning your phone off, and of course, meditating. Once you achieve a quiet mind, your spirit guides can meet you to offer help and guidance.

Pay attention to your dreams because sometimes, spirits send messages through the dream portal. Communication via dreams is a real thing. It is especially a thing with spirits who are still in the early stage of their passing. If they have successfully crossed over to the other side, the only way they can contact you is through dreams. Most of the time, they appear in your dream to let you know they are in a good place. Or they may appear to warn you of something that is yet to happen.

Finally, make writing a vital part of your mediumship journey. Some writing meditations can help you communicate with spirits. It is easy.

- Light a white candle. Sit comfortably. Close your eyes and breathe in deeply. Then, breathe out. Do this for some seconds.

- Say out loud that you would like to connect to the higher vibrational beings available to you as guides.

- Next, as a question, breathe in and out deeply and allow your hands to relax loosely. Then, write down whatever the spirits say to you. They often talk fast, so don't be alarmed if you are writing just as fast.

Follow all these tips, and you will have no trouble connecting with the spirit world. Still, it is possible to have trouble establishing a connection. Don't stress about it. Remember that the whole thing is a process, and you won't necessarily make progress on the first few tries. Just because you want to connect with them instantly does not mean you will. You might take years to perfect this practice.

How to Tune Into the Spirit World

Tuning in with the spirit world is relatively easy. It all depends on how long you have been engaging in psychic activities. Suppose you have been engaging your psychic senses and sharpening your intuition. In that case, it won't be as hard as it would be for someone new to the whole thing.

Establishing a connection with the spirit world is akin to tuning in to a specific radiofrequency. When you tune in to the spirit, you are raising your vibrational energy. But Spirits lower their vibrational frequency so you can connect with them. Both of you then meet in the middle.

There are three important rules you must never forget whenever you want to tune into the spirit world.

1. Your journey to the spirit world is unique to you. You must respect and honor this.

2. Always say what you encounter. You have no reason to hide from whatever you see when you connect to the spirit world. If you do hide, you will likely lose valuable information that could give meaning to your journey.

3. Trust whatever comes to you first as you open up the portal to the spirit world. The first thing you see is likely to be the most accurate information.

Below are five steps to tune into the spirit world.

• **Set an Intention:** You need to say out loud that you would like to open up the spirit portal to communicate and receive messages from a specific spirit in the spirit world. Clarify whether you are connecting for a personal purpose or on behalf of another person. The Universe hears as you state your intention out loud, and so do the spirits in the spirit world.

• **Meditate:** A simple meditation or breathing exercise to quieten your mind is a necessary step. Using your daily meditation technique, get your logical brain to quieten down. This is crucial for a swift and clear connection with spirits.

• **Listen:** Listen attentively for any sign, symbol, or message from the spirit world. The message may come in the form of songs, images, noise, or anything else. Sometimes, you may not even receive the message immediately. So, you have to pay attention to the events that happen throughout your day. Any coincidence that happens may not be a coincidence.

• **Draw Up a Reading Screen:** If you are a clairvoyant, a reading screen is necessary to receive the spirit's message. The screen is where you will find whatever information spirit has for you in the form of images, pictures, and symbols. Helped by your third eye, visualize a giant movie screen in front of you. Attach a grounding cord to the screen and root it to the core of the earth. Now, ask a question or ask to receive a message from spirit. Be careful not to use a demanding tone. Don't be impatient – let the answer come to you.

As you practice, you will find it easier to connect with the spirit portal. To further help you create a strong connection, here are some tips.

• Don't smudge with sage right before you connect with a spirit. Sage is an ancient herb often used to ward away ghosts and spirits. Using it before channeling a spirit confuses the spirit because they read that as you tell them to leave your space.

• Set up multiple conductors. Spirits sometimes need conduits to deliver their messages properly. Before you attempt to contact a spirit, set up different conductors that can be used for communication. Light a candle, put some water in a glass, and use incense to add scent to the room. You may also install audio and video recording devices in the room. They are effective conductors that can help with transmission from the spirit world to the human world.

Connecting with the spirit world is an opportunity for you to explore the differences between the physical plane and the realm of the dead. Use that opportunity wisely. As you advance your mediumship journey, you can finally introduce the Ouija board and pendulums into your practice as a psychic medium.

Chapter Seven: Unlock Telepathy

Suppose someone was to ask you to say the first thing that comes to mind when the word "communication" is mentioned. In that case, you'd mention things such as speaking, writing, and even chatting before you mention telepathy. Yet, telepathy is one of the best ways of communicating.

Telepathy simply means communication through the mind. Your mind is much more powerful than you even realize. Yes, science says that the mind is a powerful entity. Still, even science has yet to unravel the extent of the power of the mind. Most of us don't even understand how awesome this is.

F. W. H. Myers coined the term "telepathy" in 1882. Myers was a British researcher interested in psychical practices. When he coined this term, he was researching the possibility of "thought transference." Simply put, thought transference was firstly defined as a phenomenon in which two people's thoughts coincide, requiring a causal explanation. Later, it was defined as "a transmission of thought independently of the recognized channels of sense."

From this definition, you can tell everything that telepathy entails. Telepathy is a psychic ability that allows you to communicate with people without using known communication channels. The communication takes place through your mind. If you are a fan of mystical superhero movies, you have likely seen a depiction of telepathy before. It usually involves two or more people talking to each other inside their heads. But the movie depiction of telepathy, as with anything psychic, is somewhat exaggerated. So, don't read this chapter hoping to become Dr. Strange by the time you get to the end.

Telepathy is not a new psychic ability. It has been recorded in different cultures around the globe for hundreds of years. Some sources even say it has been around for as long as five thousand years. Some say it has been around for much longer.

You might feel like this is one psychic ability that is unlikely for you, but you do have the ability. As long as you have psychic senses and portals that allow you to access other psychic abilities, telepathy is just another ability waiting to be accessed. Everyone has the natural, inborn power to communicate through consciousness.

There are four ways telepathy can be used. The first is for reading. Reading means hearing the thoughts running through another person's mind. The second way is for communicating, which is when you interact with another person without using words. The third way is via impressing. This is when you plant a thought, word, or image into the mind of another. Last, you can use telepathy to control when you use it to influence someone else's actions.

Since your consciousness is central to the practice of telepathy, aligning your consciousness with that of another person is the key to communicating telepathically. However, that is not the only way. Energy is also vital to telepathic communication. Every single person has an inherent ability to transmit frequencies through their vibrating energy. When you can align your vibrational frequency with that of another person, you no longer need to communicate with them through the known channels or senses. Aligning your vibrational frequencies establishes a direct link for sending and receiving telepathic messages.

Twin telepathy is one of the most common forms of twin telepathy. Twins are believed to have the "special" ability to interact without speaking or using verbal cues. Suppose you have ever been around any pair of twins. In that case, you might have noticed them finishing each other's sentences or immediately sensing any negative emotion or affect. Many people believe in twin telepathy, yet they don't believe in telepathy among individuals.

Scientific studies have been conducted on twin telepathy. But most of these studies have been based on personal accounts and experiences of some people.

Telepathy comes easily to twins, even when they aren't into esoteric practices because they share the same consciousness grids. They are born on the same vibrational frequency, so they need not struggle to connect telepathically. They already operate on the same wavelength. Also, being born together means that the blueprint for their consciousness grid is similar, almost to where you can't differentiate one from the other without intense scrutiny.

Twin telepathy is proof that telepathy is indeed real and possible. But what are the signs to watch out for should you want to identify telepathy in a person?

You have likely had different telepathic experiences while growing up. At the moment, you may have passed them off as coincidences, but that was your ability showing itself. If you have ever completed someone else's sentences for them, you have had a telepathic experience. Some of the telepathic experiences may have seemed trivial to you at the time. For instance, you might have sensed that your best friend in another state isn't feeling great, called them, and found they weren't. Many people have had several instances like this, but there is a tendency to think of them as coincidences. Some people think of the experiences relative to luck.

A strong intuition always accompanies telepathic ability. The two are not mutually inclusive. If you are telepathic, you are intuitive. To unlock this gift, you have to embrace and trust your intuition. Without trusting your guts, you cannot connect efficiently with other people's vibrations. This makes telepathic communication unattainable.

Another thing about telepathy is that it often occurs when you are in a dream state. Your sleep time is the period where your brain waves at the highest frequency, allowing for a flood of data into your mind. You may believe that time is linear, but it is not. Remember that I said something about the Akashic records and how they contain a collection of every event you have experienced in your past lives. Every thought, feeling, word, and intent from your past, present, and future is contained in the Akashic Records. Therefore, when you dream of something, it is because that thing is happening in real-time in another timeline and dimension.

As a psychic, if you often get intense sensations in the middle of your forehead, that is your third eye itching to unlock your telepathic doorway. Of course, this could also be a sign of another psychic ability. Or it could be a sign of all the psychic abilities lying dormant in your psychic portals. Don't be afraid if you get more of this sensation when you start practicing telepathic techniques. They will subside subsequently.

Telepathy is interconnected with empathy. If you are highly empathetic, then you more than likely have this ability. As you know, empathy involves experiencing other people's feelings almost as real as they experience them. On the other hand, telepathy is linked to thoughts. You can read other people's thoughts inside their heads. If you are clairsentient, both of these abilities are intertwined for you. Being empathetic and telepathic means that your ability goes beyond just thoughts. It extends to feelings as well. I believe that one cannot be a true telepath without empathy.

If you always know when being lied to, that is another pointer to telepathy. Telepaths can sense when the information they are receiving isn't accurate. Usually, you don't even need to look inside someone's head to realize it. You just find you can sense what is going on in their head.

After developing your latent telepathy gifts, you will begin to pick up on thoughts. This is when your clairaudience sense comes to play. You may find you can hear people's thoughts out loud in your head. Sometimes, claircognizance is the psychic sense that comes to the forefront. You start 'knowing' people's thoughts. But the psychic sense involved does not matter. What does matter is that you have access to people's unspoken or unexpressed thoughts.

It does not stop at that. The more practice you put in, the more your ability will advance. You will get to where you can send and receive long-distance messages. You will also be able to plant thoughts, ideas, and messages into others' minds. Naturally, getting to this point requires months or years of practice, depending on how in-tune you are with your psychic side.

Exercises to Develop Telepathic Abilities

A solid meditation routine and practice is, unsurprisingly, the first thing you must put into practice if you want to develop your telepathic skills. You cannot learn telepathy if your mind is always in a cluttered state. Meditation is for getting rid of any clutter in your mind so you can receive psychic messages. A clear, free, and focused mind is your best chance at linking your consciousness with that of other people.

When you first start practicing, observe, and try to determine your strength. Are you a better sender or receiver? I make a better receiver. Not that one is better than the other, but just as you have a stronger inclination toward one psychic sense, you are also naturally inclined to send or receive more. It helps to practice with what you are better at. Then, you can progress to the opposite once you have learned it to a comfortable level.

An even easier way of determining your preference is to think about the question below.

Are you more likely to call a friend and have them tell you they were just thinking about you? Or are you more likely to think of a friend and unexpectedly receive a call from them?

If you answer yes to the first question, it means you will make a better receiver. But answering yes to the second question tilts you towards a sender.

When you have determined this, you can practice based on your strong suit. If you are naturally inclined towards receiving, start practicing how to receive telepathic messages. In your interactions and conversations with others, put in a deliberate effort to pick up on what they are not saying out loud. Note it does not always come across as words; you might pick up on it in the form of feelings. Try practicing with anyone with which you are comfortable. Tell them to think of something and see if you can determine what it is. Be sure not to do this with a skeptic, as this may cause a vibrational block.

If you tilt more strongly towards sending, practice sending people messages via extrasensory perception. An excellent way of practicing is to meet someone on the street and say "hello" to them normally. But in your mind, think "goodbye" instead. Watch their facial expression as you say and think of two completely different things. If they show any sign of surprise or confusion, it means they received your message. They likely will say nothing to you unless they are familiar with esoteric practices. Still, their nonverbal reaction will be your clue.

Below are two effective exercises for practicing sending and receiving telepathic messages.

Exercise 1: Tarot Card Technique

To use this technique, you need a willing partner and a deck of tarot cards. You may even use a standard playing deck or an oracle deck if you don't have tarot cards.

- Tell your partner to sit in a specific part of the location far from you. It should be in such a position you can't see each other.

- As the sender or transmitter, draw four cards from the deck and place them on a flat surface. Make sure that they are facing down.

- Next, flip one card over. Relax your mind and concentrate on the card's image, keeping your focus solely on that image. Send the mental image to your partner, who is the receiver. Set the intention for this.

- Your practice partner's job is to try to receive and accept the image you sent and then send it back to you.

- If you want, you can switch positions and act as the receiver instead of the sender.

Trust your gut, and don't second guess yourself.

Exercise 2: Emotion-Induced Technique

This exercise is to be practiced with someone with whom you already have an established emotional connection. Sending and receiving telepathic messages is much easier when the other party is someone you have an intimate relationship with. This is because the vibrational frequencies are more potent this way. This exercise can be practiced over a long distance, depending on how strong your emotional connection is. The stronger it is, the more they are likely to receive your message regardless of distance.

- Meditate to put yourself in a relaxed and receptive mental state. You shouldn't feel like you are forcing the relaxed state. It should feel as natural as it feels when you have leisure time.

- Make sure that your recipient is also in a relaxed state of mind. If not, they won't be able to receive any message you send. Both of you must enter a receptive and relaxed state before you begin.

- Determine what you want to send and visualize the other person receiving it. With your eyes closed, picture the other person as clearly as you can. Imagine exactly what they are doing at that moment. You may imagine them sitting in front of you. Add all the details that matter, such as the skin tone, eye color, height, weight, hair length, and sitting position. If you are doing it over a distance, look at a picture of them before you start visualizing.

- Build a mental image and visualize it, sending it to the receiver.

Start this technique with a simple word or image. Sticking with something simple helps. For example, you can imagine a banana. Visualize a banana in front of your mind's eye. Focus all your thoughts on the banana and imagine the taste and feel of it as you bite. Don't send the message until you have formed a clear mental image of what you want to send.

Whichever technique you use, be sure to ask your practice partner what they received. This will allow you to know if they did receive your message. If you aren't successful at first, don't let that discourage you. The key to unlocking telepathic skills is to keep practicing until you achieve them. Remember to use a different word, thought, or image for each practice session. As you progress, you can use telepathy to control or influence people's behavior.

Chapter Eight: Types of Divination

Divination is perhaps the most complex and comprehensive psychic ability. It is the art of finding "hidden" knowledge about the future to interpret it. This is made possible through intuition, divining tools, and the help of Divine power. It is regarded as a branch of magic, but it is also a psychic skill. It's used to foretell the future and determine the significance of an event, supernatural or otherwise. You could say that divination is a way of unraveling destiny.

The art of divination operates on the idea that everything in the universe is connected through energy. We are all connected on an energetic level. Therefore, the whole universe is similar to a massive energy grid that links all of our energy imprints. Once you understand this, it means you can access information from pretty much everything with energy. You need only to find a connector that can link you to the infinite interconnecting grid. Then, you can ask questions and seek answers infinitely.

Many divination practitioners access the infinite energy grid by using divination tools that range from runes, stones, and tarot cards to shells, sticks, and leaves. As the diviner, you can connect to your divination tools to obtain information from the grid and relay them back to yourself or another person through the tool. How clear the information you obtain is depends on your experience, conviction, and ability to clear your mind to ensure clarity when receiving your answers.

Any information that comes from the universal energy grid is a hundred percent accurate. However, it may become distorted or be interpreted inaccurately by the diviner.

Whether you want to use divination for just yourself or you would like to help other people along the way, you can learn different things. Divination can help you determine what is coming your way and when it is coming. It can also guide you when making a decision that could affect your life. Through divining, you get a symbolic message you can only interpret. Usually, a diviner is inspired via a thought, feeling, idea, or memory, then metamorphoses into an answer.

Answers gotten through divination can be subjective. You need real skills to be objective in your interpretation of the information you receive. Otherwise, you may allow your thoughts, feelings, or beliefs to get in the way. A diviner must learn to be objective, nonjudgmental, and devoid of agenda. This is the only way to keep yourself out of the way of the varying energy signatures sent to you from the cosmic wide web.

It is natural for you to have some form of doubt when you first start your divination practice. After all, divination is much more complicated than other psychic practices such as telepathy, mediumship, astral traveling, etc. But you must learn to let go of doubt. Otherwise, it will disturb the clarity of the information. If you have ever been in any divining circle, you have probably heard people say, "Give the message exactly as you receive it." This is to avoid distorting the message.

Always accept the first thing that comes to your mind when you use divination to access the cosmic energy grid. Do not be tempted to change the nuance or nature of what you receive. If you do this, you are bound to let your convictions influence the message's meaning. Avoid adding any irrelevant or unrelated piece of information or detail to the mix.

Generally, there are several methods of divination. You can't practice all these methods. But you can find one or two that appeal to you and master them. Note that none of the methods is necessarily better than the other. Some people believe that people who use tarot for divination have less talent than people who don't. This is not right.

One reason divination has varying methods is to choose whichever appeals to them the most. If Tarot divination is what you find comfortable, don't be afraid to master it. The divination method you use does not reduce or limit the quality of information you can obtain from the energy grid.

Here, I will be discussing six methods of divination. Since we have discussed Tarots, Pendulums, Runes, and Crystals in an earlier chapter, I won't focus on these. Everything discussed in Chapter three about the use of these psychic tools can be applied to the practice of divination. There is little to no difference since, in the end, the point is to receive psychic messages from a higher source.

The six methods of divination you will be learning are:

- Scrying
- Tea leaves reading
- Sand divination
- Pyromancy
- Osteomancy
- Numerology
- Automatic Writing

One by one, let's expatiate on what these divination methods entail. In this chapter, I will explain each method briefly just to know the basics. The next chapter will go into details on how you can practice some methods.

Scrying

Scrying is the divination method that involves gazing into water, fire, or crystals. There is also the full-moon scrying, which encompasses the practice of gazing into the full moon whenever there is one. It is one of the oldest methods of divination and has been around for hundreds of years. Some people call it the reflection divination. Throughout history, there have been stories of different people across different cultures staring into mirrors, water, oil, metals, and crystals to read the reflection. The practice of crystal ball reading originated from scrying.

Tea Leaves Reading

The art of reading tea leaves has been a thing since the 17th century. The technical term is tasseomancy. It has been around for centuries, even before the Dutch brought China tea to Europe. Tasseomancy is a mix of French and Greek. "Tasse" is the French word, and it stands for "cup"; "manteia" is Greek, and it stands for prophecy. So, perhaps the literal translation of tasseomancy is the art of foretelling the future from a cup. Tea isn't the only thing you can use for tasseomancy practice. You may also use wine sediment or coffee grounds. You can tailor your tasseomancy practice to fit your own needs and tastes.

Sand Divination

Also called geomancy, sand divination is a divination practice that involves reading the shapes of stones and sand for divining purposes. This practice is common with Muslim communities, especially in the Middle East. Geomancy is regarded as one of the most beautiful art forms. Like any other divination form, those who practice sand divination believe in the presence of vital energy in the sand. The "vital energy" in this context is the aura.

Pyromancy

Many people believe that pyromancy is the oldest divination form. For many centuries, the practice of pyromancy was banned in Europe, alongside hydromancy and necromancy. However, fire is just too fascinating and intriguing to leave alone. Pyromancy is the divining art of gazing into a fire to obtain psychic messages. If you are a fan of the TV show, Game of Thrones, then you should know that the red lady Melissandre was a pyromancy practitioner. Dancing around a fire can help you answer some of the most challenging questions in life.

Osteomancy

Osteomancy is also called bone divination, and is the art of reading bone for divine information. Osteomancy has been a widespread practice across cultures for thousands of years. Although it has varying applicable techniques, the goal is the same thing – to read messages displayed in the bones. This is one method you may not be able to practice because of the rarity of animal bones. But still, knowing about it may be of benefit to you.

Numerology

The basics of numerology are that numbers have substantial spiritual significance. It is believed that some numbers are more potent than others. Also, numbers can be combined to foretell the future and make crucial decisions. And numbers are also connected with planetary movements and shifts.

Automatic Writing

Automatic writing is one of the most known ways to get messages from the spirit world. It is popular among mediums who communicate with ghosts and spirits. It is the same process I described in the chapter about beginning your mediumship. You simply get a pen and paper, relax your mind, and let divine messages flow through you with no conscious effort on your part. Whatever you write down on the paper is channeled from the spirit world.

The next chapter goes more into how you can practice scrying, tea leaves reading, and more of the divination forms discussed in this chapter.

Chapter Nine: Practice Divination

This chapter will focus on discussing the techniques for practicing the divination forms explained in the preceding chapter. So, let's get to it.

Scrying

Scrying has long been a method for ancient people to put their wisdom and intuition to use. Everyone knows that water is a very potent source of vital energy. There is a connection to water that we all feel. There is a reason why we feel so energetic after having a warm or cold bath. Your mind and body are intricately linked to water.

The earth, moon, and sky are all water sources, which means that water plays a part in the lunar cycles. You need a clear sky, a full moon, and a bowl of water to practice scrying. Apart from these, you also need a flat surface, a notepad, and meditative music. The last one is, however, optional.

You may decide to cast a circle or not. That depends on you. Play your meditative music to put you in a relaxed state of mind. Gently sit in front of the flat surface where you have a bowl of water. Close your eyes and feel yourself tuning into the energy of your environment. All of your senses should be alert.

Listen as the wind rustles the tree. Smell the scent of leaves around you. Feel the energy wash over you. Focus on gathering the energy you feel. It comes as a sensation that is there for you to feel when you look for it. Feel your connection to that energy and its Divine source. Remain like this for some minutes until you are ready to scry.

When you are ready, open your eyes gently. Observe your environment. You should feel an extraordinary sense of calm, awareness, and clarity. That is due to the energy to which you are attuned. Look at the bowl of water in front of you. Visualize guidance and wisdom swimming within the water. As you visualize, see the energy swirling around the water. Acknowledge that the water can reveal mysteries to you.

Stare into the water and look at the reflection. Search for patterns, pictures, and symbols. Do not take your gaze away from the water. After a while, you will start to see pictures, words, or symbols forming in the reflection on the water. Random thoughts that don't immediately make sense may pop into your head. Take your notepad and write them down exactly as they come. Write everything down.

You may gaze into the water for as long as you want. Spend up to an hour if you wish, but a few minutes is also enough to get the information you seek. Stop when you feel restless or mundane thoughts flood your mind.

When you are done, check to see you wrote down everything that came to you during scrying, including the thoughts, feelings, and sensations. For the next few days, sit on the information and allow your subconscious mind to ruminate on the meaning until it makes sense. Eventually, you can make sense of it all.

If the message you receive doesn't seem to have anything to do with you, think about your loved ones and friends. Try to determine which of them it applies to.

If you have a natural water source near your home, try scrying with larger bowls of water. This makes messages easier to detect amidst all the energy.

Reading Tea Leaves

Reading tea leaves is one of the most iconic ways to practice divination. This method may not be as popular as some of the other ones, but it is just as effective. Plus, it is relatively straightforward. You may want to get cups that are designed especially for this divination form. Those cups have symbols and patterns inscribed, allowing for a more straightforward interpretation of any message you receive. So, how exactly does one read tea leaves?

First, you will need a cup of tea to begin. The tea has to contain all the leaves, so don't use a strainer when brewing. Using a strainer will get rid of all the leaves, and there will be nothing to read. Your teacup should be light-colored to allow you to see whatever is happening to the leaves inside the cup.

The larger the leaves of the tea, the more accurate your reading will be. So, take note of this when making the tea. Use a loose tea leaf blend, so the leaves don't become too small. Go for blends like Earl Grey because they usually have large leaves. After making the tea, consume it at your own pace.

After this, all you will have left at the bottom of your teacup are leaves. Firmly shake the cup so the leaves can form a pattern. One way to do this is to swirl the cup around in a circle a couple of times. Do it three times to avoid having wet leaves around.

Next, observe the leaves and see if you can see any images in the patterns they form. This is where you start divination. Typically, diviners interpret the images in two ways. The first way is to follow a standard set of symbols passed down from century to century. For example, if you get an image that appears like a dog, it means you have a loyal friend in your corner. An apple represents education or knowledge. You can get material with information on tea leaf symbols and their interpretation. While you may find variations in the interpretations, the meanings are pretty much universal.

The second way is to use your intuition to interpret the leaves' images that appear to you. Concentrate on how the images make you feel and think. The image may be that of a dog, but it may not inspire a positive feeling symbolic of a loyal friend to you. Here, you have to trust your intuition. Intuitive interpretation requires you to trust your instinct.

Multiple images may also appear to you. When this happens, read the images starting from your teacup's handle, and go around clockwise. If the cup has no handle, start from the very top, the farthest away from you.

Don't forget to have your notepad with you as you do the reading. Whenever you practice, keep the notepad handy. This will allow you to go back to the things that appear to you in the teacup.

Numerology

The basis of numerology is the belief that numbers have powerful spiritual and magical significance. In some numerology variants, it is believed that odd numbers are feminine energy numbers. In contrast, even numbers have masculine energy and meaning. Universally, each culture has a different interpretation of what the numbers mean.

In some traditions, the meanings of numbers include:

1: Linked to the cosmic life force that connects everyone in the universe. It is regarded as a source and a grounding number. Using tarot cards, 1 symbolizes a person who takes control of his environment and achieves personal power by taking advantage of the people around him.

2: This symbolized duality and polarity. It is the number of balances. When you think of the number 2, think of yin and yang, light and dark, and other opposites. This number represents one of each thing,

3: In many numerology traditions, 3 is considered the most magical of all the numbers. It is symbolic of the realms of the sky, sea, and land. It also represents your mental, physical, and spiritual needs. Three also symbolizes action and interaction. In other traditions, it is the number for neutrality and passiveness.

4: Connects to all the four elements – fire, earth, water, and air. It also represents the four seasons and the four cardinal directions of the world. It is also a symbol of creativity.

5: Five is the number of spirits. It is symbolic of your five human senses. It is regarded as a symbol of chaos, struggle, and conflict in some traditions.

6: Represents solar energy. It is a vital source of masculine energy. It represents responsibility and security.

7: Represents lunar energy. It is connected to the moon and femininity. This number is symbolic of intuition and wisdom, representing consciousness and thought-forms.

8: Eight is associated with the planet mercury, which concerns communication and messages. It is an infinity symbol when flipped on its side.

9: Three times three is nine, which makes nine a triply potent number. It is linked with goddess energy. Nine indicates growth and change. Using the tarot represents the completion of a new process.

0: Zero represents nothing. It represents the potential you have to create something new out of nothing. Zero is a sign of the beginning.

Check through tarot divination, pendulum divination, crystal divination, and all the other divination forms we have just discussed, and choose the one you think will work best for you.

Chapter Ten: The Power of Clairvoyance

Clairvoyance is the most popular psychic sense in most psychics. Some of us have clairvoyance as our dominant psychic sense, coupled with another psychic sense. If you remember clearly, we briefly discussed its basics in chapter two. You have already learned that clairvoyance means "clear seeing." It is the psychic ability to see and read energy. Since we have already talked about its meaning and what it entails, this chapter will focus wholly on how you can hone and develop your 6th sense to sharpen your clairvoyance sense.

Clairvoyance is the one psychic sense common to all the psychic abilities we have discussed so far in this book. If you successfully hone this sense, you will find that any psychic ability you want to learn becomes easier when your clairvoyance is awakened. The key to developing your clairvoyance is to awaken your third eye. Therefore, below are six exercises you can use to awaken your third eye and open up the pathway to clairvoyance.

1. Visualization

This is one of the best ways to strengthen your third eye and intuition. There are so many ways you can practice visualization. One of these is flower visualization. Getting started is easy. Buy a flower that looks pretty and smells good. Place the flower before you and observe it for some minutes. After this, close your eyes and picture the flower with as many details as possible. Imagine the shape, size, color, and all other details.

Another visualization exercise is to imagine the number one in your mind's eye. Envision that you see the number one. Make it as big as you want with whatever colors you want. You can even imagine some sprinkle of glitter. Hold this image in your third eye for at least 10 seconds. Next, open your eyes and do a quick breathing exercise. Repeat these steps from number one to two, three, etc., until you get to 10.

2. Talk to Your Spirit Guides

Talking to your spirit guides is another way you can develop your clairvoyance ability. Suppose you interact with your spirit guides regularly. In that case, you can ask them to send you messages in the form of beautiful images. If you have never met your spirit guides, don't fret. Use the meditation technique discussed and call out to your spirit guide to talk to you. Then, wait for their message to appear to you. Don't forget that the message can take different forms. It may come as images, words, thoughts, feelings, or physical sensations.

3. Play Clairvoyant Games

There is a game we used to play when we were younger. The game is called Memory. If you played the game when you were younger, you might remember that you used to place cards face down, flip one over at a time, trying to make a match. This game can sharpen your third eye and increase clairvoyance. Before you flip each card over, use your mind eye to try to "see" which card is which.

Another fun game for clairvoyance is to have someone place ten random objects on your table. Don't stay in the room while the person is setting up the items. Now, close your eyes and visualize each object. Try using your third eye to "see" where each item is located and its color and size. Write down details about each item. Be as specific as possible about the items. When you are done writing, open your eyes. Go to where the items are and see how accurate you were.

You can practice this particular exercise alone. Go to your nearest part, study the environment, then close your eyes and visualize as many details as possible about your surroundings.

4. Practice Aura Reading

Aura is your human energy field, as I have established. It is in the form of lights and colors. Anyone can train themselves to see this energy around all living things. This makes it an excellent exercise for building clairvoyance. To practice seeing auras, you need a practice partner. Ask the person to stand in front of a white-colored wall or any other plain-looking wall. Step back some feet until you reach a point where you can see your partner's head and shoes without looking up or down. Concentrate and look through the person to the wall behind them. Focus and the outline of the aura will start appearing around their head.

5. Journal

Journals are a critical part of any psychic development journey. Before you start your journey, get a journal to record all your spiritual and psychic experiences. Any time you connect with Spirit and your Higher Self or even have a meaningful dream, write everything down. By doing this, you can connect more with your intuition and your clairvoyance sense to make sense of the messages you receive.

6. Awaken Your Third Eye

Open your third eye through third eye chakra meditation. The purpose of the third eye meditation is to help you improve mental clarity, focus the mind, and increase concentration. The meditation is brief and straightforward.

Sit comfortably in a chair. Make your spine upright, and your shoulder relaxed. Your chest should be open. Place your hands on your knees with the palms facing upward. Gently touch your index finger to your thumb. Relax your body from the face to the jaw and belly. Your tongue should rest behind your front teeth, and your eyes should be lightly closed.

Breathe in and out through your nose. Do this deeply and smoothly. With your eyes still closed, look up at the area of your forehead. This is where you have your third eye chakra. Concentrate your gaze on this spot intently. Wait until a bright purple or indigo color appears. Gently take your mind away from thoughts in your mind and maintain your focus on the third eye.

Remain in this position for at least 10 minutes while breathing in and out gently and deeply. After your ten minutes are up, inhale and exhale gently, pull your palms together and bring them both to the front of your heart. Then, end the meditation with these words, "May the Divine grant me the ability to see and perceive the truth clearly on every level." Round up and gently open your eyes before going back to your daily business.

You can do the third eye meditation every day if you want your third eye to open up quickly. However, when you start getting uncomfortable sensations in the spot where your third eye is, stop the meditation, or your third eye will open up completely and become overactive. An overactive third eye does more harm than good to psychics.

When the third eye becomes overactive, you will no longer have control over your thoughts and feelings. You might become susceptible to an influx of psychic messages, all of which will be too much to handle. So, be careful when opening your third eye.

Chapter Eleven: Spiritual Healing: Work with Energy

Energy healing is the psychic and holistic practice of activating your subtle energy bodies to eliminate blocks and create a passage for energy to flow freely. By getting rid of the energy block, your body's innate ability to heal itself of physical, mental, and emotional conditions is activated. In an earlier chapter, I talked about how blockage in the subtle bodies can disrupt energy flow through the body system, resulting in imbalance. This results in illnesses and diseases of the body and mind.

The point of energy healing is to take a holistic approach towards restoring the balance in energy flow through your body, mind, and spirit. Energy healing directly affects the physical, mental, emotional, and spiritual aspects of your wellbeing. Energy healers have mastered the art of using energy to treat various medical conditions, particularly those that concern your mental health.

They do this by using vital energy to determine the root of the disturbance in the energy system. Once they locate the spot of the blockage, the flow of energy is restored. The ill person automatically becomes cured when the flow disruption is fixed. To heal with energy, you first need to master your energy body. Please refer to Chapter Four. Once you have mastered your energy field and astral form, you can use your energy to heal other people's energy systems.

Energy disruption is often caused by an accumulation of physical, mental, and emotional stress. It may also be caused by environmental stress, trauma, and negative belief systems. These are factors that act as blocks to your spiritual and personal growth. They often accumulate and store in your energy field, resulting in decreased functions.

Using energy healing techniques, you can facilitate the healing process to eliminate blocks in your field, repair and restore the balance of the chakras, and more important, repurpose energy around your body so it can return to an optimal state of functioning. From there, the body can gain back its ability to heal itself.

Besides this, energy healing techniques can also help you find and identify problems before they manifest physically as pain or distortion. Learning energy healing opens up your consciousness to whatever part of your body requires or needs healing. Doing this helps bring a sense of harmony, health, and vitality to your life.

There are different energy healing techniques. To become an energy healer, you have to master some of these techniques. Some of the most popular techniques explicitly used to heal energy are Reiki and Acupuncture. Besides these, you also have lesser-known techniques such as Chakra balancing, Spiritual healing, and Crystal Healing. The subsequent chapter focuses on crystal healing practice, so I won't be touching on that here. Remember that I have also explained chakra balancing in a previous chapter. Therefore, we won't be talking about that.

Reiki Healing

Reiki was created over a hundred years ago by Mikao Usui, a Japanese Buddhist. It is a healing therapy founded on the principle we are all guided by an invisible life force (Energy) that controls our physical, emotional, and mental wellbeing. When this life force flows freely without restriction, we can access unknown power reserves across the universe. When the life force is exposed to blockage, which is often caused by an overload of stress, trauma, or negative thoughts, it affects our system's functionality. This is the same thing I explained in the chapter where you learned about the energy body.

Someone who isn't well-versed with spiritual practices may easily discard this as magic or voodoo. Still, many nonspiritual people have attested to the efficacy of Reiki in treating physical and mental conditions. Most people who have witnessed the awesomeness of Reiki healing have reported feeling a huge positive shift in countenance, thinking, and overall vibes. Reiki is a mix of energy sweeping and light touches all over the body. It may feel like grounding for some people while, for others, it feels like emotional realignment.

The first step in any Reiki healing is to receive energy. Start by activating your energy source within your system. Close your eyes and run through a few rounds of powerful and deep breathing. Visualize your crown chakra opening up with a stream of white light flowing out. The white light is healing. Picture the light moving from the top of your head into your chakra, to your arms and hands. Ask that the light fills up the part of your body where you require the most healing.

As the energy flows from one part of your body to the next, keep breathing. Do this until the energy has touched every part of your body where you need healing. Your mind might get busy along the line. Simply bring your focus back to the sensation of your breathing as you continue. Imagine yourself as a medium for healing. Pray to the Divine so you can receive healing of the greatest quality. If you use Reiki healing to help a loved one, you have to make sure you are filled with energy first.

Reiki can help another person improve their sleep. To do this, follow the steps below.

- Ask the loved one or recipient to lie down flat on the bed while you hover around their head. Visualize a bright stream of light emerging from your hand into their system through the back of their head. Set an intention for the light to clear their mind of any discomfort building up.

- Tell the recipient to breathe in and out in several rounds. Ask them to visualize their whole memory from the day at once and show appreciation for the memory. Then, ask them to release the memory with their breath.

- Continue to channel the healing light from your hands into their energy field. Ask them to picture their body healing, relaxing, and getting heavy for a pleasant night's sleep.

Fifteen to thirty minutes is enough to practice Reiki for sleep on your loved one or any other person you wish to try it on. By the time you are done, they should be relaxed and calm enough to drift off to sleep.

Reiki may also relieve stress and anxiety, which are some things that result in energy blockage in the system. Stress and anxiety disrupt a person's breathing, resulting in shortness of breath. This also causes more stress.

Reiki's purpose for stress is to channel energy into the recipient's body to eliminate tension and release the knotted nerves.

- Place your palms on the person's shoulders for up to 15 minutes.

- Send the pure energy from your hand into their body.

- Breathe deeply and ask them to breathe with you. Let your breathing sync. This will naturally release some of the tense mental energy into their body.

- If the person is lying flat, put your hand behind their head to help them calm down and relax.

For as much relaxation as possible, keep this technique going for about 15 or 20 minutes.

To conclude, you have to seal off the energy from your crown. Offer your gratitude for the successful healing process. Cleanse yourself with the energy from your hand. Then, close the source of energy to complete the healing session. You may do something as simple as wiping your hands of excess energy and releasing that remaining in prayer. End the sessions with both of your hands raised in prayer.

Qigong

Qigong is a spiritual healing therapy used to restore the body's lost balance. This technique has existed for as far back as 4000 years. It comprises a series of coordinated body movements, which include breathing and meditation. The point of Qigong is to stimulate healthy, vitality, and spirituality in your body, mind, and soul. From the name, you can already tell this healing therapy works with energy. Qi is Chinese for energy.

This healing technique involves moving energy through the channels and centers while fixing the flow, strengthening it, and balancing it across the different energy points throughout your whole body. Its exercises can prevent illnesses, heal them, maintain quality health, and increase one's chances of longevity. One thing about this energy healing thing is that you can use it for anybody across any age. Your physical condition does not matter. Qigong can significantly benefit the quality of your overall health.

There are some basic Qigong exercise techniques.

The first is concentration. This is a technique that is geared towards increasing energy awareness. It has to do with learning how to focus and let go simultaneously. In other words, Qigong concentration helps you master how to accommodate your mind, body, and spirit's functions while being focused and undistracted by extraneous factors. In doing this, you allow the worries of your everyday hassles to drift away.

Breathing is also a Qigong exercise technique. The technique is targeted at stimulating vital energy with your breaths. The two most common breathing methods to fill your body with energy are Buddha's Breath and Daoist's breath.

Buddha's breath requires you to inhale and expand your belly with air. When you finally exhale, contract your belly and release the breath, starting from the bottom area of your lungs and pushing it out until the air deflates from your tummy and chest. As you inhale and exhale, visualize your Qi flowing through the energy channels. Using your mind, allow it to flow in an orderly way. Don't tug or push at the energy.

Daoist's breath is the direct opposite of Buddha's breath. You can repeat the steps stated above but do it in contrast. Breathe in and contract your belly muscles. Then, exhale and allow your torso and lungs to relax.

As you go through these steps, never forget that Qigong is an ongoing way of increasing awareness at the highest level. Still, don't practice unless you are comfortable. Do the exercises you find comfortable.

Below is a quick Qigong awareness exercise:

• Shut your eyes halfway. Clear the clutter in your mind and focus on your palms.

• Breathe slowly and gently, without force. You should feel like you are inducing a trance.

- Draw your hands together, with the palms touching and your fingers pointed upward. Make sure the centers of your palms touch each other. That way, you can feel when energy starts emanating from your body.

- Slowly move your hands apart until they are around 12 inches away from each other. It should feel like you are compressing air between your hands.

- You will start feeling a tingling sensation in the spot where the palms are touching.

- Start a back-and-forth movement of your hands. Let the range of the bellows vary.

This exercise can help channel energy, build awareness, and enlighten yourself. Prepare for a mindset change when you experience the powers of Qi energy for the first time.

Pranic Healing

The Indian word for Energy is Prana. Therefore, Pranic healing is just another way of saying energy healing. It is a form of healing technique in which prana, also known as the universal life force, is heightened, controlled, and used for specific healing purposes and benefits. Pranic healing can be used for yourself or the people around you, and the process entails projecting prana from a pure source into the system of people who need healing. There are different levels of pranic healing.

First, you have basic Pranic healing. It is the most basic healing level, which involves projecting your prana energy into a person's body. It further entails scanning the person's body, cleaning, balancing, and letting go of the projected energy. The healer, who is you, also has to cut off the energy cord between the energy receiver and themselves. This is to prevent contamination and speed the healing process up.

Second, you have advanced Pranic healing, when you master how to use prana energy to purge and purify a person's body to invigorate and revitalize them.

Third, Pranic psychotherapy involves mastering the ability to use colorful prana energy to cure mental illnesses and psychological disorders.

The fourth and final is the Pranic crystal healing, which revolves around using healing crystals to focus energy on someone on a more intense level.

Naturally, you have to start at the basic level. As you practice more, you can progress to other levels of pranic healing.

Here, I have the procedure involved in performing basic pranic healing meditation. It involves seven steps, all of which must be followed in order.

- Step 1: Cleansing is the first step in pranic healing. You start by performing a couple of simple exercises for purifying the energy body. The purpose of cleansing is to get rid of any accumulated energy congestion in the auric field.

- Step 2: Invocation is the second step in pranic healing. It is significant in this meditation. You simply have to seek divine blessings and guidance in your meditation. This is to make sure you have absolute protection and appropriate help during the procedure.

- Step 3: The third step is the activation of the third chakra. Do this by pressing two fingers to the area where your heart is located. Visualize and focus on your heart chakra. Imagine the earth as a little glowing ball with shining bluish-pink light and use it to bless everyone across the universe. Visualize everyone on Earth, including yourself, being filled with wonderful feelings of peace, delight, hope, and devotion.

- Step 4: The next step is the activation of the Crown chakra. Just as you did in step 3, press two fingers to the top of your head where your crown is located. Wait for a couple of seconds while focusing on the crown chakra. Send blessings to everyone across the planet and ask that they are filled with love, light, and kindness. Feel the positive flow of energy pumping through your own body and mind.

- Step 5: Envision a shining white light emerging from your crown chakra. Imagine the light flooding the entire planet. This means you are blessing the whole earth with the white light from your crown chakra and golden light from your heart chakra. This will make your blessing more plentiful and potent. Again, feel the positive flow of energy as it runs through your mind and body.

- Step 6: The sixth step is the stage where you achieve illumination, basically expanding awareness. Imagine the radiant white light on your crown chakra and chant "OM" and "Amen" together. Do this for up to 15 minutes. Chant the mantra and focus on the light simultaneously. Once it gets to a point, you will feel light explode within you.

- Step 7: The final step involves releasing the remnant energy inside you. It is the perfect closing to your meditation. Use some more additional minutes to bless the earth while allowing the energy to be released through your hand into the earth.

Before you round up your session, allow your body to return to its normal, stable self. Otherwise, you may experience a series of acute chest pain and migraine.

Quantum Healing

Quantum healing entails using a combination of breathing and visualization exercises to increase the energy level in your system. Quantum healing not only has spiritual benefits but also has a direct medical impact on your immune system. Essentially, quantum healing combines meditation and Eastern medicine with mind-body medicine and quantum physics. By shifting the vital life force at a quantum level, you can use quantum healing techniques to heal your mind, body, and spirit.

I don't advise beginners to try quantum healing on their own unless they have taken a comprehensive course to prepare themselves. So, this is not to tell you to try quantum healing by yourself. Still, there are body awareness exercises related to this technique. They are brief and straightforward, so you can try them on your own.

The core principle of quantum healing is to raise your vibrational levels using resonance and entrainment. Therefore, body awareness and breathing techniques are a good start for anyone interested in quantum healing.

Here are some exercises to try.

- **Feeling Your Finger:** Hold out your middle finger. Pay attention and be aware of the finger. Don't take your focus away from it. In the next few minutes, you will notice a tingling sensation, buzzing, heat, heaviness, and vibration in that finger. Your awareness of the finger becomes increased.

- **1-4 Breath:** Deeply and completely breathe in to the count of one and breathe out to the count of four. Do this until you start feeling dizzy. Then, stop.

- **4-4 Breathe:** Mentally do a body sweep from your feet to your crown as you breathe in to the count of four. Take one second for each count. You should start to feel waves of sensations as you bring awareness from one part of your body to the next. Breathe out to the count of four and allow all generated sensations to concentrate in your hands.

As with all the psychic abilities we have discussed so far, you have to put in practice if you want to learn all these energy healing techniques.

Chapter Twelve: Crystals for Healing and Personal Power

As you progress in your psychic journey, there are certain things you must make a constant. Crystals are part of things that can increase your psychic abilities and enhance your healing power. They are not just beautiful. They also have a lot of properties that make them a must-have. Crystals are packed with a lot of energy to bestow their owners with clarity, protection, and guidance. Other than this, you can also use them to amplify your psychic abilities.

For centuries, crystals have been used in various ways due to their powerful properties. Their powerful energy allows them to have an easy impact on the body and mind. Due to their connection with the cosmos and yourself, they are the best tools to have in your psychic development journey. Some people think that crystals are an outdated way of connecting with the spirit world. These people have no idea what they are missing out on. Forget how crystals are portrayed and used in Hollywood movies and focus on reality.

Crystals are natural minerals from the bottom of the earth. Their connection with the earth is likely why they have such potent energetic properties.

Choosing crystals for your personal use depends absolutely on what you want to use them for. But the coolest thing about them is that you don't have to choose them. They choose you. A crystal's powerful energy can connect with your own and draw you to them. When you go crystal shopping, you will just find yourself compelled to pick a particular crystal. If this happens to you, be sure to choose that crystal. Never forget that your intuition is more aware than you can fully comprehend.

Below, I will list the best crystals you can use to increase your psychic senses. But before that, there are a few things to remember. First, when you go through the crystal list, observe the ones that seem more interesting to you. Don't overanalyze; just notice which ones draw you in. There's no definitive guide to picking the right crystal. Just allow yourself to have fun.

If you go to pick out crystals in person, hold and feel them in your hands. See how they make you feel. You are bound to notice differences in how each crystal makes you feel. If you are buying the crystals online, breathe deeply, and center yourself. As you browse through the pictures online, ask yourself how they make you feel.

With this in mind, you can pick your crystals. All crystals are energetic items. They all have the power to open up your body and mind to your inherent psychic abilities. But some crystals have more powerful energies than others. Here are some of the most potent crystals for increasing your psychic abilities.

- **Amethyst:** This is a gorgeous purple stone that is incredibly powerful, purifying, and healing. Amethyst is good for third eye development. It can be used to get rid of negative and toxic energy. It also cleanses the blood, boosts hormone production, and relieves stress and anxiety. It is also said to help promote sobriety and improve a person's sleeping situation.

- **Azurite:** This is another favorite for the third eye. Azurite vibrates at the same level as the third eye, meaning it is suitable for anyone looking to hone their psychic gifts, such as clairvoyance.

- **Clear Quartz:** This is a white crystal that many psychics consider a master healer. Clear quartz crystal is said to can absorb, store, release, and amplify energy. It also has the natural ability to improve focus and concentration. It can also cleanse and balance the immune system by stimulating it. You may pair this stone with other stones to amplify its energy and abilities. A good pairing is with the rose quartz crystal.

- **Rose Quartz:** This pink stone is a symbol of love. It is used to maintain harmony and trust in one's relationships. To improve your relationship and intimate connections, this is the stone to go for. It can also help build love, trust, respect, and worth.

- **Bloodstone:** Another brilliant stone for developing your psychic abilities. Feeling grounded is essential in your journey, and this is what bloodstone can help you achieve. This stone is also great for activating the root chakra. Don't forget that the root chakra is your key to staying grounded in Mother Earth. Place a grid of this crystal under your bed before you sleep and notice the difference.

- **Obsidian:** This is a very powerful stone for protecting yourself from physical, mental, and emotional toxicity. You can use it to get rid of emotional blockages in the energy system. It also helps with the detoxification of the physical body.

Each crystal has different vibrations. It does not even matter if they are of the same stone variation. Using crystals for healing and increasing your psychic ability is a way of receiving multiple benefits in one go.

Caring for your crystal is important. Cleanse your crystals regularly to ward off negativity and toxicity. You can rinse them with warm or cold water. You may also do the cleansing with sea salt or by burning sage.

The most important thing is to accept and respect what your crystals can do for you. Follow all the tips, and your psychic journey will be a smooth and seamless one.

Conclusion

Psychic development can either be a fascinating and enlightening journey if you approach it the right way. Like I said, psychic skills cannot be learned in one go. You have to put in months and years of consistent practice if you want to make progress. Be careful as your journey the world of mediums and psychics. If possible, find a mentor that can make the whole journey much more enduring and fun for you. If you don't allow yourself to have fun along the way, you may end up halting your learning abruptly. Find ways to make sure this does not happen. A genuine psychic always follows through to the end no matter how tough.

More importantly, don't forget to never compare your progress with that of another person around you. Good luck!

Part 2: Divination

An Essential Guide to Astrology, Numerology, Tarot Reading, Palmistry, Runecasting, and Other Divination Methods

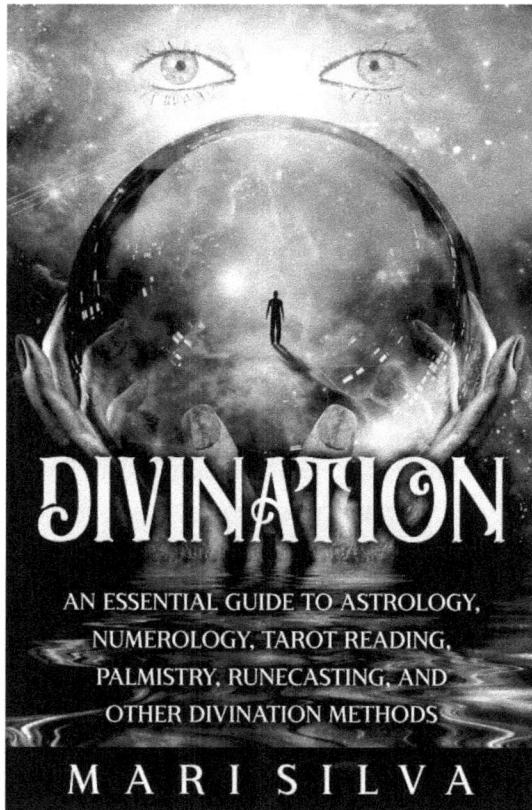

DIVINATION

AN ESSENTIAL GUIDE TO ASTROLOGY, NUMEROLOGY, TAROT READING, PALMISTRY, RUNECASTING, AND OTHER DIVINATION METHODS

MARI SILVA

Introduction

Do you know what divination means? Do you ever wonder what you are destined for? Are you curious to learn about your future? Imagine if you could quickly sneak behind the curtain to see what is in store for you. Do you seek your true purpose in life? If you answered "Yes," here's some good news! When you harness the power of divination, you can unlock the secrets and mysteries of the cosmos. All the information you need to obtain this goal is presented in, *Divination: An Essential Guide to Astrology, Numerology, Tarot Reading, Palmistry, Runecasting, and Other Divination Methods.*

Divination is the art or practice of seeking knowledge about the future or the unknown. The concept is not a recent practice. It can help you understand the hidden significance or the fundamental cause of events in your life, and it can be used to foretell the future. Ancient cultures across the world have their own traditions and practices to understand the divine or the unknown. They use this information to make sense of everyday events. Do you want to learn how to do this? Well, this book will act as your guide every step of the way while you explore the fascinating world of divination and all that it entails.

You will learn about simple and effective time-honored techniques used to strengthen your intuition and harness universal energy. When you access your unconscious and use divination, you can lift the veil between the realms to peek into the future.

You will learn what divination means, the different tools to use, and how you can use it to sneak a glance at the future. Not only that, this book will introduce you to the basics of astrology and how to read a birth chart in an easy to understand manner. This will act as your introductory guide to using divination tools such as numerology, palmistry, runecasting, and tarot reading. Learning about this is not only interesting but can be instructive. Knowledge is power, and once you are equipped with the information given in this guide, you will be able to determine your life's purpose much easier.

So, if you are ready to begin, turn the page!

Chapter One: Is It Really Possible to See the Future?

You can see the future now! You know how your life will take its course and where you will be in five years. You have untold riches at your feet and the ability to disappear at will. Sounds downright silly, right? Well, of course. No one can predict anyone's future. No diviner can firmly state what will happen to you in five years. Wait, so why is this entire book written about "divination"?

Well, because divination is not simply looking into a crystal ball and predicting some mumbo jumbo. It is not looking at tea leaves and telling you that you will have a great year ahead. Divination is not a science; it's the culmination of years of study and patient learning about human personality and how all aspects and factors tie in to make each person unique.

What is Divination?

Divination is not just a bunch of people sitting around a Ouija board, chanting random things and trying to summon the spirits. Though Ouija is very much a part of the practice of divination, the meaning of divination is basically "divining" or trying to ascertain the hidden causes or significance or meaning behind events in a person's life. This practice was born centuries ago. In today's context, it encompasses various methods—astrology, birth charts, tarot, runecasting, etc. Modern divination teachers and practitioners work more toward ascertaining the root causes and impact of past and present events on a person's personality.

Historical Significance of Divination

Ancient cultures such as India, Mesopotamia, Egypt, and China sought to find answers to everyday questions and understand the environmental phenomena occurring around them, like thunder and lightning, seasons, migratory activities, etc. Each culture had its specific manner of dealing with the divine or the unknown.

The Chinese used tortoise shells to read and decipher patterns. This led to the I Ching movement and the hexagrams associated with it. The Vikings favored rune stones, but the Romans had a rather gruesome method of observing the intestines spilled out of slaughtered livestock. The Aboriginals from Australia turned inward and studied inner space. Others, such as the Mexican Indians, made use of plants to study and record answers. In the Old Testament, there is a reference to a set of divine stones called Urim and Thummim, which were used to figure out the course of future events.

The widespread art of divination you see around you today is a recent development. In days gone by, this art was mostly limited to oral transmissions and cave drawings or carvings on rocks by shamans, healers, priests, prophets, etc. Only after the invention of the printing press did this knowledge of divination spread far and wide, from the ancient world into the developing world.

After the invention of paper by the Chinese and a primitive movable type created thousands of years ago, it became possible to increase literary output. The I Ching, one of the world's most respected divination systems, saw the light of the day by being put in print. Later on, Johann Gutenberg's printing press gave rise to a multitude of books, card decks, flyers, etc. As literacy grew and the world population exploded, many divination systems came into existence. The most popular and those with close connections to history include astrology, tarot, runes, numerology, and I Ching. They are also known as the "classic" divination systems. These divination systems weren't merely tools to predict silly and inane questions; they challenged people's world views, analyzed personalities, and helped everyone understand the universe and themselves better.

How to Interpret Divination

There are various schools of divination, which try to explain phenomena in their own manner. Here they are discussed briefly.

Inductive Divination

Divining things from the skies or stars is common now, but it dates back to ancient times. The early ancients used to look up to the heavens and decipher phenomena on Earth, such as weather changes or migratory patterns of birds. Lightning, clouds, and thunder were interpreted as gods being angry with humans. Weather-related disasters such as excessive rain, storms, hail, drought, and floods suggested divine control over these forces.

There is a concept known as "augury," which the ancients used to discover divine events and God's hand in nature. Sometimes, this practice was also used for rituals involving the flight of birds or sacrificing an animal. For example, the study of the liver, called "haruspicy," was used to discover the history of the creature being studied. This is akin to modern-day palmistry. There was a technique known as "scapulimancy," which is divination from a fire-cracked shoulder blade. This technique was used mostly in North America. As mentioned earlier, "tortoiseshell divination" originated in China. The Chinese ancients used to study the spirals and patterns on the shell of a tortoise and interpret them.

Interpretive Divination

In this technique, omens are studied rather than looking toward the heavens or studying animals and birds. This relies on a cause-effect scenario. Of course, events do occur randomly, too, which cannot be explained by logic, while to a certain extent, there is a cause behind every effect. Divination by studying fire and related aspects, known as "pyromancy," was one such technique. The accused would be tested or probed in front of a fire, and if the fire suddenly leaped out at them, their guilt would be "proven." This may seem highly unscientific now, but that was how things were in the days of yore. Another technique involved throwing objects into the fire and seeing how the fire reacted to it. Divination by studying water (hydromancy) was also practiced. Water was used to study and interpret reflections of objects in it.

Other related practices included cleromancy and geomancy, divination by "lots" and "maps," respectively. Frankly, these were strange practices. For instance, in cleromancy, the objects found on the person conducting the divination were used to assess and predict the person's current status and future. Dried intestines, a tooth, or a decayed piece of hair all held different meanings in the interpretation. Along with these objects, the diviner asked various questions designed to elicit a response from the asker. If the answers betrayed the question or veered off course at some point, the diviner would interpret it as being the cause of the problem.

In geomancy, most notably in Africa, along with maps, drawings, and lots, occult readings were also conducted on the person asking the question. The diviner would attempt to read and interpret the body signs of the person (phrenology). Dream interpretation was also used and called "oneiromancy."

Intuitive Divination

To perform this, the diviner or shaman uses trance states to "cure" or find solutions to the person's problems. This is done either by drugging the man or woman or using their own tribal techniques. Going into a trance could also involve occult, spirit possession, and speaking in a different language.

Sometimes incubation was also practiced. In Egypt, people thought that sleeping inside a sacred temple would mean being blessed by God. The ancient Maya civilization saw young girls thrown into a deep well. Those who managed to climb out were required to tell others about their messages while inside the well. Trances and possession are seen in modern-day divination as well. More often than not, the diviner has their "spirit" replaced by the one they are summoning. After the necessary questions and answers have been dealt with, they return to their original spirit.

An unfortunate byproduct of all this was the negative connotation attached to divination in the form of witchcraft. Innocent women were accused of being witches and burnt at the stake for no fault of their own, except perhaps they looked different or suffered from a mental illness or physical deformity. Ordeals were horrifying too. The accused would be thrown into open rivers or seas. The presumption was that if they survived, they were innocent. Similar things happened to those thrown into a fire or from a hilltop.

Today, there are numerous divination methods, namely astrology, birth charts, horoscopes, tarot cards, runes, etc. During the turn of the twentieth century, methods such as crystal gazing, chiromancy, necromancy, and palm reading flourished. As you might already know, divination has more to do with intuition and an overall reading of the person's personality, traits, quirks, and mental state—everything that makes them unique. The following chapters deal with popular methods of divination that you will study and learn.

Chapter Two: Tools of Divination

Some divination methods are more popular, some are obscure, and yet others still unknown. It depends on your preference, means, and interest! You can choose whatever tool you wish and make it work for you. It is not as if tarot is better than astrology, or runes are better than a crystal ball. It just has to be something that you are comfortable with.

Here are a few popular methods and tools for divination. You will study these in greater detail in the following chapters.

Runes or Runecasting

These have been used since ancient times as a method of communicating. Runes are small stones or symbols carved into wood or stone that are then deciphered and interpreted. Each rune has a meaning attached to it, such as wealth, prosperity, travel, negative issues and aspects, and so on. You can buy a set of runes or even carve a set out of wood. Store your rune stones or crystals in a cloth pouch, draw the runes out randomly, place them on a cloth on the ground, and ask your questions. There are several books and guides available on the Internet to help you interpret the results.

Tarot Cards

Tarot is one of the most commonly used divination methods and has been around for a long time. People usually think that tarot is used to predict their future, but just like other divination methods, tarot is a tool and guide to help you understand yourself better. Tarot has two types of cards: The Major Arcana and the Minor Arcana. The Major Arcana comprises twenty-two cards dealing with major life characteristics and situations. The Minor Arcana is made up of 56 cards, which represent everyday issues and feelings. There are various layouts and spreads to try out. Once you shuffle the deck, you can choose any of the spreads and get a reading from them.

Crystal Ball

The stuff of supernatural movies, right? A beaded, mysterious mystic sits before a crystal ball, gazes into it, and predicts something ominous for the person inquiring, which usually turns out to be true. However, in reality, this has nothing to do with predicting anything. As with the other methods, you need to study long and hard about the intricacies of crystal ball gazing and interpreting the results.

Angel Cards

Do not confuse these with tarot cards. Angel cards are used to invoke the blessings of angels in one's life. These cards are mostly positive and sunny in nature and provide insight into personal growth, wealth, relationships, love, etc. When you are doing an angel card reading, it behooves you to listen to your heart and connect it with the spirit of the angels. Focus your energy on positive outcomes.

Spirit Boards

Also known as Ouija boards, this is another staple of horror movies. Ouija boards contain letters of the alphabet, numbers one to nine, and words such as "yes," "no," "here," and "goodbye." If you wish to try this out, you place a finger or hand on a coin or planchette in the middle of the board and try to contact whomever you wish. This is still a very imprecise branch of divination, though. Be careful before trying anything like this. Things might go wrong fast!

Pendulum

A pendulum can also answer specific questions for you. It is a chain that has a cone-shaped crystal or stone attached to it. Dangle it over a parchment or vellum sheet with "yes" and "no" printed on it. Swing it and see where it settles. You can buy or make your own pendulum. This method is also popular when trying to guess the gender of an unborn child, using a jewelry chain with a wedding band placed on it.

Psychic Cup

This cup is used for reading tea leaves. The person asking the question must drink hot tea (loose tea) and leave a small amount at the bottom. The dregs contain the tea leaves, which is then swirled around and poured onto a saucer. There will be patterns and swirls on the saucer that the diviner interprets.

Palm Reading

One of the most ancient methods of divination, palmistry, involves the reading of the palms. Palms contain numerous lines and bumps, and each of the lines and the bumps has significance. Taken in conjunction with each other and various other lines, every individual can get their unique reading by the palmist. This requires a detailed and thorough analysis of the palm.

Astrology

Everyone is familiar with their sun signs, but astrology is not just about those. It encompasses a lot more. The rising sign, the moon sign, and the birth chart, along with the stars' and planets' positions at the time of your birth—degrees, angles, and cusp aspects—combine to form a complete picture of you and your being.

Numerology

Numbers have a profound effect on your life. Your life path number, name number, fate number, house number, expression number—each one tells a story about you. It is convenient, practical, and fun!

DIY Tools for New Diviners

If you think that the practice of divination is expensive and will burn a hole in your pocket, fear not! There are plenty of do-it-yourself tricks and tips available on the Internet to help you out. Here are just a few tools you can make for yourself.

Make Your Own Pendulum

1. Take a chain or thin rope. It can be any old chain you have at home.

2. Search for a ring or ring-shaped object. It must have a hole, so it can slide into the chain or rope easily.

3. Slide the ring into the chain and close it. If it is a rope, tie the ends securely. The ring must not fall off.

4. Test the pendulum out. Write "Yes" and "No" on a sheet of paper and place your arm over it, such that the pendulum is perpendicular to the sheet. You can decide on the movement interpretations; the left is "Yes," the right is "No," and the middle is "Unknown."

5. Think of a question. Say, "Is the rainbow multicolored?" Swing the pendulum over the paper and see where it lands. It should land at the predetermined answer. If not, you need to change your interpretations. Do this a few more times until the swing of the pendulum is regulated. Now you are free to ask any question.

How to Make Your Own Rune Set

The most common Runic alphabet is known as the Elder Futhark (covered more extensively later on). It is made up of twenty-four letters. Some runes in a set come blank—or are called "Wyrd runes." Do not think of these runestones as tools for predicting the future, but as something to guide you on the journey.

Materials: Runes are often made of naturally occurring materials, so they usually aren't expensive. You can choose between wood, stones, pebbles, old bones of animals who have died of natural causes, clay, etc. You can carve your runes on these materials easily.

You will need twenty-four pieces of whatever material you choose because the Elder Futhark is made up of twenty-four alphabets. They must be similar in size. Also, they should not be so big that you cannot hold them and work with them. Once you gather your materials, it's time to paint or carve the runes onto them!

To begin with runecasting, you need to find a peaceful spot and time when you are the most energized from within. Take a candle and light it. Pick out a rune, think about its meaning, meditate for a while, and pass it near the candle flame. Place it to the right on the cloth that you are using. Do the same with the other runes. Now, you are ready to begin reading!

Make Your Own Tarot Cards

Wow, isn't this wonderful? A set of your own tarot cards made out of old poker cards!

- Your supplies should include an old set of playing cards, white paper, glue, labels, a pen, and most importantly, tarot card details.

- Organize your cards by suits and put them in ascending order, beginning with Ace and ending with King. The Joker cards go in a separate pile.

- Cut out the paper to fit the cards. Make 54 pieces.

- Now, you have to write! Write out tarot information on each suit of cards. For example, for all Heart cards, write "Tarot suit Cups." Then make a brief note of what that symbolizes. In the case of Cups, it means "emotions, deeper feelings, love, relationships." For all Diamonds, it will be "Suit of Pentacles," all Spades will carry "Suit of Swords," and all Clubs are "Suit of Spades." Find out the meaning of these tarot suits in the books listed for you at the end of the chapter.

- Organize each of your suits in ascending order, beginning with the Ace and ending with the King. Every number has a meaning attached to it, which you will find in the books listed later on. Write the corresponding traits on the cards. For example, three stands for development, self-expression, and growth, while four means stability, solidity, and a foundation.

- Congratulations! Your deck is ready. You can attempt a reading now.

Book Recommendations to Help You Start Your Practice

- *A Practical Guide to the Runes: Their Uses in Divination and Magic* (Lisa Peschel)

- *Seventy-Eight Degrees of Wisdom: A Book of Tarot* (Rachel Pollack)

- *Divination for Beginners: Reading the Past, Present, & Future* (Scott Cunningham)

- *The Complete Idiot's Guide to Numerology* (Jean Simpson)

- *A Little Bit of Numerology: An Introduction to Numerical Divination* (Novalee Wilder)

- *Numerology and the Divine Triangle* (Faith Javane and Dusty Bunker)

- *The Easiest Way to Learn the Tarot – Ever!!* (Dusty White)

- *The Ultimate Guide to Tarot Card Meanings* (Brigit Esselmont)

- *365 Tarot Spreads: Revealing the Magic in Each Day* (Sasha Graham)

- *A Little Bit of Palmistry: An Introduction to Palm Reading* (Cassandra Eason)

- *Runes for Beginners: A Guide to Reading Runes in Divination, Rune Magic, and the Meaning of the Elder Futhark Runes* (Lisa Chamberlain)

- *Futhark: A Handbook of Rune Magic* (Edred Thorsson)

- *Runecaster's Handbook: The Well of Wyrd* (Edred Thorsson)

- *Rudiments of Runelore* (Stephen Pollington)

- *The Secret Code on Your Hands: An Illustrated Guide to Palmistry* (Vernon Mahabal)

Chapter Three: Understanding Astrology

Astrology is the study of how distant planets and stars influence lives on Earth. It is not just making silly predictions based on one's whims and fancies. It considers the position of the sun, planets, and stars to form a complete picture of a person and their personality, relationships, career paths, and other aspects.

The most common thing people usually ask and know is their "sun sign." Your basic everyday newspaper and popular columns usually consider only the sun sign because it is the most basic form of astrology. Sun sign astrology only requires your date of birth—sometimes just the month of birth. For a more accurate and better reading, you need to study each planet's and star's position at the time of your birth. Not just this, the House position, angles, degrees, cusps, aspects, etc., come together and present a detailed and accurate picture of you, your personality, career, relationships, attributes, etc.

All ancient cultures practiced their own version of astrology. Some of the oldest among these include the Vedic, Chinese, and Tibetan practices of astrology. This is not a definite science; even in Western astrology, you will find various interpretations and philosophies.

A common categorization that is based on the end result is as follows:

- *Mundane Astrology* — This branch deals with world events, current affairs, predictions about the economy and general political climate, etc.

- *Interrogatory Astrology* — This branch of astrology refers to the more commonly known method of making predictions and analyses about people

- *Natal Astrology* — This is what astrology is all about. Looking at a birth chart and calculating the position, angles, degrees, and aspects of planets and stars accurately at the precise moment of a person's birth and then making predictions based on this.

Noteworthy Facts About Astrology

- Astrology came into being before the Copernican revolution. It assumed that the Sun moved around the Earth.

- The term "zodiac" comes from a Greek term used to identify animal sculptures.

- Ancient Egyptians were the first to identify and name the constellations in the night sky.

- The Ancient Greeks created today's modern zodiac sign. The Babylonians also had twelve signs, similar to what exists today.

- A book written by Ptolemy, called *Tetrabiblos*, made it possible for the Greek zodiac to gain popularity among the ancient world.

- Do you know what "horoscope" means? It literally means "hour watch."

- Astrology is not just a mumbo jumbo of predictions. To create an accurate birth chart and horoscope, one needs to calculate the planet's angles using geometry principles!

- Ancient Romans used mnemonics to remember the long lists of fortunes or fortune headings to be recited for someone's horoscope reading.

- Almost all ancient civilizations, such as Egypt, America, Greece, and Rome, believed that the stars and planets influence human life.

- The Roman Emperor Augustus used to have his Capricornian profile etched onto coins.

- There is a branch of study known as meteorological astrology, which tries to predict the weather based on the zodiac.

- Astrologers say that almost all the mighty empires in the ancient world, such as Britain, Rome, Egypt, and Germany, flourished because they were under the influence of Aries, the sign associated with creativity and birth.

- Former U.S. First Lady Nancy Reagan used to have her horoscope read regularly!

Sun Signs

"What is my Sun Sign? What does it signify?" These are common questions most people have, and they associate astrology with only the Sun sign. To calculate this, you only need your month and date of birth—yes, it's that simple! It gives you a fair idea about your personality without digging deeper.

The Sun is at the center of the solar system, and similarly, your Sun sign puts you at the center. It not only provides an overall view of your traits and life path, but it also tells you about your core and basic personality and passions. This sign is your identity in life.

Your Sun as an Air Sign (Libra, Gemini, Aquarius)

You are an intelligent being who also loves to party, have fun, and generally have a good time. You love socializing and are often found at large gatherings. People love to be around you.

Your Sun as a Fire Sign (Aries, Leo, Sagittarius)

You are drawn to power and ambition. You are fiercely protective of your loved ones and friends and will go to any lengths to keep them from harm. You also enjoy physical activities and outdoorsy events!

Your Sun as an Earth Sign (Taurus, Capricorn, Virgo)

You are practical, committed, and love material comforts in life. You love having beauty and order around you.

Your Sun as a Water Sign (Cancer, Scorpio, Pisces)

You are an enigmatic and mysterious person, stubborn as a mule and deep as a lake. You are uncannily intuitive and go by your emotions and darker desires. You prefer intimate connections with people rather than large groups.

Moon Signs

The Moon is associated with the cool, calm, and silvery peace of the night. It relates more to your inner being, private desires, dreams, thoughts, etc. To calculate your Moon sign, you need a full date of birth, exact time, and year.

The Moon is the ruler of beauty and emotions. It reveals things that you keep hidden from most people and tell only very trusted people in your life, like deep feelings, sentiments, intimacy, etc. If the Sun brings out your outer mind, the Moon reaches into the subconscious mind.

Your Moon as an Air Sign (Gemini, Libra, Aquarius)

Any changing experience or life event is dealt with by evaluation and not mere emotionality. You feel in charge when you rationally think things through.

Your Moon is a Fire Sign (Aries, Leo, Sagittarius)

Your inner world is characterized by action and excitement. You feel most alive and open when you can express your ideas and feelings confidently, without straying into negativity.

Your Moon as an Earth Sign (Taurus, Virgo, Capricorn)

Stability and solidity are the cornerstones of your inner being. Any change in this pattern will lead to anxiety. You are happiest when you are working toward a productive goal.

Your Moon as a Water Sign (Cancer, Scorpio, Pisces)

You are deep, sensuous, mysterious, and highly emotional. You love having your feelings involved with something and also love to probe other people's feelings!

Rising Signs

These are also known as your Ascendant Signs because they rule the First House of your natal chart. This is the most significant portion of the chart astrologers look for and study. It represents your physical side, body, and how you seem to others. It also depicts a fine balance between your inner and outer sides. The Rising Sign determines your overall outlook toward life.

Your Rising Sign as an Air Sign (Gemini, Libra, Aquarius)

You are loquacious, inquisitive, mentally agile, and very friendly. You know exactly what you want from life and are deliberate with your movements and actions.

Your Rising Sign is a Fire Sign (Aries, Leo, Sagittarius)

You are driven by power and ambition, focused, detailed, and blunt with people. Your physical energy astounds others around you, and you shine with vitality.

Your Rising Sign as an Earth Sign (Taurus, Virgo, Capricorn)

You focus more on the luxuries and material aspects of life. You are to the point, dependable, and stable. Others look to you for guidance.

Your Rising Sign as a Water Sign (Cancer, Scorpio, Pisces)

You are very emotional, dark, sensitive, and lash out when hurt. You keep secrets hidden so well that you sometimes have trouble trusting any other person. You are also easily influenced by the environment.

What the Planets Mean in Astrology

We all know how planets travel in the sky. As they move through the different imaginary zodiac zones, their energies at any given point of time are different from those at other points in time. A birth chart is most helpful while giving out the exact time, angle, and degree of the planet and zodiac at your birth's precise time, giving you a unique reading. If you know what planets live in your birth chart, you can examine their relationships with the other planets, aspects, and signs and determine your personality and future.

Now study the interpretations of the planets in astrology.

Sun

As said earlier, the Sun is at the center of the solar system. It gives life to Earth, which is why the Sun signs are so important in astrology. The Sun represents creativity, positive vibes, purity, and life forces and is mainly the driving force behind everything we do. The Sun naturally rules Leo.

Moon

The Moon represents the feminine side —nurture, empathy, compassion, security, emotions, expressions, etc. It brings out the maternal side. There are certain parts of your personality that you do not like to show others. The Moon brings all that out. It shows you your need for security, protection, comfort, and emotional wellbeing. The Moon naturally rules Cancer.

Mercury

Mercury is, as you guessed it, mercurial! It is the planet for communication, intellect, multi-tasking, reasoning, and powers of expression. Usually, Mercury is associated with its topsy-turvy retrograde periods. But even so, it affects how you infer and transmit information, communicate, and what your travel and exploration style is. Mercury naturally rules Gemini and Virgo.

Venus

Venus is the planet of love, beauty, romance, sensuality, and everything to do with these aspects. No wonder writers and poets fawn over it! Named after the Greek goddess herself, this planet concerns itself with aesthetics, beauty in every form, and, surprisingly, money. It defines luxury in terms of expensive things and baubles, such as chocolates, trips, and jewels. Venus naturally rules Taurus and Libra.

Mars

Mars is usually associated with aggression and drive. It was named after the God of War, so naturally, it is full of raw drive, energy, temper, action, and fighting spirit. Mars shows you how to tackle problems in life and work toward your goals. It also lives up to its moniker, the Red Planet, by being associated with sexual aggression and intensity. Mars naturally rules Aries.

Jupiter

Jupiter is the planet representing optimism, good fortune, and abundance. This is the largest planet in the solar system and carries with it a great deal of positivity. It indicates positivity, growth, opportunity, and good vibes in general. It also represents philosophy, teaching, education, broadening of minds, etc. Jupiter teaches you to keep working toward your goals and dreams and not give up. Jupiter naturally rules Sagittarius.

Saturn

Tough old Saturn is all about life, lessons, code of conduct, discipline, criticism, and tough decisions. Just like the Moon is all about maternal instincts, Saturn is about paternal instincts. It represents challenges and restrictions, boundaries and limits, and roadblocks. These can feel suffocating but remember: There can be no easy way through life. Saturn naturally rules Capricorn.

Uranus

Uranus represents an awakening within oneself. This might happen due to an external or internal revelation or progress in life or just letting your subconscious mind do its job. It indicates forward thinking, creativity, and changes. These changes can be abrupt, leading to a completely different way and thinking pattern of life. Uranus is also thought of as a lightning bolt, which jolts a person awake from slumber and gives them deep insights. Uranus naturally rules Aquarius.

Neptune

This planet is all about your dreams, mystic realm, idealism, intuition, psychic dealings, and astral aspects. Neptune is a dreamy-eyed planet, ethereal and full of calming colors. It represents artistic expression, spirituality, meditation, escapism and works toward lifting a person from life's banalities into something outwardly! Neptune naturally rules Pisces.

Pluto

Pluto, having been downgraded to a dwarf planet, is still a tremendous force in astrology. It represents a brooding, dark mind, the underworld, occult, intensity, and moodiness in general. Pluto is intense and quiet, deep and dark. It represents the extremes — light and dark, day and night, ending and beginning. Pluto naturally rules Scorpio.

Zodiac Signs

There are four elements in astrology, each corresponding to three signs, making a total of twelve. These are Fire, Earth, Air, and Water. These elements act like building blocks of life. Now you will delve into the elements and how the signs are connected to them.

The Fire Element

Aries, Leo, and Sagittarius fall into this category. Fire signs signify assertion, candid behavior, and spontaneity. Fire is usually impulsive and does not reflect first. It also signifies passion, courage, creativity, and immense pride in one's work. An outer spirit most likely guides it. Fire signs are the life of any party. They are idealists and love to take the lead. For instance, Aries is innovative, enthusiastic, and always ready to take on challenges. Leo is a Fixed Fire sign; it is more loyal, passionate, and fierce. Such people make particularly good managers and teachers. Sagittarius is a Mutable Fire sign, which means it is more flexible, but it is also fiery when aroused. Such people do well in spiritual endeavors. Fire signs fall under the masculine aspect.

The Earth Element

Taurus, Virgo, and Capricorn fall under this category. Earth signs are known for their reliability, solidity, and practicality. They build things, collect valuables, are pragmatic and sensible, materialistic, and like to surround themselves with fine luxuries. They need to feel in control of their immediate physical environment. They also make excellent managers and administrators because it ties in beautifully with their ability to manage others, see results for themselves, and also keep others in some semblance of control! Earth signs are feminine.

The Air Element

Gemini, Libra, and Aquarius are Air elements. These signs are fun, curious, intellectual, and, most importantly, fair-minded. Air signs are socially active, excellent communicators, and humanitarian by nature. Libra is a Cardinal Air sign, Gemini is a Mutable Air sign, and Aquarius is a Fixed Air sign. Of the three, Gemini is mostly adaptable to any situation. Libra thrives on action, comparing ideas and dreams and generally raring to go. Aquarius is the most steady and loyal of these signs. It tends to dwell on things rather than be impulsive and rash about decisions. Just like Fire signs, Air signs fall under the masculine category.

The Water Element

Cancer, Scorpio, and Pisces are Water Signs. As is their name, these signs are known for their intuitive powers, deep and emotional nature, and fluidity. Just like still waters run deep, these signs are emotionally deep and dark. They rely on intuition and gut feelings. Of the three, Cancer is caring, nurturing, and more focused on other people's feelings. Scorpio is magnetic, mysterious, psychic, and the keeper of all secrets. There is not much that escapes the canny Scorpio. Pisces is dreamy, spiritual, and full of starry dreams, compassionate to a fault, and easily influenced. Water signs are feminine and are very deep, private, stubborn, and highly secretive too. They do not see things on the surface level— they prefer to dig deep and find out the real meaning of things and feelings.

Now that you have a basic understanding of the effect of planets and stars on human beings on Earth take this knowledge forward to the next chapter and apply the principles and interpretations there.

Chapter Four: How to Read a Birth Chart

Most people love to read their horoscope, right? But have you ever wondered how the stars and planets foretell your story so succinctly? There must be something behind all that. To understand how a birth chart works and how to read one, you need to understand the basic concepts, as detailed in this chapter.

The Houses

What this means is the sky at the time of your birth. The houses are the backbone of the birth chart. In a typical birth chart, the left corner is known as the "ascendant" or rising. You read the chart from here and progress in an anticlockwise movement. Usually, there are twelve houses in a typical birth chart. Opposite to the ascendant is the "descendant" part of the setting.

The first house in the chart depicts your daily life areas: goals, self-esteem, appearance, behavior, etc.

The Signs

The signs depict the characteristics of the sky at the moment of a person's birth. What was the rising sign? What was the setting sign? What was the neutral sign? This is also where the individual aspects of every person's chart come to life.

The Planets

These are not just fiery heavenly bodies revolving and rotating in the sky. They can mirror the experiences and characteristics of people on Earth. Planets show the personality traits, strengths and weaknesses, and overall life path of a person.

So, how do you read a birth chart? By reading the major components listed above and other elements such as aspects, cusps, degrees, ascendants, and descendants.

Any basic birth chart comprises four elements: an individual's Sun, Moon, Ascendant, and Chart Ruler. So, look at the sign and house position of these four elements and try to read the birth chart accurately.

The Sun and Moon Elements

Not only are these the basic chart elements, but they also foretell a person's basic traits. The Sun concerns itself with the personality's expressive and masculine side, while the Moon is connected to one's innate self and feminine side. These two, like yin and yang, provide a wholesome picture of one's personality. Identify your Sun and Moon element in your chart with this symbology. The house and sign meanings will give you a picture of your inner and outer self.

Ascendant and Chart Ruler Elements

These two elements look toward the ongoing and upcoming phases in your life and shape your whole personality in the future. What your life experiences teach you is revealed by your Ascendant. This particular element is associated with the First House, and therefore, only has a sign attached to it, no aspect or planet.

Your Chart Ruler is the planet you are governed by. If you look at your Chart Ruler's or planet's sign and house position, it tells you much more about who you are and whom you may turn out to be. When looking at your birth chart, locate this planet, and look up the sign and house placement.

Aspects of the Chart

The associations that form between the mentioned components are called "aspects." For a detailed analysis of the birth chart, you must learn about the aspects detailed in this chapter. After that, look into the planetary readings. Just remember that the ones closest to the core of your chart will determine your personality and future. Those in the periphery are just faint layers of what makes you a whole human being. All in all, consider what you analyze in the First House, as that is a vital component of your entire being.

The Twelve Houses of the Zodiac

A typical birth chart is circular and divided into segments. The first wheel in the circle represents the twelve Houses of the zodiac and the second wheel represents the twelve signs of the zodiac. This is different for everyone, depending on where his or her house-cusp falls. Houses one to six are your "personal houses." Houses seven to twelve are known as "interpersonal houses." Each of these houses has its own planetary ruler and sign—and this is different for everyone. A general ruler of the chart and your own personal ruler of the chart might be entirely different. Now, look at what each house represents.

First House: Self

Ruled by: Aries and Mars

Interpretation: Also known as the "ascendant," the first house is all about you. What makes you—your self-esteem, goals, leadership, initiatives, and appearance. It ties in very strongly with all the beginnings and "firsts" in our life.

Second House: Finance and Value

Ruled by: Taurus and Venus

Interpretation: This is the house for physical and tangible things such as immediate physical environment, sensory experiences, property, possessions, and wealth. It also concerns itself with your attitude toward these things and the value you attach to things and yourself.

Third House: Communication

Ruled by: Gemini and Mercury

Interpretation: This deals with your method of expression and communication with the outside world. How you interact with people, experiences, places, and things fall into this gambit. It also governs how you use logic to your advantage, how you manage relationships within and outside the family, and how well or poorly you make your points.

Fourth House: Home

Ruled by: Cancer and the Moon

Interpretation: Quite literally the cornerstone of any person's life, this house is all about your foundation. It represents the home, family, parents, stability, nurturing, emotionality, comfort zones, and nostalgia. It also stands for the time in your life when you felt the happiest and the most secure, your memories, and sometimes ancestors.

Fifth House: Creativity and Pleasure

Ruled by: Leo and the Sun

Interpretation: This house is about fun! All of your creative pursuits, hobbies, passions, interests, romances, drama, affairs, etc., fall under this. It also represents children, luck, heart, and love.

Sixth House: Health and Service

Ruled by: Virgo and Mercury

Interpretation: Your work ethics, service to others, everyday tasks, organization, dedication to work, etc., come under this house. It also represents your health and lifestyle, diet, nutrition, exercise, and whether there is any personal quest for self-improvement.

Seventh House: Partnerships

Ruled by: Libra and Venus

Interpretation: This is opposite to the first house (Self). It naturally follows that this house is about service and connections with other people, instead of the self. It governs relationships, marriage, commercial partnerships, contracts, etc. In a converse direction, it can also represent negative partnerships like enemies, lawsuits, or divorces.

Eighth House: Sex and Transformation

Ruled by: Scorpio and Pluto

Interpretation: This house has a mysterious aura about it, no doubt because the ever-enigmatic Scorpio rules it! It represents death, dark sides, wills, investments, inheritances, occult, losses, sacrifices, and above all, transformation. Something begins when something ends. It's an inevitable cycle. This is a house of transformation and personal growth.

Ninth House: Big Ideas

Ruled by: Sagittarius and Jupiter

Interpretation: The third house reveals basic thought processes. The ninth house, opposite it, is all about higher thinking and philosophy. It represents adventure, travel, exploration, and a constant search for deeper meanings to life and challenges oneself for growth.

Tenth House: Public Image

Ruled by: Capricorn and Saturn

Interpretation: This is sometimes known as the "Midheaven" in astrology. How you cultivate your image in public, reputation, and life path are determined and revealed by this house. It connects itself with fame, tradition, honor, achievement, authority, and influences in your life and career path.

Eleventh House: Community and Friends

Ruled by: Aquarius and Uranus

Interpretation: This house is about groups, community, networking, friendships, teamwork, humanitarian causes, originality, astronomy, inventions, etc. It governs the need for social justice and a collective goal to achieve something better in life and contribute to society.

Twelfth House: Subconscious and Secrets

Ruled by: Pisces and Neptune

Interpretation: This represents the evolution of the soul. It depicts secrets, fantasies, desires, endings, karma, traumas, separation from society (imprisonment, institutionalization), paranormal and occult energies, old age, the afterlife, subconscious desires, etc.

Sister Signs of the Zodiac

Each sign of the zodiac corresponds to a different sign, and they might be opposites or share similarities. These signs also share modalities and congenial elements, as you will see in the following segment.

Modalities

In the Zodiac, Taurus, Leo, Aquarius, and Scorpio are known as the Fixed Signs. They are the most stable, stubborn, and deliberate signs.

Gemini, Sagittarius, Virgo, and Pisces are known as Mutable Signs. They are remarkably easygoing, flexible, and tend to go with the flow.

Aries, Capricorn, Libra, and Cancer are known as the Cardinal Signs. These signs are known for their bossy nature, and such people usually take the initiative much quicker than the other signs.

Elements of the Zodiac

Active Elements

The Air Signs (Gemini, Libra, and Aquarius) and the Fire Signs (Aries, Leo, and Sagittarius) are the active elements.

Passive Elements

The Earth Signs (Taurus, Capricorn, and Virgo) and Water Signs (Scorpio, Cancer, and Pisces) fall in this category.

Even though they might be polar opposites, Sister signs fulfill each other's weaknesses. Now see the sister sign pairings in the zodiac and understand their interpretations.

Aries (First, Cardinal, Fire) and Libra (Seventh, Cardinal, Air)

An Arian is almost always spontaneous and the life of the party. They can be volatile and hard to handle. They are also filled with excitement for new things in life. Libra is the total opposite. They are gentle, patient, warmhearted, and like to stay out of chaos.

These two signs balance each other out and together make a strong team.

Taurus (Second, Fixed, Earth) and Scorpio (Eighth, Fixed, Water)

Taurus is a bull, stubborn and unyielding. So is Scorpio. Taurus loves beauty, taste, and class in his life. So does Scorpio. Taurus and Scorpio are both very intense signs. The difference lies in their way of processing these personality traits. Taurus is upfront and gives it back in a transparent manner. Scorpio bides their time and plans revenge carefully. Both signs are totally impervious to outside influences when it comes to their life and career.

Gemini (Third, Mutable, Air) and Sagittarius (Ninth, Mutable, Fire)

Gemini is all about gregariousness and knowing as much about the world as they possibly can. Such people are usually curious about all aspects of life, and others sound them. Sagittarius tries to make sense of the world. They are the kind of people that seek meaning and a greater purpose in life. Both signs are paired together because each can bounce off the other to gain a new perspective.

Cancer (Fourth, Cardinal, Water) and Capricorn (Tenth, Cardinal, Earth)

Cancer is mostly about care and nurture. This nursing and motherly instinct is very strong in this sign. They are also intuitive and introspect a lot, so they can usually tell when someone is feeling down or low. They will always be there for you and have your back. Capricorn, on the other hand, believes in tough love. When in relationships or forming strong feelings for someone, such people will feel responsible for that person. In their misguided zeal, they might try to steer the other person in the direction they feel is most appropriate. It works well with Cancer because, while both are caring types, Cancer will intuitively pull Capricorn out of tight spots.

Leo (Fifth, Fixed, Fire) and Aquarius (Eleventh, Fixed, Air)

Leo is fiercely protective and connects with people at a very basic level. Their emotions and actions will always tend toward the protective nature they possess. On the other hand, Aquarius also believes in love and protection, but at an emotional and mental level. A Leo connects more with the physical aspect; an Aquarius connects with the mind.

Virgo (Sixth, Mutable, Earth) and Pisces (Twelfth, Mutable, Water)

A Virgo is sensitive, honest, and values authenticity in all aspects of life. They value truth and transparency. A Virgo is also intelligent and stable. Unlike this, Pisces is a dreamy-eyed person, with loads of plans and activities bouncing in their heads. They live in castles of air most of the time. But even so, their imagination and creation make them fun to be with. Both the signs bounce off each other splendidly.

Now that you have covered the basics of houses, signs, and sister signs in the zodiac, it is time to delve a little deeper into the reading of a birth chart. You will study other factors such as aspects, angles, and cusps.

Planetary Aspects

The distance between any two planets and zodiac signs is known as the "aspect." Aspects are measured using geometry (degrees and angles). Seven major aspects are classified as "soft" and "hard." Soft aspects include conjunct, trine, and sextile. Hard aspects include semisextile, square, quincunx, and opposite.

The Seven Major Aspects

- Conjunct
- Semisextile
- Sextile
- Square
- Trine
- Quincunx
- Opposite

So, how does this work in a birth chart? For instance, if you find that Mercury and Venus appear in the chart with a soft aspect, this means their powers are blended, and you may have an excellent love interest and communication with that person on the horizon. Conversely, if the two planets form a hard aspect, you might struggle in either area.

Now, look at each of the aspects in brief detail.

Conjunct: Two Planets in the Same Sign (Zero Degrees Apart)

Such planets will blend their energies, form a powerful alliance, and boost the people within their ambit. For example, if you have Neptune and Mercury in this formation, this can mean an extremely creative person who is sometimes absentminded. If three or more planets are in conjunction, it is known as "stellium." The formation of the planets is also important. If it is Uranus or Mars, it might mean stress and tension for the person involved.

Semisextile: One Sign Apart (Thirty Degrees Separation)

These planets might not have anything in common, making the proximity a bit difficult. For example, if one planet is in Sagittarius, the other in Scorpio, look at what happens. Scorpio is a fixed water sign and highly emotional and introverted. Sagittarius is a mutable fire sign and extroverted. As long as these two are semisextile to each other, the discomfort will continue.

Sextile: Two Signs Apart (60 Degrees Separation)

This is a highly compatible situation. Though not strong individually, they bring with them cooperation and friendly interactions. Such a formation means a lot of compatibility factors for the individual. Pleasure, companionship, and camaraderie are promoted with this sextile. If two planets were sextile in your chart, that part of your life would be stress-free. It might be anything— your career, love life, marriage, or children.

Square: Three Signs Apart (90 Degrees Separation)

This is a classic tug-of-war situation, which is why this is one of the "hard" aspects. A battle of wills is almost always the consequence as neither planetary characteristic is willing to budge. For example, if Jupiter falls in Virgo, forming a square with Venus in Sagittarius, this might mean that your micromanaging tendencies are brimming to the hilt, obsessing over what everyone says to you. But that would also mean that with Venus in your Sagittarius, you rush off and indulge in impulsive romantic acts, which might not always be the best thing to do. If your natal chart has squares in it, that will reveal parts of your nature, which you need to reflect and work upon.

Trine: Four Signs Apart (120 Degrees Separation)

This is normally considered the best aspect since there is harmony, ease of interaction, and luck amongst the planets involved. Sharing the same elements promote the same goals and energies. If you spot a trine in your birth chart, look closely at what it says. A trine in stable earth elements makes you a solid, dependable person who is also a hard worker.

Quincunx: Five Signs Apart (150 Degrees Separation)

This is an eccentric angle, so to speak. This aspect denotes much awkwardness and discord because the signs have nothing in common and feel like strangers at a party. Major cooperative activities will need to be attempted if these signs are to work well together. For example, if Mercury lands in meticulous Virgo, it forms a quincunx with Mars in the impatient Aries. You already see the problem! Detail-oriented does not go well with "go with the flow." Such quincunxes have different interpretations. Some planetary formations make you take risks, others make you independent, some drive you crazy, and yet others might help you overcome your fears.

Opposite: Six Signs Apart (180 Degrees Separation)

These signs are polar opposites, the meeting of two extremes. Conflict is guaranteed, but so is balancing and mirroring of the signs and personalities. There is a reason why opposites attract. It's because of the tremendous learning potential the two offer each other. The strengths and weaknesses of each sign can be used to fulfill those of the other.

Cusps, Degrees, Signs, and Interceptions

One cannot talk about these three points in isolation; they have to be understood together. A cusp is not merely the overlapping point between two Sun Signs. At the moment of your birth, the Sun was in one sign. Because the Sun moves from sign to sign every year, the cusp actually means that imaginary lines separate the houses in the horoscope, not the signs.

Sometimes referred to as "angles," four of the cusps have different names.

- First House Cusp: Ascendant

- Fourth House Cusp: Nadir

- Seventh House Cusp: Descendant

- Tenth House Cusp: Midheaven

As you already know, the houses represent various areas of the sky. The first house is for the east, the seventh is for the western horizon, the tenth is for the highest point in the horizon at any given point, and the fourth is for its opposite point.

For example, if someone were born with twenty degrees of Sagittarius rising, it would mean that in the imaginary 360-degree clock or circle of houses, the first house hand points to the middle of the sign if someone were born near the equator and the second house hand points in the middle of Capricorn.

Now, say Sagittarius is on the cusp of both the first and second houses. This means that Capricorn is entirely omitted from the reading, and the third house gets Aquarius instead. This sort of situation is known as an "interception." Of course, this does not mean that Capricorn has vanished! It is merely hidden in the second house.

Planets are divided into two categories as per your planetary chart: outer and personal.

The outer planets of the chart are Jupiter, Saturn, Uranus, Neptune, and Pluto.

- Jupiter represents your personal and higher growth.

- Saturn represents integrity, rules, and ambitions.

- Uranus stands for your imagination.

- Pluto represents how ready you are for a change in your life.

Personal planets are the Sun, the Moon, Mercury, Venus, and Mars.

- The Sun tells you about your overall personality.

- The Moon tells you about what you think and feel.

- Mercury is all about your perceptions in life.

- Mars represents your ambition and willpower.

See where the planets appear in your birth chart and under which sign. For instance, if you see Uranus in Aries in the fourth house, it means the following:

- Uranus = growth, potential, imagination

- Aries = fiery, passionate, charming

- Fourth House = family, property, relationships

You now know that planets, stars, and their precise alignments combine to give you a holistic and complete picture of yourself. The answers to questions, sometimes, can indeed be found in your planetary position.

Chapter Five: Numerology — See Fate Unfold Through Numbers

Numerology — What Does It Mean?

A study of numbers in your life is called numerology. Each number conveys deep meaning. The field of numerology is universal, as numbers are universal in nature. Numerology isn't a stand-alone field. It ties in neatly with astrology and other similar divination methods. This field's basis lies in the fact that almost everything tangible in the universe can be broken down into the simplest form of numbers.

The History of Numerology

Some of the earliest numerology records come from Egypt, Babylon, Rome, China, and Japan. It is universally agreed that the great mathematician Pythagoras, also a Greek philosopher, first put forward radical ideas about numerology. Of course, it wasn't known by that name centuries ago. It was Dr. Julian Stenton who came up with the nomenclature.

Positive and Negative Numbers

Just as there are positive and negative integers on a number scale, numerology refers to the balance of positive and negative energies the numbers have on your life and other aspects related to it, such as career, relationships, and health.

Master Numbers

11, 22, and 33 are known as the master numbers in numerology. Taken together with the overall context, these numbers have deep meanings. As with any other divination form, you need to look at the holistic picture before interpreting anything. Usually, when the numbers totaled, if you are left with a double-digit number, say 52, 5+2 becomes 7. This gives you your primary number as 7. But if your total ends up being either 11 or 22 or 33, you don't add these up to get 2, 4, and 6. You let the master number be as it is.

Strengths and Weaknesses from Numbers

Numbers do reveal a lot about you, including what you are good at and what you need to work on. For many people, numerology provides their life's purpose!

Combinations of Numbers

When you look at the number chart and the traits associated with each number, you get a better sense of clarity as to why certain things happen to you. For instance, if you keep fighting with your best friend or sibling, if you do not share a warm relationship with your loved ones, or if you feel magnetically drawn toward someone, an in-depth look and analysis of the numerical relationships between you and your friends and family will reveal a lot!

Numerology and Your Birth

Sometimes, people change their birth name and hope to expect success and riches. It does not work that way. Sure, adding or removing letters from your name will change the numerology of your birth and life number, but when you were born, the alignment of the stars and planets, the angles and degrees they made, and your birth name all add up to a powerfully unique number to "make you."

Numerology — What Is It?

Basically, many calculations! It is not just simple addition, though. These calculations can involve several levels and sequences. Even basic reading involves a lot of hard work. After a detailed analysis, a numerologist can arrive at your birth number, life path number, soul urge number, expression number, etc. The following explains the meaning of each of the numbers first and then goes on to the other aspects of numerology.

Number 1: These people are usually at the top of their game. Leadership skills, charisma, initiative, and entrepreneurial spirit are associated with this number. Yes, such people also have little patience to deal with others and may sometimes come across as brash and arrogant. In matters of love and romance, 1s try to be alone for a long time before finding someone!

Number 2: They strike a delicate balance between all areas in their life. They crave harmony. Because of their magnetic and easygoing personality, they are a favorite with people everywhere. But they also need to put their foot down when needed, as their sacrificing nature keeps getting in the way! For business, life path number, and any agreements requiring peacekeeping abilities, number 2 is a sure shot guarantee of success.

Number 3: This number corresponds to generous spirit, teamwork, and social aspects. They are the life of any party, and people love their witty banter. They also tend to stick with the mundane or shallow pleasures of life instead of learning new things and sticking with something more profound. They are also prone to having more than one romantic relationship. 3s are known for bringing people together and keeping the social fires going.

Number 4: 4s make amazing planners, administrators, organizers, and managers. They have excellent attention to detail and can get along with anyone. They are also adept at getting work from people. When such people wish to date, they must make sure that the other person can keep up with their spirit. Otherwise, it might seem as if the 4 is taking charge everywhere.

Number 5: If your life path number is 5, that means you do not care to be bound to any one thing or person. You are a free spirit and want to do things your way—be it a freelance career or a penchant for travel. You are flexible and open-minded. You need someone similar in thought or the exact opposite to balance out the yin and yang.

Number 6: Sincerity, warmth, and affection are the hallmarks of 6s. These people speak and do things from their hearts. Their natural warmth and love make them a popular choice for careers like teaching, therapy, pediatrician, or social work. When such people make relationships or embark on a new project, they throw themselves completely into it. 6s need to understand that too much of anything might not be that good. They need to learn moderation.

Number 7: Such people have excellent analytical skills and coupled with their intellectual pursuits, it makes them perfectly suited for careers in education, philosophy, detective, or police work. These people work more with their heads, not the heart. Emotions and expressions do not come naturally to them.

Number 8: This number corresponds to hard work, motivation, sincerity, and a sense of purpose. Such people almost always have a great mind for numbers and do well in accounting, finance, and economic advisers. They are methodical and patient. Such people find it easy to make and maintain relationships—although they might find it hard to let go.

Number 9: 9s are all about a humanitarian approach and leadership. They also tend to keep giving until they don't have anything left, but they need to look out for themselves more and stop putting others first.

The Master Numbers

11, 22, and 33 are considered the master numbers in numerology because 1, 2, and 3 form a Triangle of Enlightenment. The other numbers, 44, 55, 66, 77, 88, and 99, are known as Power numbers.

Master Number 11: The most intuitive and analytical of all numbers, 11 corresponds to number 2 in many aspects—insightful, mysterious, deep, emotional, stubborn—but with more leadership and charismatic qualities.

Master Number 22: This is one of the most successful numbers and is also known as "Master Builder." 22 mirrors some qualities of number 11, but it also complements those by its innate nature of 2 and 4—making it more analytical, practical, and idealistic. 22s must learn to be practical; otherwise, they will waste their potential.

Master Number 33: This is the "Master Teacher" and most spiritually and aesthetically sound number. It contains all the qualities of the 11 and 22, along with those of 3 and 6—making it powerful and magnetic! 33 is considered active when found in your life path number, expression number, or personality number. That is when it is most effective.

The Secondary Numbers

Number 10: Indicates the completion of a portion of your life cycle or karmic cycle. Usually considered a good omen.

Number 12: Completing something, rewards, and fortune.

Number 13: Ill luck, sickness, death, bad omens, and restrictions.

Number 14: Mental and physical upheavals, trials, break-in fortune, delays, and curbing of freedom.

Number 16: Intellectual pursuits, emotional coolness, cold attitude toward something or someone.

Number 19: Selfish behavior, laziness, anger, aggression, and powerlessness.

Number 40: Finality in something, the beginning of a new project or relationship.

Now, look at the different aspects of numerology, namely:

1. Life Path Number

2. Year Number

3. Name Number

4. Fate Number

5. House Number

Life Path Number

This is the most important number, which forms the basis of your life and everything you do in it. It reflects who you are, your traits, where you are strong, and where you can improve.

To calculate your life path number, do the following:

Add all the digits in your complete birth date. For example, say Rachel Jones was born on April 6, 1998.

Break it down as:

4+6+1+9+9+8=37

Add 3 and 7. You get 10. Further, add them. You get a single digit 1. This is Rachel Jones's life path number. If your total comes up to 11, 22, or 33, do not add them further. The Master Numbers have different interpretations.

Year Number

Every year brings a different meaning to your life. To calculate your current year number, do the following:

Add the current year to your date of birth. For example, if the current year is 2020, and your date of birth is November 5:

5+1+1+2+0+2+0=11

Your year number is 11.

Name Number

Use the table given below and convert the letters of your name into numbers. Then add them up to get your name number. This reveals your characters and traits.

For example, your name is Rachel Jones.

R=9, A=1, C=3, H=8, E=5, L=3

J=1, O=6, N=5, E=5, S=1

So, Rachel Jones translates as numbers into:

9+1+3+8+5+3+1+6+5+5+1=47

Further, 7+4= 11

So, Rachel Jones gets her name number as 11.

Inner Personality: Add up the vowels in your name.

R A C H E L J O N E S= A, E, O, E

A=1, E=5, O=6

1+5+6+5= 17

1+7= 8

The inner personality number is 8. This is what governs her inner self.

Outer Personality: Add up the consonants in the name.

R A C H E L J O N E S = R, C, H, L, J, N, S

R=9, C=3, H=8, L=3, J=1, N=5, S=1

9+3+8+3+1+5+1= 30

3+0=3

The outer personality number is 3. This is what her public persona is.

Fate Number

To calculate your fate number, add your birth number and name number. If you continue with the above example, you'll see that Rachel Jones has a life path number (birth number) as 1. Her name number is 11.

11 +1= 12

1+2=3

So, Rachel's fate number is 3.

House Number

You simply calculate the numbers in your address. Leave out the street and building names. Reduce it to one single digit. Here are the interpretations:

If your house number is:

1 — Represents self-reliance, quarrels with neighbors, dissatisfaction

2 — Represents harmony and building of good bonds between residents

3 — Represents an outgoing and open-minded nature of people

4 — Represents entrepreneurial spirit, home businesses, life improvement

5 — Represents quiet, energy, activities, and relaxation mode in residents

6 — Represents family, domesticity, and harmony between people

7 — Represents students, introverted nature, stubborn attitude

8 — Represents a need for more money, balance, unexpected arrivals, a bit of strife

9 — Represents intellectual pursuits, music, joy, fortune, new projects

Numbers, just like other aspects of life, have hidden meanings. You can cultivate the wisdom and growth needed to understand and interpret them!

Chapter Six: Palmistry — The Basics of Palm Reading

Reading palms is often a favorite pastime at gatherings or get-togethers. It is mostly fun, but there is a deeper meaning behind all those squiggly lines and bumps on your palm. Palmistry refers to reading hands or palms and assessing someone's personality, future aspects, fortune, etc. This practice is also known as "chiromancy." However, palmistry is just not reading palms; it takes into consideration your fingers, fingernails, and arms too. Every single bit of the palm adds together to bring a whole meaning to a person's character traits and personality.

Palmistry Origins

This ancient practice has its roots in India, Rome, and China. Other countries such as Persia, Greece, and Egypt also use ancient palmistry recordings in their day-to-day lives. Chinese history suggests that palmistry began there almost three thousand years ago. A comprehensive detailing about the practice originated in China during 202 BC–9 AD during the Western Han Dynasty's rule. Xu Fu wrote this treatise.

Aristotle, one of history's greats, elaborated on the practice of palm reading in his book, *De Historia Animalium*, which translates to *"History of Animals."* He believed that the lines etched in the human hand mean something and are not there without any reason. Now delve into this fascinating ancient practice, which still finds many serious takers today.

Major Palm Lines — What They Are and How to Read Them

If you look closely at your palms, you will see a crisscross of numerous lines. Some may be parallel, intersect, twinning, and yet others might be single. Each line of your hand says something. Time to find out what:

Life Line

This is one of the three major lines in your palm. It begins from the edge of the palm, resting between the thumb and forefinger, and extends toward the thumb base. In general, it tells you about the life energy of the person. The absence of a lifeline is not a good sign. It means you will suffer ill health and possibly have a short life. Frequent accidents are also predicted for such people. In contrast, a deep and long lifeline indicates that the person is highly resistant to ill health and disease and may enjoy a long life.

A thick lifeline may mean that the person is more suited to jobs involving hard physical labor than a desk job. These people will also be good at physical activity and sports. A thin and weak line indicates gynecological problems in females and unsatisfactory career paths in the initial stages of life. A secondary line running parallel with the lifeline means a good, strong vitality for the person involved. He or she may also recover very quickly from illnesses.

Any branches or forks in the lifeline indicate many things: upward branches might mean more opportunities, chances, fame, and prestige in life. Downward branches can mean less energy, so getting diverted from one's goal and loneliness in later years.

Heart Line

This is also known as the "love line" and is of extreme interest to most people! This line usually indicates how a person responds to love and affection. Your personal relationships and how to deal with them become clear with the heart line. A good line is considered deep, unbroken, curved, and extending for a long way without a break. If it has two or more forks at its end, it's all the better!

Length of the Heart Line

Short: A short heart line indicates ruthlessness and narrow-mindedness. Such people act without thinking and, therefore, face problems due to their impulsive nature.

Long: This indicates a certain stubbornness in dealing with people. Career-wise, success is seen, but at a personal cost. In matters of the heart, romance and heartbreak seem to go together. Major troubles can be seen, which are mended with the person's resolve.

Culmination at the Mount of Jupiter

This shows many dreams, love, and great expectations from oneself.

Culmination between the Mount of Jupiter and Saturn.

If the line ends below the forefinger and middle finger, it indicates the purity of one's love.

Curvature

Straight: This indicates a stable, mild, and approachable personality. In romantic overtures, this person is shy and passive. It also indicates a harmonious and stable family life ahead.

Curved: If it is an upward curve, it indicates a lot of eloquence for the person. He or she may be excellent at speaking out and creating a favorable romantic atmosphere. A downward curve, on the other hand, shows a negative temperament. Others might feel uneasy around you due to your inability to show your true self and feelings. Some drama and twists are predicted for this personality's love life.

Islands

Any islands in the heart line indicate changes in your love life, most commonly, emotional and romantic distress. Your love life might experience some sort of breakdown, unwilling attitudes, and other causes for concern.

Broken Lines

If the gap is large, there are indications of a break or hardship in the relationship.

If the line breaks under the little finger, the results indicate stress and hardship in both your material and romantic life. It also indicates an inability to stick or stay faithful to one's partner, thereby causing the relationship to break up.

If the line ends where the ring finger and little finger meet, this sadly indicates a failed relationship or failed marriage. However, all is not lost. It also shows happiness and another true love after the disaster.

If the two broken lines are concurrent, you are more than likely to suffer poor blood circulation and other related ailments.

If none of these and the broken line seems to go on in the direction of its own, it usually means that the person is a bit neurotic, impulsive, and hard to love. This person will most certainly enjoy his or her life the way they want.

Head Line

This line begins from the edge of the palm and extends across it, between the life line and heart line. The head line indicates a person's state of mind, beliefs, the way they think, self-control, etc.

A long head line shows that you have clarity of mind and are considerate and responsive. It would also indicate overthinking.

A medium-length line means that you are smart. You have a talent for doing things in a way that others can't.

A short line extends only up to the middle finger. Such people usually are hasty, impulsive, and careless. Conversely, such people can also be counted upon to finish tasks quickly and creatively.

The Degree of Bending

Straight. This usually indicates that a person is practical and dedicated. He or she is typically an idealist and does well in commerce, science, and math.

Curved. Such people do well in PR, mass media, psychology, and sociology. They have a realistic bent of mind.

Downward. You have a highly creative and artistic ability. Vocations such as painting, murals, poetry, and creative writing will be most suitable for such people. Conversely, people with this kind of line are also quite impulsive when it comes to handling money.

Relation to the Life line

Joined. If joined and then split toward the end, it usually shows the strength of character. If they overlap, it means that the person is shy and thoughtful.

Separated. Such a line depicts an extroverted personality, which is highly independent.

Other Important Lines and Their Interpretations

Marriage Line

One of the aspects usually troubling people is their marital life and status. This line shows your marital situation quite clearly. Some people have a single line, others might have multiple, and yet others might have crossed lines or no lines at all. In the case of a marriage line, the length usually determines the outcome. Of course, apart from that, there are other aspects to interpreting the marriage line too. So, keep reading!

Length

Long and Straight

This is the ideal line, indicating a deep and strong bond of love. A happy and stable family life is interpreted with this line. If this kind of line touches your sun line, the outcome is not only a happy marriage but a successful career path too.

Short

A short line will mean that you are not as passionate about the opposite sex as you should be. If the line does not run deep, it means there is reluctance toward pursuing romantic relationships. Such people also usually marry late in life.

Curvature

Curve Downwards

Ominously, this might mean the death of a partner earlier than your death. A sudden dip in the line might mean an accidental death. A line curving downward and touching the heart line means that you will have clashes and fights with your partner. This is also the line that indicates separation or divorce.

Curve Upwards

A serene love life is the reading for this line. You are stable and happy in your relationship and do not have any financial worries about the future. This kind of line indicates a happy marriage.

Broken Line

A broken line indicates that you will have reservations when it comes to your marital life. Quarrels will be the mainstay of this relationship. If it reaches a certain point, divorce is almost always on the cards.

Crossroads or X sign

In palmistry, anything that has a crossroad or an X sign is considered to be inauspicious because it indicates trouble in paradise. Such people tend to have a greater chance of marital unhappiness and arguments. They may also seek love affairs outside their marriage, which further worsens the situation.

Overlapping Lines

Such lines usually mean that you have a less than ideal relationship. You have ideas and dreams about your mate that are hard to fulfill in reality. If unmarried, you will stay single for a long time. If married, you will find yourself seeking outside pleasures and interests.

Fate Line

The fate line is another major line that runs up the palm near the middle finger's base. It can begin from anywhere. It is also known as the "career line" because this line indicates how well you will do in your chosen career. This line also indicates changes in your work life and career path. If it is clean and deep, you can consider yourself blessed with a great career path and fortune. This line is also referred to as the "line of luck."

Timing of the Fate Line

From the base of the palm, the fate line begins at age five.

The fate line and headline intersect at the point for age 35, and the heart line's intersecting point is for age 55.

If the point for the fate line comes to the Mount of Saturn, it points at age 75.

Absence of a Fate Line

This does not mean that you will not have a fruitful career. It merely means that you tend to keep job-hopping due to your nature and do not wish to maintain any permanency in your career.

The Shape of the Fate Line

Long and Deep

This kind of line usually shows a strong entrepreneurial spirit in the individual. He or she is strongly capable of running their own business.

Narrow and Thin

If this goes from the middle part of the line toward the end of the line, it means that you will have a rewarding career in your early days but get progressively worse during your later years.

Shallow Line

Hard work, albeit with some twists, is indicated for this line. If it is shallow and wide, you will work hard but will fail to reap the benefits of the hard work.

Oblique Line

This shows that the individual has a unique thought process and gives a very refreshing perspective to general ideas and views at work.

Fate Line and the Heart Line

If the heart line stops the line of fate, it usually indicates that your emotions cloud your thinking. You rule with the heart rather than the head. This may affect your career chances.

A fate line that emerges from the Mount of Venus (surrounded by the lifeline at the base of the thumb) and ends near the heart line denotes a marriage with a person of fame and repute.

Fate Line and the Head Line

An early divorce or separation of parents might be the outcome if the head line stops the fate line.

If it merely brushes by the head line and does not penetrate it, it indicates fame and fortune. It also shows that the person does not see a project through. These people would do well to save money from an early age.

If a fate line is stopped at the head line, you stop working of your own free will. Even though you have the talent, a false sense of judgment about your abilities will make you do so. Don't lose heart, though. After age 35, you will have some sort of breakthrough in your work life.

Sun Line

This line begins from the Mount of Moon, which is at the base of the palm on the side of the little finger and goes upward to the Mount of Sun, below the ring finger.

The sun line depicts the kind of talents individuals may possess, their capabilities, and their liabilities. People with a long sun line generally fare better than those without it. A good, strong sun line boosts the fate line.

Some Pointers

If the line is clear, it indicates that the person has a refined taste in literary and artistic pursuits.

If the sun line is short or not present, it indicates an ordinary and placid life. A complete absence would mean a lack of success for the individual.

If the line is thin and narrow, it usually indicates a life of frustration and possible problems in marital life.

Doubled Lines

This shows that the individual is versatile and open to suggestions. This person has varied skills and has a good head for business.

Multiple Lines

If there are more than two sun lines, that means you do not have a head for finance and may lose money. Your expenditure is more than your income. You will need to start saving early and learn a few financial concepts.

Sun Line and Fate Line

If both these lines are parallel in your palm, it is a particularly good sign. This spells success, fortune, and a good reputation for the person throughout their life.

Money Line

The money line can be found under the ring and little finger.

If the line is clear and straight, it indicates that the person is a smart investor and makes smart money decisions. In conjunction with a clear sun line, it could mean that the person will gain both money and fame later in life.

If the money line is wavy, the person's wealth in life will not be stable. There can be troubles in their work or career.

Any other curvature in the line indicates a weathered fortune ahead. If this kind of palm belongs to a generally short-tempered person, it will mean a lot of difficulty in earning wealth and prestige.

Money Line and Sun Line

Sometimes, a sun line branches off and extends toward the little finger, which is also the money line. This kind of line signifies commercial success and a great head for money-related matters.

If the sun line and money line are intertwined or connected, this person enjoys an unexpected windfall later in life.

When a short line crosses the money and sun lines, it would indicate enemies in your life who wish to sabotage you and rob you of your wealth.

M Sign

According to Chinese palmistry, the M sign in a palm is significant. This happens when the career line passes through the head line in an upward formation, and its endpoint touches the heart line, forming an M shape. For individuals having this line, great riches are foretold.

Money Line — Upward Branching

This kind of line means that the person can manage money and handle business or commerce-related aspects. This person would be the go-to for any money-related advice.

Health Line

The most important line for any person! Located at the base of the little finger, it can travel almost anywhere in the palm. It may or may not join any other lines.

There is a slight catch to this line. Although known as the "health" line, its mere appearance on the palm signifies that something is wrong with the bodily systems. Of course, not all health lines are bad. If it is a straight line that does not touch the lifeline, it is considered good. Surprisingly, the absence of a health line is a good sign!

The Shape of the Lines

- *Wavy:* This warns the person of digestive, liver, or gallbladder problems in life. This person might also suffer from gastrointestinal issues.

- *Broken:* Again, the digestive system is at play here. Terraced lines or those with a sharp break spell doom for the GI tract of the individual.

- *Short Lines Cross Over:* This kind of individual may be accident-prone and suffer ill health over a long time.

- *Multiple Short Lines:* This person is usually weak-bodied and sick for a large part of their childhood and adulthood.

Length of the Health Line

Crossing the Head Line

A long health line doesn't necessarily mean good and robust health. In fact, if this crosses the head line, it could mean that one's health might be affected by excessive mental strain.

Reaching Over to the Mount of Venus

If the health line extends to the Mount of Venus, it means there is something wrong with the circulatory system. Such people are more prone to heart and cardiac-related ailments and diseases.

Touching the Life Line

This is usually interpreted to mean an inauspicious sign of health, contrary to the connotation. It indicates a poor circulatory system and a weak heart.

Palm Mounts

Now that you have covered the palm's major lines, it is time to review common mounts in the palm and understand what they mean.

Palm mounts are raised bumps on the flesh of the hand. In Chinese palmistry, there are seven mounts, each named after a different planet and which stand for different characteristics of the individual. These mounts can be found in the following places:

- *The Mount of Jupiter*: Base of the forefinger, above the Mount of Inner Mars.

- *The Mount of Saturn*: Base of the middle finger.

- *The Mount of Apollo*: Base of the ring finger.

- *The Mount of Mercury*: Base of the little finger, above the Mount of Outer Mars.

- *The Mount of Luna or the Moon*: Base of the palm, on the side of the little finger.

- *The Mount of Venus*: Base of the thumb and surrounded by the life line.

- *The Mount of Mars*: Inner Mars is between the mounts of Jupiter and Venus. The Outer Mars is between the mounts of Mercury and Luna. The plain of Mars, a neutral ground, is located in the center of the palm.

Interpretation of the Mounts

The Mount of Jupiter

A well-developed and significant elevation here indicates that the person is career-minded, ambitious, and responsible. This mount displays authority, self-respect, honesty, and reliability in an individual. Such people are naturally predisposed to jobs in the government or with the armed forces. If this mount is underdeveloped, it indicates a lack of honesty, morals, and timidness in the person concerned. This kind of person also shies away from fame and honor. Conversely, if this mount is extra prominent, it means that the person is pretentious, snobbish, and overly ambitious.

The Mount of Saturn

This mount corresponds to perspective and integrity. A well-developed mount in this location shows that you are sincere, independent, and extremely intelligent, more so than average. Such people are good scholars and efficient organizers. If the mount is too depressed and shallow, you might be a lonely person, tending toward superstitions and religious views. On the other hand, if the mount is too high or pronounced, you tend to be a show-off and might not care for others' opinions. If the mount appears to be too large, it means you tend to be more pessimistic than average.

The Mount of Apollo

Apollo translates to beauty, emotions, and wealth. A well-developed mount here signifies a strong affinity toward art and culture. You will be someone who loves the beauty around you. Such people are also compassionate and work for others willingly. A low mount here signifies a lack of interest in the arts.

The Mount of Mercury

This mount represents your ability to think and make decisions in life. A well-developed mount here means that the individual is resourceful and can adapt to any situation in life. Such people do well in emergency services and management-related studies. But the pitfall is a prominent mount—it mounts to bravado and fluff, no substance. If the mount is low, that indicates that the person is negative in predisposition and will not pull together in teamwork.

The Mount of Luna

Much like the Moon, this mount represents mystery, imagination, and many intrigues. If this mount is developed, it signifies a great deal of intuition and imagination and the ability to dream far and wide. Such people are prone to depression, too, because sometimes their sentiments get the better of them. A low mount means the person isn't open to new ideas. A higher mount means the person is highly emotional and open to love and romance. Conversely, if the mount is low, such people do not show any interest in love or commitment. Their lives are rather humdrum.

The Mount of Mars

Inner Mars: Related to an adventurous streak in individuals, a strongly developed mount indicates courage and fearlessness. A mount higher than average could also mean aggression and fighting tendencies. A lower than average mount usually indicates indecisiveness on the part of the person.

Outer Mars: Sometimes also called the Mars Negative, this mount represents self-control. A strong mount here means that you sail through life without any major fears or dangers holding you back. You persevere through setbacks. You are someone who doesn't like taking monetary risks.

Plain of Mars: It is called a plain as it is never too high nor too low. If it's without any crosses or squiggles, it's a good sign. It means clear sailing in life. Any other lines on it indicate that you will have to fight off obstacles to lead a good life.

The Mount of Venus

Much like the Greek Goddess, this mount relates to love and affection. If it is prominent, it shows that the person enjoys companionship and is highly sentimental. If too low, it indicates that the person lacks energy and is coldhearted. If too high, the person becomes overly energetic, which might lead to complications in their love life.

Left vs. Right Hand

Having read this much about the practice and study of palmistry, now look at the difference between the left and right hand.

In palmistry, the left hand is considered to be passive, and the right hand dominant. This applies to most of the population. If your dominant hand is right, you should ideally present that for the reading. If you are left-handed, this hand should be presented for the reading. However, usually, most practitioners read both palms for a better understanding of you.

The Left Hand Reveals: Your wealth position, family, opportunities, potential, personality traits, quirks, and fears.

The Right Hand Reveals: Your action potential, drive, destiny, and future goals.

Reading of both hands is important because both halves make up a full you. You cannot read one and leave the other because that would mean only half a reading. Beware of cheap and pretentious psychics who read only one palm and rattle off predictions. That is not how palmistry works.

Now that you have a basic understanding of the palms' lines and mounts read on to discover yet another delightful and interesting method of divination: the Runes.

Chapter Seven: Runecasting I: How to Cast the Runes

What is Runecasting?

Runecasting is another method of divination that has been around since ancient times. Runes are cast in specific ways, spread, and then interpreted. Now, just like other forms of divination, runes do not give you the exact and literal meaning of your life events. Nothing like "Who am I going to marry?" or "When will I get a promotion?" Like everything else, runecasting is simply a guiding tool. You will find answers here, but do not take them at face value. This method suggests and offers various options and variables to you regarding your issues and problems. You have to look inside yourself and find the answers.

Origin of Runecasting

According to Nordic legend, the Norse god Odin is credited with the discovery of the rune alphabet. Its origins are as deep and ancient as the Norse gods themselves. Runes are alphabets known as the "Futhark." It remained popular in Scandinavian and German countries before spreading out into the outside world. The word "rune" means a mystery or secret. They are mostly made of stone. The runic alphabets are a diverse collection of symbols that represent several meanings. These rune carvings can be found all over the Scandinavian countries. These carvings date back to the Early Bronze age!

The oldest alphabets are known as the "Elder Futhark," which contains twenty-four runes. Over time, this alphabet was modified and transformed into Anglo-Saxon English. A newer version of the runic alphabet is known as the "Younger Futhark." Because of alphabet variations, it seems safe to assume that migration and emigration of people around the world spread the method of runecasting everywhere.

The first six letters of the Elder Futhark literally spell "FUTHARK." Have a look below:

- F for Fehu — wealth, domestic cattle, prosperity, or gain

- U for Uruz — wild ox, determination, or life force

- T for Thurisaz — giant, thorn, problem, force, or unexpected change

- H for Hagalaz — hail

- A for Ansuz — ancestral, one's own god, communication, or knowledge

- R for Raidho — chariot, wagon, vehicle, travel, or movement

- K for Kenaz — torch, beacon, guiding light, fire, or energy

As mentioned earlier, the Runic alphabet evolved to form the English language alphabet. As you might be aware, the word "alphabet" is derived from two Greek words, "alpha" and "beta." The Elder Futhark is the oldest and most recognized alphabet system because it also happens to be the most ancient form of writing, a complete symbolic system, which appeared in Sweden around 400 B.C. Evidence suggests that more than fifty runestones were discovered in the Viking era (950–1100 AD). These stones spread throughout Denmark, Sweden, Greenland, Copenhagen, and Germany.

Cast Runes

You can either buy a set or runes or make your own. In ancient times, runes were made out of a certain wood, but today, there are different types of wood available, such as oak, cedar, or pine. Rune symbols can be carved onto wood, stone, or even painted. Other rune-making materials include metal, bone, pebbles, or crystals. When you are just starting out, a basic and simple set of runes is recommended.

After a while of practicing the craft, you might want to graduate to a special set of runes. See where your inner light guides you, and choose that particular set of runes to be with you on your journey! Like with any other divination method, choosing your rune set and casting with it is a deeply personal choice and should not be influenced by anyone or anything. It is what you do with it that matters, not the material itself. When you get yourself a set of runes, most likely, it will be accompanied by clear and precise instructions. The information tells you what each rune is, what the alphabet means, what the symbols represent, and how you should interpret the meaning by looking at the overall picture instead of focusing only on one symbol or idea.

A Rune Cloth

This is a piece of fabric where you place the runes while doing a reading. Typically, a rune cloth is white and not too big. Do not worry about getting an exquisite and expensive piece of cloth for the runecasting just because you read somewhere that rune casting is a magical and exotic idea. The cloth is only to prevent your rune stones or crystals from becoming dirty. Dust is a deterrent in runecasting and any other reading, so the cloth helps keep the runes clean.

How to Cast Runes

There is no one specified method to do this. However, there are some established patterns and spreads for you to try out.

You need a quiet place and time to begin your reading. Any outside disturbance will cast a shadow on your inner being and add to the turmoil, leading to an inaccurate reading. You need a clear mind to focus on the subject at hand. Take deep breaths and calm your entire body and mind. Think about any issue or question that has been nagging your mind. If you wish, you can say a silent prayer to the god or deity of your choice. Lay your rune cloth in front of you and place the runes upon it.

Just like in tarot, there are several different spreads and layouts for runecasting. But if you are trying this for the first time, go simple. Pick out one rune and analyze it completely. If you get comfortable with a simple spread, you can then try out the other variations.

Before you place the runes on the cloth, move your hand around in the bag and shake them up. This is similar to shuffling the cards in a tarot deck. Like other divination methods, runecasting looks at all influences—past, present, and personality—to come up with a guiding light for the person. In a three-rune cast, you need to pull out three runes from the bag, one at a time, and place them on the cloth. The first of these indicates an overall summation of your situation or issue, the second one deals with the problems you might face in the course of your action, and the third one represents what you should do to overcome these obstacles and sail through to your goal. Another kind of spread is the nine-rune layout.

In Nordic mythology, nine is considered a magical number! For this reading, shuffle your runes and take out nine of them, one by one, and just scatter them on the cloth. There is no set pattern as to where these runes should fall. Now open your eyes and see what pattern has been formed by the runes. Which ones are facing up and down? Are some near the center of the cloth? Some might be toward the far end. See where each rune has fallen and its direction. Then interpret it, keeping in mind your past and present influencers.

How to Interpret Runecasting

As per the Runic alphabet, you will find that each symbol has more than one meaning. Therefore, experts emphasize that you should never simply go by the meaning provided, but instead figure out the overall picture and then make an interpretation. For example, Ehwaz means "horse." It also means "wheel" or "luck." So, does that mean you are getting a horse? Or a new set of wheels? Or maybe you will just get lucky? Could be. However, add that to the other runes and look at the past and present influences and the person's personality. It could mean anything. He or she might have some luck in their travels. Maybe they could gallop in the wind like the horse and find their stable, i.e., their true goal. Sometimes, these three meanings can point to something even better—maybe an unexpected bonus or promotion at work!

Do not worry if you do not get satisfactory results straight away. It takes time, patience, and years of study before you can begin to really understand the runes and their meanings. There are several books and online resources available to guide you in your quest. Please look at them and try your own readings. Of course, as with any other method of divination, you have to rely on your powers of intuition and deduction for a rounded analysis. And just like with tarot cards, an upside-down or sideways rune can have a completely different meaning compared to an upright rune. Make sure you consult your guide to figure out the correct meaning.

How to Take Care of Your Runes

Generally, rune stones or crystals are stored in a small pouch tied with string. The pouch is soft and keeps the runes safely in one place. Alternate means could include a rune box or a rune chest where you can keep your cloth and runes together. Just make sure you clean them after every reading.

Sometimes, blank runes come in a rune set. That could leave ample room for interpretation, but traditional practitioners of the craft have said that they have never encountered anything like a blank rune in their castings. If you wish to remove them from your reading, that is fine too!

Now that you know what runes are and how to cast them look at some layouts and spreads of runecasting in the next chapter.

Chapter Eight: Runecasting II: Layouts and Spreads for Divination

Here are some popular spreads and layouts and their interpretations.

One-rune Layout

The classic and the simplest. You pick one rune out of the bag and lay it on your cloth. This represents your overall attitude and feelings regarding your question.

Two-rune Layout

You pick out two runes and lay them on the cloth. It represents the idea of what was and what could be. The first one could mean aspects of your life, which are unfolding right now, and the second might lead to events in the future and how you feel about them.

Three-rune Layout

This refers to the past, present, and future layout. The first one is the past—things or events that have occurred already, whose influence you are now acting under. The second one is the present, which deals with events currently taking place. The third one is all about the outcome of what you have asked or wished for.

Four Directions Layout

The four directions represent different aspects of your life. The North (Nordri) influences the past, the West (Vestri) the present, the East (Austri) the future, and the South (Sudri) represents all the possible outcomes of this reading.

However, do not interpret this to mean that your future is predicted or that you have a clear look into what will happen. There will be multiple options and outcomes for you, based on how you take the answers.

Five Cross Layout

The first rune represents the question you have asked. The second rune is about all aspects related to the question, which also includes the past. The third rune represents something hidden or overlooked in the question you have asked. The fourth rune tells you about the life forces associated with the question. The fifth rune provides answers or multiple options for the question.

Midgard Serpent Layout

In mythology, this beast was believed to have lived in the ocean and was extremely long. You don't need to place your runes in the same formation, in a flowing curve, as the figure suggests. The figure merely symbolizes a snake; you begin with the tail and slowly advance toward the head. While making this journey, you will climb metaphorical hills and fall into ravines and stumble. There will be periods and patterns of rewards and rest. This is basically life's journey.

The first rune represents your past and your feelings attached to it. The second rune is about what you have undergone concerning particular painful events of the past. This is also related to obstacles and roadblocks. The third rune represents your present—your state of mind and attitude to confront the past and its challenges and overcome present obstacles. The fourth rune tells you to renew your journey. There is a higher hump here, signifying even more problems. The fifth rune gives you a glimpse into your journey. You see your goal and are exhilarated! The sixth one tells you that you need to work hard and put in more effort to reach your goal. The last one represents the snake's head. Symbolically, this is your goal.

Be aware that this does not merely represent a timeline of events for you to reach your goal; it is also a cycle. Once you complete the journey, there is another one waiting for you. This teaches you not to be complacent and placid.

Bifrost Layout

According to Nordic mythology, Bifrost refers to a bridge connecting the world of humans to the world of gods. With this kind of layout, the runes make a deep connection between the material and the astral world.

The layout is like a rainbow, with the VIBGYOR (violet, indigo, blue, green, yellow, orange, and red) colors. Each color means something.

- Red — past attitudes and feelings
- Orange — what you see and perceive in the present
- Yellow — your present attitude
- Green — the effects of your mental state on your present actions

- Blue — what attitude you will hold for the future

- Indigo — the effects of your present attitude on your future

- Violet — the total of your outcome

Grid of Nine Layout

Take the runes out and place them in a grid. The first rune you pick out will go in the middle of the third row, the second rune toward the right corner of the first row, and so on. Adding up the numbers from any of the columns or rows gives you fifteen.

Read the third row first—this is all about your past experiences and feelings about things and people.

The third row contains three runes in order 8, 1, and 6.

- 8 — corresponds to hidden meanings and influences of the past

- 1 — corresponds to basic past instincts

- 6 — corresponds to the present-day attitude and mental state

The second row contains runes in order 3, 5, and 7.

- 3 — corresponds to present influences that are partly obscured

- 5 — corresponds to events that are currently taking place and shaping your life

- 7 — corresponds to your attitude and feelings toward these events

The top row is the last one to be read. It contains runes in order 4, 9, and 2.

- 4 — corresponds to the outcomes of the future, delays, or any roadblocks

- 9 — corresponds to the question at hand and its implications

• 2 — corresponds to what you really feel and think about the problem or question you have asked

Odin's Nine Layout

Historically, this layout represents Odin's body as he hung from a tree. To read this layout, follow these steps:

Think of the layout as having four columns.

The first one has numbers 1 and 2 in it.

- 1 — hidden influences of your past
- 2 — your present attitude to past events

The second column has numbers 3 and 4 in it.

- 3 — the action of obscured influences now
- 4 — your attitude and mental state for events happening currently

The third column has numbers 5 and 6 in it.

- 5 — any obstacles that might prevent you from seeing the outcome
- 6 — your response to the outcome

The last column contains 7, 8, and 9.

- 7 — indicates the powers you already have or will need for the first column
- 8 — indicates the powers you already have or will need for the second column
- 9 — indicates the powers you already have or will need for the third column

The last column, which shows Odin's spear, represents the powers you have or need to deal with each of the previous three columns.

Celtic Cross Spread

This is similar to a tarot layout. In this layout, concentrate on the placement of the first two runes. Ideally, you can have the person casting the runes pick out a specific rune related to their question— love, career, relationships, health, life, etc. If you can, draw a picture depicting this rune and ask the person to concentrate and focus on it during the reading. Another method involves picking out a random rune from the bag and drawing it on the paper. This will be a random one and not necessarily connected to the question the person wants to ask. The second rune should be placed above the first one. However, if not possible, lay it next to the first rune.

- 1 — the issue or question at hand
- 2 — the outside influences that might pose obstacles
- 3 — the hidden influences that affect the issue
- 4 — the personal influences of the person asking the question
- 5 — any fears or misgivings the person has with regards to their question
- 6 — influences from family and friends
- 7 — the dreams and hopes of the person asking the question
- 8 — the anxieties or negative feelings associated with the future
- 9 — the person's handling of their past and present influences
- 10 — the outcome of the entire reading

Egil's Whalebone Layout

This layout is based on a mythological tale in Iceland, telling the story of a poet, Egil, who cures Helga, who fell ill due to incorrectly carved runes. Egil scraped those off and carved healing runes into the stone, which made her better. In this reading, instead of reading each rune individually, they are divided into four groups of three. The interpretation is as follows:

Group 1: Rune Numbers 1, 2, and 3

In the tale, the original carver knew exactly what he was doing. This tells you that when you are looking at the first set of runes, you know what you want from life. You know your intentions, goals, desires, and feelings. You need to keep those in mind as you go ahead.

Group 2: Rune Numbers 4, 5, and 6

Helga, the girl in the tale, falls ill because the carver carved the wrong runes into the stones. This group indicates that if your intentions are wrong or maleficent—if you just see the goal and not the journey leading to it—you might be led astray.

Group 3: Rune Numbers 7, 8, and 9

Helga's father is Thorfinn, and naturally, he was worried about his daughter becoming sick. This group of runes suggests that there will be outside obstacles and thorns in your path. These can be outright roadblocks, or some might come in disguise. Say you need some financial help. You might suddenly receive monetary assistance from someone you never thought would help you. Or, if your goal is to save for the future, your spending habits may not allow you to do so, leading to problems and frustration. The key here is to keep an eye on what you are doing.

Group 4: Runes 10, 11, and 12

Egil, Helga's savior, rubs out the wrong runes and carves healing ones. This rune group tells you to overcome all self-doubt and march toward your goal. Keep all the comments in mind but do not take them to heart.

Now that you have a basic understanding of runes and their meanings, it is time to study another popular divination method: tarot.

Chapter Nine: Tarot Reading I: The Major Arcana

Tarot cards were initially used for fun games during the fifteenth century, but it was only at the beginning of the eighteenth century that they began to be taken more seriously and used in conjunction with divination. Antoine Court and Jean-Baptiste Alliette did some major groundbreaking work to popularize tarot in Paris, from where this all began.

What do You Need for a Reading?

First, you need a deck of cards. There are many different ones to choose from, the most popular being Rider-Waite. Each Tarot card deck has 78 cards divided into two categories, the Major Arcana and Minor Arcana. The twenty-two cards of the Major Arcana refer to major aspects and influences in one's life. The Minor Arcana deals with everyday matters. The 56 cards in the deck are divided into wands, swords, pentacles, and cups. Usually, wands are symbols for creativity, swords for intellectual pursuits, pentacles for money-related matters, and cups for emotional matters. You will read more about the Minor Arcana in the next chapter.

Card Reading — Basics

There are several spreads of the cards. The most common is the "three card spread," the "Celtic Cross," and the "seven day spread." In a three card spread, you shuffle the cards, and the reader pulls three cards from the deck. The first is for the past, the second for the present, and the third for the future. Another common reading is the "daily card reading." A single card is pulled from the deck, and its meaning for the day is interpreted.

Notable Facts About Tarot

- Everyone has a Tarot Birth Card. Want to know how? Add up your birthday! For example, February 10, 1980. That would be 1+0+2+1+9+8+0, which equals 21. 2 and 1 equal 3. That means your Birth Tarot is the Empress!

- The myth that you cannot buy your own tarot card deck, and it has to be gifted, is completely untrue. You can definitely buy your own deck and do a reading.

- Anyone can read the tarot; spirituality is only one aspect of it, but you will need intuition for the reading.

- There are basic elements associated with the tarot. In the Minor Arcana, water is associated with cups, earth with pentacles, air with swords, and fire with wands.

Here are some apps for Android and iOS phones that you might find useful. Try them out sometime!

- Tarot Life and Numerology
- Tarot Card Reading and Astrology
- Astroguide
- Tarot Card Reading
- InstantGo
- Yes or No Tarot

- Free Tarot Reading
- Labyrinthos Tarot
- Trusted Tarot

The twenty-two cards in the Major Arcana of the tarot represent everyday situations, with specific meanings and messages. They are not just cards; they are a storytelling device. The following twenty-two cards represent your life journey and the lessons you learn. Without further ado, it is time to jump into this!

0. The Fool

Upright Position

The first card in the tarot deck, the Fool, is considered a good omen because he is a childlike being, uncorrupted and unaware of life's challenges that lie ahead (just like a child). He is innocent and full of joy and wonder. This card in your reading encourages you to take on the world and its challenges openly. Recognize your potential and act on it.

Reverse Position

If this comes up the other way around, you may encounter another side of yourself, which you haven't explored until now. This part could be hidden in the shadow of ego and ignorance, or you may harbor ill feelings toward someone or have psychological blocks that need to be cleared.

1. The Magician

Upright Position

This card is all about you—your unique nature and skillset that sets you apart from others. If this comes up in your reading, it means you already possess all the skills and tricks needed for you to accomplish your dreams and goals. Nothing is going to hold you back now.

Reverse Position

Conversely, an upside-down card would mean that you are your own worst enemy! You might be unconsciously sabotaging your efforts. Maybe you feel that your thoughts and ideas are too forward and shocking to put into action, or perhaps you are just not aware of what qualities you possess, or you lack the courage to find out.

2. The High Priestess

Upright Position

This might be the most intuitive card of the deck. It deals with your conscious mind, awareness, and also the subconscious. If you get this card, it is telling you to look inside and listen to your inner voice. Your gut already knows what is right and wrong. You just have to trust it and listen to it. In the tarot story, this card appears when the Fool decides to see what kind of powers and skills he can develop.

Reverse Position

This card appears to tell you that you are so immersed inside your life, thoughts, and ideas that it has now become an unhealthy obsession. There is another world outside that needs equal exploration. This card tries to teach one about balance.

3. The Empress

Upright Position

The most feminine card in the deck, this card in a reading depicts love, beauty, and tenderness. It also denotes fertility and Mother Nature. The Empress is also called "The Great Recycler" because she can reanimate and restore any havoc and upheavals, which distort and destroy your peace.

Reverse Position

If seen in reverse, this card represents nature—unleashing storms, tsunamis, and hurricanes, symbolically speaking. It suggests a surge in repressed emotions that may trigger untold misery if not checked early.

4. The Emperor

Upright Position

This card denotes power, ambition, and leadership. The Emperor is a force to reckon with, as he has weathered many a battle. He also represents authority, structure, and solidity in his being.

Reverse Position

If you get a reverse card of the Emperor, it usually denotes a tendency of being bossy, argumentative, and behaving like a tyrant. You might love being flattered and praised a lot for your good work. This is not a good sign in the long run. You may lose friends and only end up with sycophants for company.

5. The Hierophant

Upright Position

He is a heavenly messenger. His job is to bring spirituality and mystic lessons to people on Earth. This particular card in a reading means that you need to understand and follow the rules. You are also encouraged to find some spiritual outlook.

Reverse Position

This indicates rebellion from your side. However, be aware that the very tradition against which you are rebelling also serves as a soothing and calming influence at times.

6. The Lovers

Upright Position

If this card comes up in your reading, it usually means that relationships in your life and love life need some attention. Apart from love, this card can also mean a crossroads in your life, where you need to assess all choices before making a decision.

Reverse Position

This means that you are facing resistance, or maybe someone is opposing your relationships. You may also have vested interests in the opposition. You have to come clean to yourself if you want to come out of this situation.

7. The Chariot

Upright Position

This card denotes determination and a drive to succeed. It lets the person know that, along with determination, a powerful mind and thought process can make them successful and happy.

Reverse Position

If the Chariot is reversed, it could mean that you need to take charge of certain aspects of your life and bring them up to level with the rest of your personality or life events. You may also need to address your inner resistance to change and overcome it.

8. Strength

Upright Position

This card is not just about physical strength; it is also about your mental strength and aptitude, your heart's courage, and your ability to take life on its own terms. If this card arrives in your reading, it denotes that you are willing to face life on your terms and are ready for everything.

Reverse Position

Conversely, this card may mean that you do not have the power of persuasion. You will need to work hard to overcome the out-of-control and wild mental tendencies you have to succeed.

9. The Hermit

Upright Position

A hermit wants to be alone. This card signifies that you wish to withdraw from the outside world's noise and chaos and seek meaning within. The only challenge here is recognizing a teacher when you see one—as the teacher may be silent, invisible, or speak in a different tongue.

Reverse Position

This could mean a fear of being alone or a resistance you feel before going down the path of wisdom because you fear the awesome power of your intellect.

10. The Wheel of Fortune

Upright Position

This wheel is revolving like an actual wheel. The appearance of this card means that nothing in life is permanent. Everything is cyclical—good, bad, love, hate, riches, and poverty. Everyone has to go through these stages. The only constant thing is change.

Reverse Position

Reversal of fortune is usually depicted in this card. This means you need to go back and start from the beginning. Remember, this is good because the only way from rock bottom is up!

11. Justice

Upright Position

There is an equal and opposite reaction to each karma that you do in life. Life gives you right now what you did in your past—whether it is a punishment or reward. In other words, what goes around, comes around. If this card is in your reading, you need to take stock of your actions and check whether you are doing things right or not.

Reverse Position

A reversed card won't immediately be clear to you because sometimes, there are reasons beyond your capacity to understand. You will need to have patience and wait for the truth to be revealed to you.

12. The Hanged Man

Upright Position

This card reveals a limbo position you might be in. You are confused about something and cannot decide where to make a move. It might also indicate a lack of stability in your personality and lesser energy.

Reverse Position

This could mean that you wish to sacrifice your happiness and want something for someone else's greater good. With no apparent benefit to you, this is almost a selfless act of altruism!

13. Death

Upright Position

Perhaps the most misunderstood card ever, death does not mean an inauspicious card at all. It means a new beginning! It represents the ending of a project, plan, or relationship and hints toward a new one.

Reverse Position

Conversely, this might imply that you have held onto something for a long time and fear letting it go. You fear the consequences or the future and do not wish to change your regular patterns.

14. Temperance

Upright Position

A card like this means moderation, patience, and peace. If this appears in your reading, it means you are on the right path in that particular aspect of your life, and you should definitely go with the flow.

Reverse Position

But beware! If this card is reversed, it could mean that you are tired of yourself and wish to give up. There is a lot of apathy and self-neglect too. You only look at the negativity and chaos in your life and find it difficult to enjoy the sunny spots in your life.

15. The Devil

Upright Position

Ah, speak of the Devil, and he appears! This card indicates certain overpowering feelings of powerlessness in your being. You feel as though you are stuck in a particular situation in your life, and there is no hope. Your internal compass surges on the negativity of the situation.

Reverse Position

On the contrary, if this card appears in the reverse position, you could be a troublemaker! You usually enjoy being in the thick of things and may even be the cause of chaos. This card tells you to monitor your behavior.

16. The Tower

Upright Position

This card is feared for a good reason because it represents the destruction of something that you love. However, keep in mind that a weak structure cannot withstand life's forces. Something has to crumble for something else to rise in its place.

Reverse Position

Breathe a sigh of relief! The worst is over. This card indicates the upheaval in your life is drawing to a close and new beginnings are around the corner.

17. The Star

Upright Position

Just like stars in the night sky, this card signifies hope, calm, and healing. This is a sure sign that the universe is working with you and wants you to succeed.

Reverse Position

It could mean that you are diverted from your own nature, goals, and skills. You may feel alienated from yourself at times. This is the time to refocus on your talents and gifts and put them to good use.

18. The Moon

Upright Position

This card appears if you are feeling anxious, fearful about something, tense, and unusually miserable. It is also connected to your soul and subconscious mind. It tries to tell you the state of your inner being.

Reverse Position

This card indicates that you might be lying to yourself or trying to delude yourself in some way, which does not hurt your ego and keeps it safe. There is a strong temptation to be swept away, but you have to exercise control before it overpowers you.

19. The Sun

Upright Psition

Just like the bright and cheerful sun in the sky, this card embodies happiness, vitality, and pure freedom. If this card comes up, rest assured that things are going well for you.

Reverse Position

This implies that you need to be humble and grateful for all the blessings and successes coming your way.

20. Judgment

Upright Position

A crucial card; this is where the past, present, and future are tied together. As with a real judgment, here you are reminded that your present actions will determine your future. It is also known as the Resurrected card.

Reverse Position

This usually means that there is something external that keeps blocking your success. You need to face these restrictions head-on if you want any chance of happiness.

21. The World

Upright Position

If this card comes up in the reading, it means you are exactly where you are meant to be in life. Be it your career, life, marriage, love, health—you have arrived at that particular aspect. This is like your ultimate realization.

Reverse Position

This is a slight bump in the road for you, nothing serious. You just need to meet these minor obstacles with a smile and get on with your life.

Had fun with the Major Arcana? It is now time to dive into the even wider pool of the Minor Arcana cards!

Chapter Ten: Tarot Reading II: The Minor Arcana

You learned what the Major Arcana cards mean in the previous chapter. Now, you will read about the Minor Arcana cards, which means "minor secrets." Therefore, this aspect deals with things and ideas that fall under the day-to-day realm, small-scale projects, minor issues, etc. However, just because these cards do not deal with the personality at large does not mean they are any less important than the Major Arcana cards. Little details make up entire beings, and so, these cards are equally important to people.

There are 56 cards in the Minor Arcana, which can be categorized as follows:

- Suit of Wands (fourteen cards)
- Suit of Pentacles (fourteen cards)
- Suit of Cups (fourteen cards)
- Suit of Swords (fourteen cards)

Each of these is similar to a regular deck of cards, beginning with the Ace, continuing until 10, and then the four special cards: Page, Knight, Queen, and King. Now it is time to dive into the study and interpretation of the Minor Arcana cards.

Suit of Wands

This card is associated mostly with the fire element and the solar plexus chakra. It relates closely to those passions and dreams that you want to accomplish with great fervor and intensity. Whether you make plans and stick to them or give up easily in the face of obstacles is what these suits of cards show you. Wand cards show where you lack: balance in life, the confidence to tackle issues, leadership skills, and inner strength. Each of the cards holds the power to change the reading instantly—from positive to negative and vice versa.

Ace of Wands

Upright Position

This usually denotes a step of immediate consequences that might lead you toward or away from your goal. It indicates a new beginning in life or endeavor and also whether you possess the necessary drive to complete the project. It shows that you are now ready to take a new step forward—either in your career, relationship, or any other important aspect of your life.

Reverse Position

This can mean that you do not like change and resist it actively. But it also prods you to understand this scenario and gives you the courage to overcome the odds.

Two of Wands

Upright Position

This is the second step in your life's journey. This card signifies that you need to come out of your comfort zone and take on something new. A decision also needs to be made. Sometimes, it also indicates that you are at a crossroads or dead end in your life. When this comes up in your reading, it means that you need to assess all your options carefully before going ahead. If you don't, it can mean many regrets later on. You need to understand all the implications of your decision or action before taking a step forward.

Reverse Position

This indicates that you are stuck momentarily in deciding something, and you need a slight nudge in the right direction to steer you toward your goal.

Three of Wands

Upright Position

This card indicates that you already have an inner balance, which lets you test the waters before putting your toes in. This also signifies that you are capable of taking calculated risks and accomplish lofty goals. In a reading, this card urges you to look around and keep your eyes open for opportunities and chances, which you would typically miss.

Reverse Position

On the other hand, this card also indicates a temporary lack of willpower in some people. You might have already reached the burnout stage.

Four of Wands

Upright Position

This card usually means teamwork. It indicates the laying of a cornerstone, in harmony and together with other people. It denotes a home renovation activity, marriage, relationship, big project, etc. Start-up companies and entrepreneurial ventures are suggested when this card is revealed in your reading.

Reverse Position

A reverse position in this card means that you need to brush up on your people skills, team-building skills, and problem-solving skills. You need to actively work on it because not doing so will cause problems in your projects and life.

Five of Wands

Upright Position

This card signifies ambition, competition, and even aggression—to some extent. When this card appears in your reading, it means you should ask yourself some tough questions: *Why are you fighting this particular battle? Against whom? What do you expect to gain from it?* If your answer is: "Personal gain and making others feel low," you need to check your priorities. Winning is not everything in life.

Reverse Position

In reverse, this card points out that you are egotistical and cannot form friendly bonds with others. You have great difficulty being a team player. When this happens, you need to ask yourself: "What can I do to make this situation better? How can I make others feel comfortable around me?"

Six of Wands

Upright Position

This represents recognition and acknowledgment for your earnest effort. If you think of a victory parade or joyous celebration, that is the card's picturization! It is a message from above that's encouraging you to believe in yourself, not give up, act with grace and dignity, and accept the praise that comes your way. This is also a card that denotes celebrations and relaxation.

Reverse Position

You might be uncomfortable taking on a leadership role in the community, but this card denotes that you should—because of the great learning experience!

Seven of Wands

Upright Position

If this card comes up in your reading, it means that you will most likely be successful in all of your endeavors. You will be recognized for your talents and accomplishments. However, you also need to beware of the pitfalls of fame. You cannot afford to be smug and proud about this. By all means, enjoy your success, but do not let the ugly head of conceit devour you.

Reverse Position

This card indicates a lack of motivation, self-esteem, and pressure. You might need to figure out why you are resisting the very same factors that will make you successful. Being honest with yourself will help. Find out what is holding you back and fight it.

Eight of Wands

Upright Position

Events and things in your life are moving at a quick speed now. This card indicates change and that change is necessary for the evolution of human beings. Things do seem out of control but do not waste your time and energy trying to pin it down. Go along with the change, and you may be surprised at the new turn your life takes!

Reverse Position

With this card in your reading, it usually means there are a lot of changes ahead for you in your life. You cannot assume that everything is fine and dandy and carry on in the usual manner. You need to accept and acknowledge these changes if you want to achieve your goals. Otherwise, you'll be stuck in a rut.

Nine of Wands

Upright Position

This depicts the need for rest, recuperation, and restoration of your energy. Step back and let others be the hero for a change. They are just as capable as you are to fight challenges and rise to the occasion. Let them be in the spotlight for a while. Help others who need you right now. If you see this card, it depicts someone who is too exhausted to work but, at the same time, too proud to ask for help. Do not be this person; instead, let others help you out for a change.

You need to seek new perspectives on something that is bothering you or something you have been working on, or even a totally different point of view in life. Be true to yourself.

Ten of Wands

Upright Position

In contrast, this card is all about energy and action. There is no time to relax! You have to plow on and see the project or event until its very end. Even if this means giving up what you love doing, you have to complete your task. Wisely, this card reminds you to take up only one thing at a time—multitasking is not indicated here because this card represents a total and undying commitment.

Reverse Position

This indicates that perhaps you have lost your sense of direction and perspective in life. You aren't objective enough to see where you are going wrong. When this card appears, you need to take a step back and reevaluate. Remember why you are doing what you're doing. This might give you a clearer perspective.

Page of Wands

Upright Position

This indicates someone who is a non-conformist and an independent and solitary individual by nature. He or she is an innovator or a rebel. This card indicates freedom, power, passion, and development. This is an exciting card because it denotes the interests and passions of the person involved. Even though the person may appear to be simple, they possess the qualities to become a great leader.

Reverse Position

You may be concerned about what your image is like in society. You always put your best foot forward in public and worry about it in private.

Knight of Wands

Upright Position

This is a feisty person who is easily provoked. This card in your reading reminds you to keep a check on your temper and attitude. Sure, you can be intense, but make sure that this intensity does not get the better of you!

Reverse Position

This indicates that the person seeks some change and transformation within themselves or the situation around them. Others may not take too kindly to this, but instead of flying off in a rage, it would be better to understand their points of view too.

Queen of Wands

Upright Position

This person is a born leader who works well with people and sees to it that everyone is cohesive and works together. Their energy is infectious and all-consuming! This person gets things done by using the magic of people working together harmoniously. Such people make excellent managers because they know exactly what their team members are capable of, and they give them wings to fly. Another side of this person is that you can gain no sympathy from them. If they ascertain that your role is over and you can no longer be productive in that setting, they will let you go without hesitation.

Reverse Position

If this card comes up in a reading, it indicates that the person might be bossy and controlling. Others around them may not take too kindly to this kind of persona and may rebel, causing even more damage. The learning here is to trust other teammates and give them confidence.

King of Wands

Upright Position

This card indicates that you wish to lead, are ambitious to a fault, and are practical. You are the center of attention, and you love to surround yourself with your loved ones and lavish love on them.

Reverse Position

This card indicates an imminent danger in you becoming proud. You may undermine others' authority and try to stake a claim in every aspect. Not everyone likes this kind of domination. You should learn to curb such tendencies and nip them in the bud.

Suit of Cups

These cards indicate the state of your emotions, relationships, and how intuitive you are with the people around you. They deal with guidance in love and romance, friendship, and other partnerships.

Ace of Cups

Upright Position

This shows a hand with a cup containing an endless supply of fluid. It signifies your open heart, overflowing with love and concern for others. This indicates the healing and soothing areas of your life.

Reverse Position

Conversely, this could mean a loss of optimism in you or a lack of self-esteem. When this happens, reflect on what is making you feel that way. It might be external or internal factors. Try to make fewer moves here until you are sure of what you are doing.

Two of Cups

Upright Position

This usually means bonding, union, soul mates, partnership, romance, etc. This card indicates a karmic connection between people, a deep understanding. You need to focus on your relationships and make them work.

Reverse Position

This means that perhaps you are putting too much time and effort into your relationships. Your sense of identity and importance comes from external factors. You should stop that and instead work on internal validation.

Three of Cups

Upright Position

This denotes some sort of agreement, teamwork, and bonding with others in your life. It indicates that you are surrounded by like-minded people who are working toward a common goal. You need to acknowledge and appreciate these people in your life. Reconnect and stabilize with them.

Reverse Position

This might imply a lack of trust and understanding on your part for the people in your life. You may feel left out and out of place or out of sync. Try and communicate with them and clear out any misunderstandings.

Four of Cups

Upright Position

This is quite a dispirited and restless time in your life. You may be dissatisfied with something, want a change, or are feeling stagnant. However, this card also tells you to be aware that you may lose out on the simple joys of life that are right in front of you in your reckless abandon. You need to be open and willing to let new things and events enter your life.

Reverse Position

This may manifest as passive aggression on your part. You need to recognize the symptoms and try to wean yourself from them.

Five of Cups

Upright Position

Emotional disturbance, grief, upheavals, messes, expectations, etc., are indicated by this card. You may be disappointed with an outcome or sad over the loss of something. The only way forward is to forgive, forget, and heal from within.

Reverse Position

In an interesting combination of factors, this card indicates that what you perceive to be the worst thing to happen to you might be a blessing in disguise! If you have any phobias, fears, negative experiences, expectations, etc., this card helps you understand and deal with them.

Six of Cups

Upright Position

This card indicates openness, innocence, learning, and optimism. This takes you right back to your childhood. This card tells you to be open and carefree like a child and enjoy fresh experiences with a fresh mind.

Reverse Position

You have a wonderful chance to let past things, events, and hurts go and look forward to a new chapter in life. Revisiting old wounds will be easier because you now know how to deal with them.

Seven of Cups

Upright Position

This card deals with imagination. You dislike your present life and imagine another life where all your dreams may have come true. Though this card indicates that you can change your destiny, it also warns you not to lose sight of reality.

Reverse Position

Your lack of purpose in life has given rise to problems like lack of curiosity, joy, ability to dream, etc. This card encourages you to get all that back. Do not dwell on your current state of mind but work toward getting your mojo back!

Eight of Cups

Upright Position

This indicates betrayal, heartache, and emotional disappointment. This card in a reading is a message for you to walk away from anything that does not seem to be working, even after many trials.

Reverse Position

An event has set you back or hurt you perhaps, but you refuse to let it affect your life. Your resilience and cool attitude will definitely help you out of this spot.

Nine of Cups

Upright Position

A happy card signifies fulfillment and contentment. This is also known as the "Wish Card." You know things will get better if you get this card in a reading.

Reverse Position

Surprisingly, this means that you get what you thought was right for you, but ultimately that is not the case at all. It usually signifies that your dream isn't making you feel as happy as it should, and maybe it is time to set a new goal.

Ten of Cups

Upright Position

This is one of the most joyous cards you can ever get because it signifies togetherness, family, and celebrations!

Reverse Position

Conversely, this card indicates that harmony and togetherness in a group or family are decreasing slowly. There are judgment and criticism. The only way out is through communication and meditation.

Page of Cups

Upright Position

This indicates a very imaginative, idealistic, open, young, mystic, and sensitive person. If this turns up in your reading, you may be at the beginning of a relationship or something new at work.

Reverse Position

This suggests those around you have been indulging you for some time, even though they don't have to. Try not to force yourself on them, and make sure to reach out to them, communicate, and give their needs some consideration.

Knight of Cups

Upright Position

This person is profoundly educated, charming, and a smooth talker. There is a lesson here to balance your inner and outer world, your dreams and realities, and practical aspects and thoughts. Great emotional fulfillment is indicated here.

Reverse Position

This person keeps making excuses and blaming others for things going wrong in their life. It's a message to take responsibility for your actions. This card also offers up a major life lesson this way.

Queen of Cups

Upright Position

This person is well balanced, intuitive, and stable. He or she relates to others at a deep level. This card reminds you to trust your inner self.

Reverse Position

This card indicates that you block your pain by not dealing with it. That is not the answer. You need to be honest with yourself and work through the pain. That is the only way to heal.

King of Cups

Upright Position

This person is balanced, intense, and intuitive. This card suggests that you dig deep inside yourself to figure out the how and why of your relationships with people.

Reverse Position

This card indicates that you might be sour toward someone or hold a grudge. Learn to admit the wrongs and the hurt caused by the person and forgive them.

The Suit of Swords

These cards depict challenges, conflicts, and how you overcome them. They correspond with the Air element. They have a deep connection with truth and reason and, therefore, are associated with fairness and justice.

Ace of Swords

Upright Position

This represents your vision in life, optimism, guiding light, and hope. If it turns up, that means you are beginning something new. You need some clarity to go on with the task.

Reverse Position

It could mean that you are obscuring your vision and not seeing the matter at hand clearly. That could be due to your illusions or biases. You need to reexamine your perspective before moving on.

Two of Swords

Upright Position

This indicates that you have two conflicting ideas that you need to examine before you decide on something. You are unsure about what path to take.

Reverse Position

This card could mean that while you can definitely move forward, sometimes, it is better to consult with other people before deciding on something. Take more input and feedback.

Three of Swords

Upright Position

You might know this card very well. It represents sorrow, unhappiness, or separation. It usually indicates that sad times are coming, or you might already be grieving over something. But though painful and sad, this card also teaches you about experiencing pain, going through it, and coming out stronger.

Reverse Position

This suggests that some of the sadness in your life could be dissipating, and there is mending on the horizon. Conflict resolution seems to be the mainstay of this card.

Four of Swords

Upright Position

If this card turns up in your reading, it means you need to take some time out for yourself, maybe retreat into a safe and relaxed place for a while. If not, you will suffer burnout. You need this rest.

Reverse Position

If you have been single, lonely, and solitary for a long time, it is now time to enter the social world. You should balance both solitude and interpersonal relationships. This card teaches you about being in a socially and emotionally balanced state.

Five of Swords

Upright Position

This card represents tension, conflict, aggression, anxiety, and loss. You need to evaluate what kind of battles you are fighting in your life, against whom and how wise or unwise they are. You definitely need to think before you spring into action.

Reverse Position

You are beginning to take success and failure in your stride. You gain some control over your aggression, and you have also learned to take criticism with a pinch of salt.

Six of Swords

Upright Position

This is a tricky card. If you get this in a reading, it could mean that you are attempting to walk away from a difficult situation, which, on the one hand, feels burdensome, but you're also afraid to walk away from it. Maybe you fear what lies ahead but trust yourself and go anyway. You will reap the rewards later.

Reverse Position

This card urges you to put your brain to its fullest use—logic, thinking, reasoning, and analysis; everything has to be used by you. You are somehow not doing so, resulting in apathy and limitations in your ability.

Seven of Swords

Upright Position

This card indicates betrayal and deception. There may be someone in your life that isn't whom they seem to be. Beware of such people. This card also tells you that it is better to be a smart worker than a hard worker. Not only will you save time, but you will also learn new skills in the process.

Reverse Position

This card suggests that there will be setbacks in your life, despite your dedicated efforts. The lesson is not to let that get in your way or blame yourself.

Eight of Swords

Upright Position

When you see this card in your reading, it means that you are stuck somewhere, maybe bound to something. You may have also trapped yourself in your limitations and assumptions. You have to break free by opening your mind and self to new possibilities.

Reverse Position

You tend to blame others for your problems, or you rationalize your defeat in some way, rather than taking accountability for yourself. You need to face your inner self and be honest here if you wish to make any progress.

Nine of Swords

Upright Position

This card indicates loss of control, anxiety, and fears. But look at it closely, as all this stress is self-caused. You need to work through the worry and stress by eliminating negative thinking.

Reverse Position

This usually signifies a chance to banish negativity and depression from your life. You are now ready to embrace the light and leave the darkness behind.

Ten of Swords

Upright Position

This card is all about finality and limits. When this card comes up in a reading, it means that whatever you were working on or a relationship you were holding onto has now reached its natural end, and it's time to let go.

Reverse Position

You need a reality check at this point. Maybe you have begun justifying and dramatizing your problems and fallacies to gain sympathy. You need to snap out of the dream state and accept responsibility for your actions.

Page of Swords

Upright Position

This card in your reading urges you to slow down and take a look at facts before rushing off to implement your plans. Enthusiasm is great, but misinformed enthusiasm will present trouble. You should also beware of people with an ulterior motive.

Reverse Position

You tend to lecture others about their faults, or you may be very prejudiced. You need to curb some of your critical tendencies if you wish to work with others.

Knight of Swords

Upright Position

This card indicates a "bursting to go" quality. However, you need to ask yourself where exactly you are going, your intentions, and how you will treat your success and failure. There is a danger here of jumping to conclusions and not thinking before acting.

Reverse Position

A slightly unfortunate card, this suggests that you may avoid conflict altogether by sweet-talking your way out of tight spots. You may also overpromise and under deliver and make promises you can't keep. Come out of these situations by being honest with yourself.

Queen of Swords

Upright Position

This person is honest, wise, independent, and generally self-aware. It is a message to stand up for and fight for yourself and your rights. Do not let anything and anyone brainwash you into something you are not.

Reverse Position

You might not acknowledge your deepest feelings about something or someone. But you do need to accept them if you want to avoid isolation. Bring your natural compassion out by being open and helping loved ones.

King of Swords

Upright Position

This card indicates truth, happiness, intelligence, candor, and wisdom. You may find yourself in a position in life where others look up to you for guidance and truth. You are powerful and supremely content with yourself.

Reverse Position

Alas, this card offers up a suggestion that you are impervious to conscience and integrity. Something less noble has taken their place. Fight with yourself to awaken your inner goodness before it becomes too late.

The Suit of Pentacles

These cards are related to work, career, money, health, and family. They are used mostly to answer questions about these aspects and to learn more about your personality and connections with each of these elements. Pentacles are also referred to as "coins," so do not get confused if you read "coins" instead of pentacles in the interpretations below.

Ace of Pentacles

Upright Position

This represents the first step you put toward your goal, support provided to you, and fulfillment. It has a deep connection with the earth. It tells you that if you hone and polish your talents and craft, you can grow exponentially. The card suggests winning and control over your emotions.

Reverse Position

You need to reconnect with yourself and the values you prize. You have to look within yourself to understand what drives you. If not, success won't come to you easily.

Two of Pentacles

Upright Position

This is usually depicted by a juggling figure where two pentacles swoosh around the figure, unclear where to go. If this card comes up in your reading, it means that there are some changes about to happen in your life, and you need to have the patience to see and understand what they are. Until you do so, you will always be in a tizzy.

Reverse Position

You may have to let go of certain thought patterns. For instance, you may be too polar about an issue where you actually might benefit from being neutral. However, yes, when it concerns helping others, you have to take charge and be proactive.

Three of Pentacles

Upright Position

This can be called the card of the genius. More often, this indicates a master at work, creativity, and fulfillment. Stay focused on your task at hand and see it through. It also indicates collaboration and improvement in the task.

Reverse Position

You may be afraid of sharing your gifts and talents with the outside world, fearful of the comments and reactions of others. Maybe you think it is not worth doing all that. Please keep in mind that only a few people are ever given the gift of being a genius. Try and spread the divine inspiration around.

Four of Pentacles

Upright Position

This is the card of the classic catch-22. You have material comforts and are fully secure, but with that comes the dreaded responsibilities. In your reading, this card is a message to make a rational judgment and not waste your wealth—spiritual or material. You may be holding on tightly to something. Perhaps it's time to let it go and discover what contentment really means.

Reverse Position

This card indicates that you let resentment and an overbearing attitude get in the way of reaching your goals. You may be worried about something, or a task does not go well according to your standards. But that is mainly due to your attitude. Change it, and the world changes!

Five of Pentacles

Upright Position

This card suggests that you should think before setting your goals, especially those that involve short-term or temporary gains. You will definitely feel resentment and anger if your short-term goals aren't met. This card is a reminder that apart from money, there are other untold riches around you. Don't let money run your life. There's more to it than you know.

Reverse Position

This indicates that perhaps you need to be more honest with yourself. You are deceiving yourself or trying to hide from your truth. Instead of daydreaming about potential gains and riches, you need to look at yourself and figure out what you want.

Six of Pentacles

Upright Position

This card is all about giving and receiving generous spirit, knowledge, and support to others. When this card appears in your reading, this is the time for you to give rather than receive. You need to pay the kindness back, pay generosity back, and help someone else. This maintains the karmic cycle of checks and balances.

Reverse Position

Conversely, it could come to mean that you are focused on the idea of getting things back—both literally and figuratively. Your idea of payback is now all-consuming. This has become more important to you than actual giving, which may affect your karma too.

Seven of Pentacles

Upright Position

Traditionally, this card means "to cultivate something." When this card comes up in your reading, it tells you that you need to be extra vigilant with your life—projects, career, home, relationships, or family—to reach your goal. You cannot harbor any excuses. Keep your head down and race toward the finish line.

Reverse Position

This suggests that you like taking risks and gambling with your life. You have somehow lost your direction and way in the world and are willing to risk everything you have for another stab at a chance. Beware of such actions. Do not attempt anything rash at this point.

Eight of Pentacles

Upright Position

This card encourages you to expend more energy, get a fresh perspective on life, and create a balance. This card is about working hard and trying out new ways to improve one's self. Yes, there is a temptation to become a workaholic, which you must curb. You will begin to think of yourself as indispensable, whereas the reality is quite different. Strike a balance.

Reverse Position

Your work begins to take on a large part of your identity and spills into every other aspect of your life. This isn't healthy, and you need to make time for other aspects as well. Work is work, not life.

Nine of Pentacles

Upright Position

This card carries a message that you need to slow down and see if you are just working too hard and not balancing it with other life aspects. This card indicates money, financial stability, and independence. It's important to balance your monetary needs with other desires in life.

Reverse Position

You are possibly in indulgence mode. You feel lethargic and apathetic to your life situation and events. This card indicates that a boost of external energy is coming your way to spur you in the right direction!

Ten of Pentacles

Upright Position

This represents the amalgamation of a lot of effort for achieving your goals—be it a house, car, new promotion, or more money. This card also represents happy and close families, knowledge, comforts, and long-term thinking.

Reverse Position

You may have to start over from scratch after having experienced losses in certain areas of life. While it may seem tedious, starting over can be a blessing too!

Page of Pentacles

Upright Position

This card indicates someone who wants to learn, experiment, do research, learn from their mistakes, grow from experiences, and learn how to deal with failure. Quite an important card!

Reverse Position

This suggests that maybe you doubt your skills and talents. You are unsure whether you can be of service to society. It can also mean that you do not like being social to this extent—but give it a try as it won't hurt anything. You can cultivate more discipline that way.

Knight of Pentacles

Upright Position

This card comes with a message that you need to be patient, methodical, dedicated, and persevere with your efforts. This is the most peaceful card in the entire deck. You have to see the bigger picture and ignore the small fallacies in your path. Sure, the work may not always be up to your standard, but there are dignity and grace in all types of work. Rewards will surely follow.

Reverse Position

In life, you will encounter certain people who do not appreciate you or your worth. This card tells you just to ignore those people. Instead, focus your energy and time on those who love and appreciate you.

Queen of Pentacles

Upright Position

This card indicates healing, education, problem solving, encouragement, and compassion. If this comes up in a reading, it means that you need to take care of yourself and work toward giving yourself and your loved ones a comfortable and nurturing environment.

Reverse Position

It is a warning against becoming too attached to something or someone. You may have been addicted to something or someone in your life, with a negative outcome. This card tells you to break free of this habit.

King of Pentacles

Upright Position

This card is all about accomplishments, financial power, respect, and strength. This card also represents the attainment of your long-term goals. If this comes up in your reading, the message is to work even more methodically so that your gains are higher. Not just in material terms, but spiritual gains too.

Reverse Position

This suggests that perhaps, over time, you have become rather self-centric. Now is the time to switch back to self-discipline and control your desires and mold your abilities. Do not bite off more than you can chew.

In this chapter and the previous one, you have learned all the Major and Minor Arcana cards from the Tarot. In the next chapter, you will study the types of card spreads and how to read and interpret them.

Chapter Eleven: Tarot Reading III: Spreads and Layouts

Now that you have a fair understanding of the Major and Minor Arcana cards, you can begin your own reading. You can buy a set of cards or maybe have someone gift them to you!

Before you dive into a reading, it is important to ask yourself, "Why am I asking the tarot this question?" You need to figure out your real intentions first because the universe knows everything. You cannot bluff it. A simple "yes" and "no" type of question-answer might be useful for beginners, but it will not answer the deepest desires of your heart. For yes/no questions, you might be better off with a pendulum.

Tarot cards are specifically designed. Each card contains its own interpretation, and when combined with other cards, they reveal a wealth of information and guidance for you to follow. Take advantage of this inherent nature of the cards and ask deep and insightful questions.

Here are some of the most popular tarot spreads and layouts for you to choose and try.

The One Card Spread

The most basic reading of all, this layout is as important as the others and is usually favored by beginners. For this reading, you need to shuffle your deck and pick out a card. It represents a question you have in mind and have been wanting to find the answer to for a long time. For more clarity, it is recommended to do this every day by reshuffling the deck.

Three Card Spread

The next one is the three card spread. After shuffling the deck, you take out three cards one by one and put them in front of you. In a basic reading, this would mean your Past, Present, and Future. The first card represents all the elements and influences your past has had on your present. The second card is about you in the present—your current situation and mood. The third card does not show you the future but guides you toward figuring out what you need to do to let go of negativity and embrace your life goals.

This spread can also be interpreted in the following manner:

Instead of the past, present, and future, the variables can be:

- Set One — Body, Mind, Soul
- Set Two — Subconscious, Conscious, Superconscious
- Set Three — Inner Being, Needs, Methods

The Celtic Cross Spread

This can be thought of as the most detailed and analytical spread in the tarot layouts. Because it is a bit complex in arrangement and interpretation, this spread may appear daunting to beginners. However, once you get used to this, you will love it!

After shuffling, place the first card on the table. This represents you or the situation at hand. The second card goes across the first one. This card shows whatever problem or obstacle you are facing. The third, fourth, fifth, and sixth cards are arranged around the first two, with three and five directly below and above, and four and six to the left and right, respectively.

Three represents the situation itself—its basis and how you came to be in it. Four represents the events and mental state of the past, which led to the present situation. Five is for the present. Six indicates what can happen in the near future.

The next four cards are placed in a vertical column, with the seventh card at the bottom and the tenth at the top. Seven represents what abilities, talents, and skills you possess to deal with your situation. Eight is for the people in your life and what effect they have on your decisions and feelings. Nine represents any fears or anxieties you have and also shows you your hopes and desires. Ten represents the overall outcome of your reading.

The Five Card Spread

Shuffle the deck and pick out five cards. There are many layouts for this kind of spread but learn how to interpret the card number first.

- Card one — your question

- Card two — what you already know about the question or situation

- Card three — tries to point you towards the direction of a solution

- Card four — contains advice or pointers for the question

- Card five — the outcome of the question asked

If you wish to ask something related to the past or something bothering you about someone, try this method of interpretation:

- Card one — about your past
- Card two — about the recent events in the past
- Card three — conveys the present state
- Card four — guides you to the future realm
- Card five — outcome or far future

Here are two popular five card spreads:

Layout One: Five Card Cross

Put three cards in the middle and put one card above and one below it. You may designate it as three, five, and four in the middle and one and two above and below. Or, you may have two, one, and three in the middle and four and five above and below.

Layout Two: Relationship Spread

Place your first, fourth, and second card in the middle row and place the fifth card above and the third card below the line.

- Card one — your perspective and feelings about the relationship
- Card two — your partner's perspective about the relationship
- Card three — why you two got together in the first place; the very foundation of you as a couple
- Card four — present state of your relationship
- Card five — variable outcomes for the relationship

The Seven Card Spread (Horseshoe Spread)

The cards are arranged in a horseshoe formation, beginning with card one in the lower left corner and ending with card seven in the lower right corner.

- Card one — the events and feelings of the past, which are now influencing the present

- Card two — the present and the events, activities, feelings, desires, etc., associated with the current issue or question at hand

- Card three — hidden influences or under the surface currents that impact you. These are the unseen yet strongly felt feelings

- Card four — the person who is asking the question. This card reveals your entire being, attitude, personality, quirks, positive aspects, negative aspects, etc.

- Card five — how others influence you. Do they have a positive or negative effect on you? Why do you react to their words and actions? And how is that impacting your present?

- Card six — the course of action the person should take. It offers some possibilities and routes that the person might consider taking to reach their goal.

- Card seven — the outcome of all that the previous cards suggested. It is the culmination of the question and the arrival at an answer.

The Astrological Spread

This is an interesting spread, combining the zodiac signs and the tarot. In this spread, each card represents a zodiac sign and has its own meaning tied in with the tarot. There is no need to ask a question with this spread because the cards represent particular qualities and aspects of your life.

- Card one — Self

- Card two (Aries) — your current state of mind and how much you value yourself

- Card three (Taurus) — your current financial condition

- Card four (Gemini) — communication and travel

- Card five (Cancer) — family, parents, care, concern

- Card six (Leo) — productivity, pleasure, fierceness, competition

- Card seven (Virgo) — your health, partnerships, relationships

- Card eight (Libra) — marriage, love, romance, money, inheritance

- Card nine (Scorpio) — death, mystery, magnetism, emotional depth, secrets, philosophy

- Card ten (Sagittarius) — an attitude of giving, education, dreams

- Card eleven (Capricorn) — community, career, ambition

- Card twelve (Aquarius) — friendship, relationships, strong affinity to the inner self

- Card thirteen (Pisces) — fears, rebellious nature

In some interpretations, the centermost card, thirteen, is seen as the culmination of all the other cards and their meanings.

The Seven Day Spread

This is quite simple to read; all you have to do is shuffle the deck and place eight cards upon a surface, beginning with one and ending with seven. The last card, eight, can either go up or down. This spread tells you what your coming week is going to be like.

This is read from left to right. Each card stands for one day of the week. There is no intrinsic meaning attached to each position. Whatever cards you draw, they will be set according to this layout and read. One represents the current day; two represents the next day; three represents the day after; and so on.

The Six Month Spread

In this spread, four cards are used for insight into the next six months of your life.

The first card you choose is your Immediate Environment card. This card also signifies isolation, worries, insecurity, loss, and sadness. It symbolizes the loss of the skill to live life to the fullest and how you're struggling to make others understand you.

The second card is Exterior Influences. This section of the spread indicates communication, celebrations, success, happiness, reunion, affairs, gatherings, or any other influence you might have on your present.

The third card is of Past Circumstances. This represents illusions, imagination, dreams, choices, an inability to choose properly, selfishness on the person's part, or any other past circumstances that have prevented a present fruitful life.

The fourth card is Future Motivation. It reveals aspects that make you reach your goal. Your personality traits, prejudices, positive points, issues, attitude, and mental state—you get to know all of that in this section.

The Twelve Month Spread

This is another basic yet interesting spread. Shuffle the deck and select twelve cards from it. Place them in a circular position on the cloth or surface and try to remember what card you have placed in each position. Begin with card one and go clockwise.

- Card one (The Self) — you: your projection, perception, appearance, etc.

- Card two (Money) — your material wealth, finances, windfall, skills, worth, and potential

- Card three (Mental activities) — your intellect, grasping power, work, education, and career

- Card four (Emotions and feelings) — your emotional wellbeing, security, comfort level, new activities, home, and relationships

- Card five (Creativity) — your artistic ability, affairs of the heart, your relaxation activities, etc.

- Card six (Daily routine) — what you do in a day, your routine activities, job, recreation, colleagues, friends, and family

- Card seven (Work) — business matters, work, career, partners, work ethic, and business practices

- Card eight (Possessions) — your money, jewelry, inheritance, wills, bonds, shares, and any other precious commodity

- Card nine (Education) — studies, higher studies, stipends, internship, travel, and long-distance travel

- Card ten (Reputation) — your reputation in public, how people perceive you, your contributions toward other lesser fortunate people, and people in your family

- Card eleven (Goals) — your dreams, goals, wishes, and vision for the future

- Card twelve (Spirituality) — your innate psychic ability, dreams, escape mechanism, and spiritual growth

Conclusion

Congratulations on reaching the end of this book. Hopefully, you had a good time studying the various facets and aspects of divination.

A word to the wise, divination is still a budding field. While prevalent all over and practiced since ancient times, you still need to study and understand the divination methods completely and be open to learning at all times. Your intuition is all you need to guide you toward the right path. Do not lose sight of it, and do not ignore your gut feeling about anyone or anything. Ultimately, it is your thoughts, feelings, and intuition that will keep you on the right path—no book or person can do that for you. You need to ask questions, interpret the answers after looking at all aspects, and then decide on a course of action for yourself. Sure, there may be books and people to help you out but remember you are your own true friend.

All the methods given in the book are fun to try out and experiment with but do not get carried away by the answers you get. Take them at face value and try to keep improving yourself. It is not always necessary to absolutely believe the outcome predicted by the cards or runes or any other method. They are just guiding tools; they will certainly not predict the future with certainty. You can make your future better by making the present count. That is the lesson you must take away from this book. Please do not fall prey to unscrupulous people out there who will scam you and rob you of your peace of mind.

Trust yourself and live life to the fullest! The universe will definitely help you on your journey if your intentions are good.

Part 3: Mediumship

The Ultimate Guide to Becoming a Spiritual Medium and Developing Psychic Abilities Such as Clairvoyance, Clairsentience, and Clairaudience

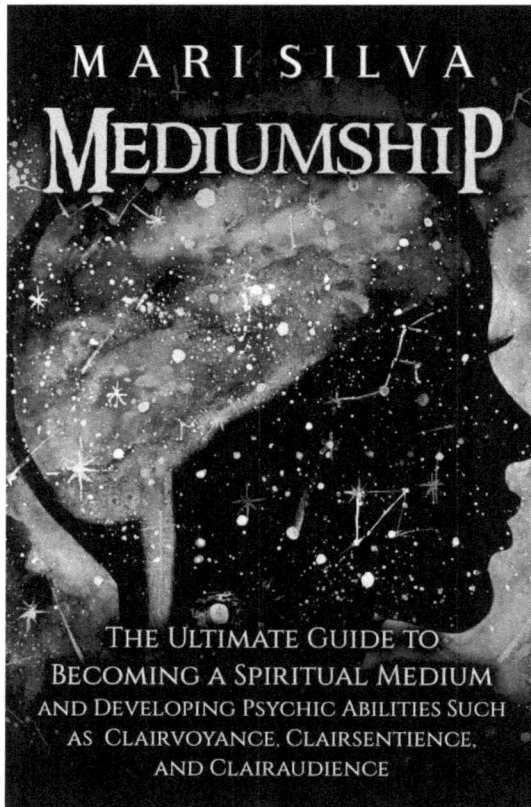

Introduction

"Who is a Medium?"

If someone asked you that, what would come to mind? Think beyond movies, plays, and fictional stories; how would you describe a medium? You probably have an inaccurate impression of mediums and mediumship, thanks to the media's misrepresentation. The typical depiction of mediums is that of a lone soul living in an isolated stone manor, surrounded by ghosts and spirits. In the movies, they look pale and frightening with an almost unearthly appearance.

A medium is just a regular person like you and me. Contrary to what many people believe due to conditioning, mediums are respectable people from different walks of life. The reality contrasts with what we all learned growing up. Unfortunately, the practice and its practitioners have been subjected to excessive dramatization for entertainment.

Mediumship is the ability to mediate between the spirit and human worlds. Mediums act as intermediaries between humans and spiritual beings on the "other side." The difference between you and a practicing medium is that they have trained themselves to be psychically attuned to the physical and spiritual planes.

Every human is born with the inherent gift to see beyond this material world into other dimensions. We tend to lose our connection with this natural gift as we grow older. The less we use the ability, the more we forget the basics. By the time we are adults, we have entirely cast the powers aside. Mediums can still access this ability, and that separates them from everyone else.

A medium is an earnest individual with spiritual knowledge, belief, desire, and patience, keen to make a difference in this world by connecting with ethereal beings in the metaphysical world.

Many people are skeptical of the paranormal because humans find it hard to understand things not supported by science. Yet, several established stories and reports about people who have genuinely had contacts with spirits and the spirit realm exist. Ask those people, and you will realize that science does not have all the answers.

This book aims to redefine your perception of mediumship and help facilitate an awakening of your inner psychical gifts. The ability to communicate with spirits is not farfetched if one stays within the realms of reality and possibility. This book sets a realistic expectation of what the journey is like for new mediums. Intended as a practical guide, it takes a sound approach in unraveling the fundamentals of mediumship. This pragmatic and down-to-earth guide is the right resource to launch your self-discovery journey.

This guidebook is for people who want practical tips that can be applied to their day-to-day lives to trigger remarkable personal and spiritual development. This is for those who need a resource that will change their lives. If you want a book that will teach you how to gain superpowers, this is not for you.

But do you want a practical handbook that can help you cultivate and hone the natural gift of mediumship that is embedded within your DNA? In that case, this is the book for you. Before you get started, make sure that you are ready to acknowledge there are more dimensions and realms beyond the one you see with your physical eyes. When you accept this, you will begin your attunement to your inner psychic!

Chapter One: Are You a Medium?

"We are all connected to spirit, in our physical manifestation and our soul."

—Linda Masanimptewa

Are you a medium? How do you know if you can contact spirits and ghosts? Are there signs you can observe? These are the most critical questions you must answer before you begin your mediumship.

Individuals new to this practice often want to know how they can strengthen their gifts. What they fail to realize is that this is not the starting point. You have to start by making sure that you indeed have the facilities to be a medium. Before I dive deep into how you can discover this, I want to clarify what mediums do.

Like the introduction made clear, mediums can psychically communicate with deceased people on the other side. The general belief is that mediums speak to the dead, but this is a misconception. There is no "death." The dead do not exist. If death were real, everyone would disappear into oblivion after their souls pass on to another realm. What we know as death is the transition of humans from physical entities to a spiritual state.

Mediums are the people who are intuitive and sensitive enough to access information from the dimension where spirits transit to using their psychic senses. These allow them to see, feel, and hear any communication attempt from spirit realms.

Now, it's time to go back to establishing whether you can connect with spirits or not. I have pointed out that we are all born with inherent psychic ability. But you can be psychic without being a medium. One of the most common misconceptions is that psychics and mediums are the same. There is an essential distinction between them. Understanding this is the foundation to becoming an authentic medium.

A medium may be psychic, but a psychic isn't necessarily a medium. This distinction is one that people tend to ignore, willfully or otherwise. I started this chapter by highlighting this difference because it is the right place to begin. I have met many people who confuse the two, and this often affects their psychic development journey.

Many people think that mediumship should come to them naturally because they have the gift of intuition. The fact remains that unless you are a natural-born medium, you have to put a lot of work into developing this ability.

The difference between a medium and a psychic is that mediums can raise their vibrational frequency to where they connect with the spirit world. But psychics can access information about the past, present, and future, but not by connecting with the other side; a psychic uses their ability to communicate with the higher planes.

Some people are psychic with the gift of mediumship and are called psychic mediums. A psychic medium has a double ability to speak to the deceased and learn information from the higher planes.

Furthermore, there are natural-born mediums and latent mediums. A natural-born medium has always been in tune with their abilities. Even though they may not realize it, natural-born mediums tend to see signs that point to this gift throughout their childhood into adulthood.

In contrast, a latent medium is someone whose ability stays dormant until it is developed later in life. Most people I have met tend to be latent mediums. Typically, latent mediums get signs and can use their ability from childhood. But as they grow older, the gifts become dormant and lost to them.

Anyone who is psychic has a propensity for spirit channeling. If you have psychic senses, then you can speak to ghosts. Being psychically attuned from birth makes no difference in this context. What matters is your willingness to learn and your eagerness to try.

How to Tell if You Are a Medium

Communicating with those who have passed away is the hallmark of mediumship. One way you can tell is if you have already seen ghosts, apparitions, or spirits in your life.

The first step is to look back into your childhood. Growing up, you must have had specific fears. Examine them. You may find that your childhood fears are tied to your inclination toward psychic ability. You might be a medium if:

- You had a fear of the dark as a child. Usually, predisposed children have a persistent fear of the dark, resulting from their subconscious awareness of the paranormal.
- You dreaded sleeping in a room alone due to vivid nightmares.

Then consider your play patterns as a child. What did you like to do? When you don't remember, ask your parents. Without realizing it, you might have had individual experiences that tilt toward the supernatural. Ask your parents if you had an imaginary friend while growing up. Supposing the answer is yes, it could mean you always interacted with a friendly spirit (or spirits) then. Often, adults see their kids seemingly interacting alone and conclude that they have "imaginary friends."

Examine Your Interests - If you had a strong interest in understanding meaning and religion, this could be another sign of your psychic connection. As a child, you might have:

• Asked parents or guardians to explain different religious beliefs to you.

• Engaged in activities that involved playing with psychic tools like tarot cards or a Ouija board.

• Read spiritual-themed or supernatural-themed books.

The older you grow, the more profound the signs become. Reflect on your middle age. Mediums tend to see auras and symbols around living people and objects. An aura is an invisible energy field surrounding everything in the universe. Most people cannot see the aura, but those in touch with their psychic side can. Seeing an aura is a sign of clairvoyance, one of the significant psychic senses that mediums have. So, think about the thing (s) that you see around others.

Understand the feeling you get when you are around other people. Can you sense people's presence in a room even before seeing them? If you can do this, it is a sign you are clairsentient. Like clairvoyance, clairsentience is also a dominating psychic sense in mediums. It is the ability to feel or sense people's energy and moods. As a clairsentient:

• You are deeply intuitive about people's feelings, thoughts, and moods.

• Touching or holding an item owned by another person makes you feel an overwhelming connection to their emotions and experiences.

Most mediums typically have personal experiences relating to death. Having a near-death encounter is how people discover their gifts. If this has never happened to you, remember the loved ones you have lost. If you have medium powers, losing a loved one can trigger strange occurrences.

An example of this could be odd sensations and feelings or something as dismissible as suddenly slammed doors. Suppose you have experienced something similar before. In that case, that might have been the spirit of your deceased loved one trying to communicate with you.

Realizing the gift you have is no easy feat. It is a long and complicated process. So many people are still unaware of their abilities. For some people, their gifts might not become clear to them until they are at a certain age. Most have experiences they believe are familiar to everyone else.

Suppose you persistently sense and feel things that rarely mean anything to you. There, they could make a difference in the lives of people around you. The messages you receive from spirits may or may not have anything to do with you in particular. Sometimes, souls choose specific people to relay messages to because they are accessible to them.

You may not relate to any of the signs mentioned above; that takes nothing away from your potential to be gifted. It does not mean you don't have the ability – it only suggests that you need to tap into your subconscious and awaken that part of you.

Everyone can connect with their loved ones who have passed away. Spirit is always willing to interact with anybody. You have to make yourself more open to the connection. To do this, you have to strengthen your awareness and pay more attention to the things around you.

Certain things could happen to you like a coincidence or a strange occurrence, but you may find they remind you of someone you have lost if you pay attention. These are often signs and symbols. Unless you immerse yourself in your environment, you will miss out on these cues from spirit.

Not all mediums know their abilities. Some require a little nudge to awaken their potential. If you fall under that category, there are things you can do to find your psychic muscle. Knowingly or unknowingly, you might even have been doing things to tap into your intuitive senses.

The number one thing that obstructs an individual from learning of their gifts is fear. Fear hinders you from opening yourself to your innate skills. Once they see supernatural signs, many get so scared that they subconsciously shut it out. But it is vital to understand these experiences are not scary. You shouldn't fear what you don't comprehend. Instead, actively try to make sense of it.

Psychic skills shouldn't cause you to fear. They are there to assist you on the path to awakening and higher consciousness. Thus, the first step to tapping into your potentials is opening yourself up to the possibilities. Embrace your otherworldly capabilities. Let the universe know that you are ready to explore your gifts. Do not allow fear to dictate your reaction to the knowledge of the ethereal.

The second thing you can do is to be more attuned to energy. When you meet someone new, there is a "vibe" you get. The "vibe" in this context is the energy. Everyone has the intuitive ability to sense someone's energy. That is how you can tell whether the stranger you meet is trustworthy or not.

Sensing a person's vibe is a manifestation of your inner psychic intuition. It indicates that you indeed have the ability, and you need to exercise it more. Strengthening that skill is all you need. So, challenge yourself to read and interpret people's energy purposively. Look beyond the appearance and disposition to find the true person. Tapping into a person's energy will give you more information about them than you will find anywhere else.

How, you might wonder? Be in their presence and be mindful of the way you feel. Understand how this reflects on them. You don't even have to see or interact with the person to do this. For example, if you are in a queue to enter a cinema, deliberately tap into anybody's energy around you and see what you find. Then start a conversation to substantiate the findings of your little energy probe.

Clairvoyance is one of the dominant psychic abilities in mediums. Practicing psychic seeing is another method for tapping into your inner potentials. One of the best ways to practice is to use a remote-viewing exercise. You practice "seeing" things from a distance. Whenever you have to visit a new place, try remote viewing ahead of your visit. Close your eyes and visualize the location in your head. Try to "see" this location, then put down whatever appears in your mind's eye.

Later, when you get to the actual place, compare your imagined description of the area to its real look. Don't be surprised when you discover that you got some of the shapes or features right. Your visualization may be precise, with certain things in the exact spots you imagined them.

To further tune into your gifts, facilitate contact with spirit guides. Spirit guides are higher-dimensional beings that are assigned uniquely to you. They exist to support and guide you in every endeavor, and many have survived multiple lifetimes on this plane. You have different spirit guides, ranging from angels to spirit animals. Each guide offers a distinctive blend of knowledge, wisdom, and skills.

Usually, one gets up to six guides that serve different purposes. One spirit guide may be for protection, another for healing, and another to help you achieve an objective. They also exist to aid you in developing your psychic gifts. That is the guide to call upon when striving to unlock your latent medium. In a later chapter, I will elucidate more on how you can contact your spirit guides.

Now, you may be wondering exactly why one could want to establish a connection with the spirit world. What do you stand to benefit from contacting otherworldly beings? The answer to this question is at the very heart of mediumship.

Being a medium allows you to lessen the pain and grief of the bereaved. With your ability, you can offer them comfort. Merely knowing that the spirits of their deceased loved ones are around to watch over them can assuage the guilt felt by grieving families.

Mediumship allows you to pray for or help to transition a departed soul. Sometimes, souls become anchored to the Earth and cannot transit to the other side. That often happens due to something else acting as a tether to keep them bound here. By communicating with a medium, these spirits can solve the anchoring issue and move on to eternal peace.

Acting as an intermediary between this world and the spirit world is a way you can gain and improve esoteric knowledge. To undergo full spiritual awakening and enlightenment, talking to spirits who have been in other dimensions might be the place to start. Channeling energies is also a way for you to establish a dialogue with the metaphysical world. You can create a bridge between this world and the spiritual ones.

In some instances, the departed comes seeking to communicate with the living. They do this for several reasons, which include:

- Assuring their loved ones they are okay. This mostly happens when the departed lose their souls through an accident or other equally traumatic events.
- To provide help and assistance to the living.
- Curiosity and interest.
- See an unfinished business to the end

There are several other reasons spirits initiate contact with the living. These are just a few of the most common ones.

Do not be discouraged if you haven't experienced or witnessed anything that might be remotely related to psychic ability. You have probably had one or two experiences unknowingly. Using the tips given above, you can tap into your inherent psychic senses to trigger a fresh experience.

The most important thing is to make sure that mediumship is something you want for yourself. Look within yourself for the answer because that is the only place you will find it. If you proceed, be ready to believe and open yourself to all possibilities. Belief is essential. Without a robust belief system, your heart and mind will remain closed to spirit, making channeling impossible.

Last, understand that becoming a spiritual medium is a long process that requires you to study, practice, and, more importantly, be consistent. Learning a new skill requires consistency. Think of mediumship as a new skill you are just starting to learn. I guarantee you can completely redefine your perception and idea of this life when you reach a specific knowledge level in this field.

The next chapter dives deep into the different types of mediums and what makes each unique. How do you know which one you are? Let's find out!

Chapter Two: Types of Mediums

"Mediumship channels guidance from those who have gone before, not only for the sake of those who are here but also for those yet to come."

—Anthon St. Marteen

Mediumship is a far cry from what most people believe it to be. It manifests in people differently. Hence, there are various types of mediums. Although the end goal is to obtain information from the spiritual plane, all mediums are different. There are four types of medium. The kind of medium you become depends on your dominant psychic trait.

Humans intuit in four ways – through thoughts, feelings, energy, or the physical body. A person who intuits through emotions is an emotional intuitive. A mental intuitive absorbs thoughts and mental energy. A spiritual intuitive intuits via the human energy field, and a physical intuitive intuits by absorbing energy into the material body. Most people have all four means of intuition. Yet, there is a tendency to be more predisposed to one or two than the others.

As a medium, you connect and interact with the spiritual dimension through these intuitive channels. Your medium type depends on which of the four intuitive channels you use to communicate with the other side. In other words, your innate intuitive type determines the kind of medium you are. Knowing this is vital because it is the key to further developing your gifts.

Naturally, you are likely to have a predominant medium type. Still, you have probably experienced the distinctive connection phenomena of all four types. Below is a detailed insight into the different types of mediums based on the four intuitive modalities.

Emotional Medium

An emotional medium absorbs the emotional energy of spirits, often without realization. They can feel the range of emotions and feelings expressed on the other side better than any other medium type. Suppose you have ever had an influx of healthy, loving emotions with no idea of the source. There, you may be an emotional medium.

Have you ever been overwhelmed by a higher love that seems to come from another place? Do you continuously get vivid memories of a departed loved one that invoke a powerful emotional reaction in you? When spirits are around you, they invoke feelings of warmth and happiness that make you feel like someone else is in the room with you.

The above are ways that emotional mediums attune to the spirit world. Unknowingly, they connect with those who have passed on to the other side.

Emotional mediums are empathetic and compassionate, with a strong desire to make a difference in others' lives. They are in tune with the highest planes where divine love originates. They tend to be natural-born empaths, which makes clairsentience their predominant intuitive sense.

Being an empath makes them feel other people's emotions just as intensely as they feel their own, or that sometimes happens when they think those feelings are theirs. Not only can they tune into the emotional energy and feelings of physical dimensional beings, but they can also tune into the auras of those in the higher spiritual realms to access emotional information.

The primary way emotional mediums receive messages from the spirit world is through feelings and emotional sensations. Suppose you are an emotional medium. In that case, you may receive a sudden sense of warmth within you. Or you may feel unexplainably happy. When this happens frequently, it may mean that a cheerful spirit is trying to pass a positive message to you or another person you know.

To determine whether you are an emotional medium, try the exercise below.

- Comfortably sit on a chair or the ground. Close your eyes, then take a couple of long breaths. Deeply breathe in and out until you feel relaxed.

- Think of a loved one that is no more. Say the loved one's name out loud for the universe to hear. You may also say it silently. It is your choice to make.

- Continue breathing to keep yourself relaxed and calm. Feel the warmth of your breath as it goes in and out of your stomach.

- Open your heart and call your loved one's name again. Quietly, listen through your heart and wait.

- Allow your heart to receive the love and warmth your loved one's soul sends

- Listen for any other message they may be sending

- Send them a warm feeling of love from your heart

Practice this every day to sharpen your connection with the departed and the spiritual dimension. Whenever you get an unanticipated feeling, take time to observe the feeling. Try to decipher the message you are receiving. If you include this exercise in your daily schedule, it will strengthen your emotional link to the other side. Inadvertently, this will make spiritual messages more accessible to you.

Mental Medium

Although most people still can't distinguish between mediums, mental mediums are more known than any other medium type. As a mental medium, you unknowingly converse with spirits within your mind. Sometimes, the "conversation" is in the form of a vision playing out on a movie screen.

Psychic messages via the thoughts come at any time. It may occur while you are driving to work or running to the park. It does not matter what you are doing at that moment. Since communication happens through your thoughts, nothing can restrict or limit the connection.

Receiving others' thoughts is second nature to a mental intuitive. Due to this, you may not even realize when you communicate with spirits on the other side. Once you recognize and acknowledge that the conversations happening in your mind are more than just internal monologue, your ability develops more rapidly.

From that point, you can discern your thoughts from those of another being or entity. You might hear a voice that sounds like your own inside your mind, but that is probably a spirit trying to communicate. The voice may seem to you like that of a departed family member or loved one. Think back to the time when you heard someone call your name, but you could find no one in your vicinity. That is an instance of a departed projecting their voice into your mental auric layer.

Mental mediums have the gift of claircognizance, which translates to "clear knowing." The psychic sense allows you to know information and knowledge without a clue about the origin. Having claircognizance as your predominant psychic modality means you can communicate with ethereal beings through your thoughts. You may know the thoughts, ideas, and beliefs of a loved one on certain subjects without a clear idea of how you have this information.

Try the exercise below to determine if you are a mental medium.

- Close your eyes. Take a few deep breaths, then open your eyes.

- Think of an aspect of your life where you want a spiritual dimensional being's opinions.

- Write down a question or concern you want your departed friend to address.

- Then, write down the solutions and possibilities you have in mind. The point of this is to clear your mind and be open to the thought energy you are about to receive from the other side.

- Now, close your eyes again. Take a few deep breaths to keep your mind relaxed.

- Call out the name of the loved one with whom you seek a connection. Repeat the name three times.

- Ask your questions and repeat them three times. Repeating the question thrice ensures the spirits hear you correctly.

- Focus on your thoughts as you continue to relax. Listen for any message.

Write down every thought that emerges and be aware of any voice in your head. The thoughts that surface is quite possibly from the spirit with whom you are communicating.

Note they may differ from what you imagined or expected.

Spiritual Medium

A spiritual medium is capable of "seeing" spirits and departed souls. They tend to communicate with the spirit realm through dreams and daydreams. They can do this because their dominant psychic sense is clairvoyance, which means "clear seeing." Clairvoyance allows spiritual mediums to receive visual messages from the other side. Spiritual mediums typically receive intuitive drops in ways I would describe as elusive.

Being a spiritual medium means that your connection with the spirit planes may feel dreamy, almost to where you feel like it is imagined. With clairvoyance as your main psychic channel, you may have seen ghosts, spirits, and other ethereal beings and dismissed it as your eyes playing tricks.

Spiritual mediums have a depth of wisdom, which allows them to learn life lessons and purpose intuitively. As a spiritual medium, you can intuit your life's purpose and that of those around you. You need not visit psychics to discover specific things about yourself.

Having the gift of inner sight enables you to see energy, figuratively, symbolically, or realistically. You can see departed loved ones in their spirit form. This ability either happens through your inner sight or in the form of translucent beings. Sometimes, they can appear to you as three-dimensional figures in this realm.

Here is an exercise specifically for developing your gift of clear seeing and spiritual mediumship.

- Sit in a comfortable position.

- Close your eyes and breathe in deeply. Then breathe out just as deeply. Repeat the breathing exercise a couple of times to calm and clear your mind.

- Visualize a white orb of energy surrounding you. Imagine yourself hidden in the white light.

- As you keep taking deep breaths, envision the orb expanding and filling up with vibrant energy.

- Envision a loved one from the spirit realm coming into the orb. Call out the name of the person you want in the white light with you. Repeat the name a couple of times.

- Continue to take relaxing breaths as you repeat the spirit's name.

- At that moment, you may feel warm tingling-like energy passing through your nerves. Or you may see a symbol or image of the person. Sometimes, the spirit may appear as a streak of sparkling light.

- You may try to initiate a conversation with the spirit or simply open your mind to the message he or she has for you.

Spiritual mediumship is the same as healing mediumship. You can raise your vibrational levels to the height of consciousness, where you can channel divine energy from the spiritual realms. Furthermore, you can impart the energy in a living person to initiate healing. The standard way to do this is to channel the divine energy through your body to another person's body.

Many people believe that spirit mediums are the most potent types of mediums, but no medium type is more powerful than the others. The extent of your abilities depends strictly on how you train yourself. It has nothing to do with how you connect with the spiritual dimension.

Physical Medium

The defining trait in physical mediums is their ability to interact with spirits through their gut feelings. Spiritual messages come to them in the form of physical sensations. An excellent example of this is when the hairs on your arms stand up while reminiscing about a deceased loved one. Perhaps you have had gut feelings that a departed friend or family member is present. You may sense they are standing behind you or simply get a sensation of their warm hand on your back. These are just some ways that spirits connect with physical mediums.

Assume you are a physical medium. In that case, you can tangibly interact with spirits and otherworldly entities. Souls that have passed have a knack for things such as blinking lights, dropping items on our path, and ringing the doorbell for no reason. Although these happen to many mediums, they usually occur more often to physical mediums.

Physical mediums are adept at psychometry, which is the ability to intuit energy from an object. When you look at a deceased person's photo, you can get a lot of information about them if you are a physical medium. How is this possible? Physical mediumship makes you more connected to the impermeable physical vibrations from the spirit world. The connection gives physical mediums a psychic advantage over all other types of mediums.

Information intuited through physical vibrations comes as a gut feeling or knowing, a sense of a spirit's presence, or through the gift of inner sight. Any message sent from the other side triggers specific physical sensations in your body, causing you to pay attention.

Below is an exercise for physical mediums. Try this to check the extent of your physical attunement to the unseen dimension.

- Find an object belonging to a deceased family member or friend. This object should naturally be something they cherished dearly while on Earth. It could be a ring or necklace. You may also use a photo of the deceased for this exercise.

- Close your eyes and do a quick breathing exercise.

- As usual, call out or silently mutter the name of the spirit you wish to contact.

- Gently open your eyes and stare purposefully at the photo or personal item.

- Sharpen your awareness and pay attention to sensations in your body.

- You may feel or sense their presence or feel a rush of energy breeze by you. You may glimpse a silhouette of your loved one as a streak of sparkling light or color. You may also hear their voice.

Even if you receive no signs of a psychic message on your first try, don't stop the exercise. Keep trying until your first breakthrough. Remember that the ability is somewhere within you. Therefore, it is not about having it – but about *tapping into it*.

Knowingly or unknowingly, you may have experienced these types of interactions with entities in the unseen world. So, how exactly do you know which medium type you are?

In my experience, the best way to decipher your medium type is to observe which experience you have more than others. If you always seem to know things that were never in your head, you could be a mental medium. If not, you may be the other medium types.

Essentially, the one thing that matters is that you can intuit through your thoughts, feelings, energy, and physical body. Therefore, you can be any medium you want. Remember that it is okay to be predisposed to one medium type than the others. It takes nothing away from your abilities. It adds a lot to you.

As you become more self-conscious of your natural connection, you will become more confident in your medium abilities. This makes them effortless to hone. One vital thing you shouldn't forget is that you must never compare yourself to other mediums. Doing that to yourself is a way of undermining your potentials.

Mediumship is like a skill, as I mentioned before. Everyone learns a new skill at an individual pace. So, in your journey to spiritual self-discovery, don't distract yourself by comparing your success with that of another medium. Focus on your gifts and the difference you can make with them in your life and other people's lives.

Chapter Three: Beginning Your Psychic Journey

"We only receive in a psychic reading what is most necessary and beneficial to us at that particular moment in time. Nothing more. Nothing less."

—Anthon St. Marteen

Intuitive guidance and psychic abilities come naturally. Still, psychic development is a journey with a specific destination in mind. This means there are several roads you must take on your way. There are steps you must take on the path to psychic development. Remembering that mediumship is a type of psychic ability, this chapter is written from a general psychic perspective.

Having a psychic predisposition is a state of being. It is less about doing and more about being. But most people make psychic development more complicated than it is. It happens because they have had no proper guidance as beginners. Knowledge about the psychic voyage can make your path more straightforward and far less complicated than for those who do not have this knowledge.

Know there are varying ways you can incorporate intuitive development into your daily activities. It is the best way to master your abilities because everyday use strengthens your trust in these activities. It would help if you did a few things before beginning your development journey are basic things you may otherwise ignore. I have six things I always suggest people do before they get started.

It may come as a surprise, but the first thing is to declutter. That's right – you need to clear your physical and mental spaces. Relieving your living/working space and your mind of stuff that no longer benefits you is crucial to spiritual awakening. Clutter encourages distraction. Remembering that focus is essential to psychic development; you cannot have clutter anywhere around you. While decluttering your physical space, you must declutter your mind. The best way to rid the mind of unwanted thoughts and beliefs is to meditate every single day.

Meditation is food for the soul. It is the practice of sitting in silence and solitude to achieve mindfulness. During meditation, allow your thoughts to flow freely. Don't stifle, repress, or judge any of your thoughts. Let them pass without judgment. Slowly, your mind will become free of mental clutter.

Meditation is a way of grounding yourself to be present in the moment – which is present and valid – without worries about anything. When you immerse yourself in the present, you will realize there is no fear, only love. This realization offers you a more vital link to your intuitive self.

Examining your beliefs is also something you do before starting your psychic practice. Be intentional about the journey you are about to take. Know what you believe in. Acknowledge that you are affecting your world and the world at large with your energy. Make sure that your beliefs match the spiritual growth and awakening you are about to experience.

Often, intuitive development requires that one lets go of certain beliefs that have been there from inception. Fortunately, that is the thing about psychic awakening – first, realize that you have been asleep all along.

Again, expand your mind to the possibilities of the path you are on. Opening your mind is key to achieving an intuitive journey. A closed mind cannot be visited or affected by spirit. The point of a psychic awakening is to help you learn something new. It is unachievable if you don't open and expand your mind to your potential and the realms you experience.

Energy is everywhere around you, but you will find it outside more. So, prepare to spend more time outdoors. Spirit and energy are awaiting you in nature. Many people want to become psychics, yet they spend all their time sitting indoors behind a MacBook screen. How can you connect with the world if you never spend your time in it?

Connecting with nature is a surefire way to prepare for the journey. Understand that spirits love nature, so spending time in nature can help amplify your psychic portals to the spirit plane. When you connect with nature, put your mobile gadgets away to avoid distractions. Soak yourself in the quiet and solitude. You may surprise yourself.

This one often sounds odd to many but eating a healthy diet is vital to psychic development. One can write a whole book on the importance of healthy eating to psychic awakening and growth. The foods you eat can block your energy centers, resulting in an imbalance of your spiritual body. Blocked energy centers make the free flow of energy through the soul, body, and mind impossible. In turn, this leads to a limitation of your psychic abilities.

Healthy eating allows you to stay attuned to the Divine power and your inner guidance. So, add high-vibrational foods to your diet. Consume more vegetables and fresh fruit. They will keep your vibrational energy high, making it easier to connect to spirit. That does not mean you have to overhaul your whole diet; you only need to incorporate more high-vibe food. Examples include fruit, greens, and dark chocolate. You will notice a difference in how in-tune you are with your psychic abilities.

One cannot force a psychic awakening. With the right tips and guidance, anyone can go through one. But there is no definitive way to enlightenment. You cannot force your abilities to come alive, as you only do what you can do.

You may become too attached to the idea of becoming a psychic, medium, or psychic medium. In that case, your chances of experiencing it drop until it is nonexistent.

As a bonus, use your waiting time for more productive things. "Waiting time" is the period you spend waiting for the doctor in the waiting room or in the car waiting for your kids to finish school. That is a time you can use efficiently to develop your psychic senses, particularly clairaudience. Clairaudience is the psychic gift of "clear hearing." Doing this is better than just sitting around until the children get out of school or until it is your turn to see the doctor.

Once you know and understand all these things, it is time to begin your psychic journey. On your way to spiritual growth and advancement, three things must always be your companions. These include - meditation, visualization, and journaling. One by one, let's find out why they are crucial to your journey.

Meditation

I briefly highlighted the significance of meditation, but let's dive in deeper. There are many benefits of meditation for psychics. It is safe to say that these benefits are endless. There are vital advantages specifically for those on a psychic and spiritual development journey.

1. Connect to Your Higher Self

Your Higher Self knows who you are and why you are here on Earth. More important, it also knows the purpose of your psychic gifts. Meditation is the best way to connect with that all-knowing part of you. When you meditate, you open layers of yourself that you didn't know existed. It is a way of diving deep and focusing on your inner self. Since your Higher Self is the spiritual part of you, meditation automatically brings you there.

2. Remove Negative Energy

Psychics must always attract positive energy. Just like you clean your house, your energy field also requires daily cleaning. Meditation is the best way to rid yourself of harmful and toxic energy. It is a way to get rid of internal cobwebs and clouds of dust so you can refocus your mind on what is truly important. Not only does meditating kick negativity and toxicity to the curb, but it also raises your vibrations. This ushers in the sense of calm and grounding that is attractive to spiritual beings.

3. Achieve Emotional Balance

Emotional balance is crucial when one is on a spiritual journey. Again, it is a way to raise your vibration. Meditation helps take your focus from your past so you can focus on your present as it is. That fresh perspective triggers emotional balance, resulting in an alignment of your logical self and spiritual self. It is proof that psychic practices do not counter logic in any way. If anything, they promote the use of reason.

4. Heighten Your Intuition

Intuition is the channel through which the nonphysical part of you communicates with Spirit. Daily meditation can help enhance your intuition by bridging the gap between you and your Higher Self.

The question is, how do you meditate?

You have to meditate to get the benefits discussed above. So, how do you meditate the right way? There are no benefits to gain if you do your meditation incorrectly. If you have never meditated before, starting with a guided meditation can help make sure you get it right. It is a way to make things easy for yourself.

The best thing about it is that you don't have to think or worry about anything. It is all spelled out for you. Just follow the instructions. There are apps for guided meditations you can easily find online. Try the different apps until you find one suited to your liking.

Meditating is straightforward. Find a quiet and comfortable place where you can be in solitude. You can choose a specific area in your home for daily meditative practice. It is all about grounding yourself in the moment. One way to do this is to focus on your breathing and calmly allow your thoughts to pass through without distracting from your breath. Besides that, you can also focus on a specific mantra. The endgame is to fully immerse yourself in the present, up to where you are aware of everything happening around you.

During meditation, your mind may wander to other things. It is usual for this to happen. Redirect your mind back to the object of concentration whenever you find it wandering. The three tips for using guided meditation are:

- Sit in a comfortable spot with a good headphone plugged in your ears
- Focus entirely on the guided meditation
- Bring back your mind to the guide whenever it wanders

If you would rather meditate the traditional way, follow the steps below.

- Sit quietly on a chair or the ground. Choose a position comfortable for you.

- Allow your thoughts to leave your mind. Visualize them floating on little clouds away from your mind.

- Place your palms on your tummy.

- Take deep breaths in and out. Focus on the rise and fall of your belly each time you inhale and exhale.

- Do this until your mind is clear and free of clutter

If the above makes you susceptible to incessant mind wandering, consider counting from 100 to 1 as you inhale. You can also chant a mantra as you meditate.

Tools that can make meditation better include:

- Meditation beads (Malas)

- Salt lamp

- Essential oils such as Lavender, Rose, Frankincense, Patchouli, and an oil diffuser

- Meditation mat

Having the items above can make meditation a fun and enlightening experience for you.

Visualization

Most people argue that visualization is just another type of meditation, but it is much more than that. Yes, you can integrate it into your daily meditative routine, but it can stand on its own. It involves using imagery and visuals to achieve mindfulness. It has all the benefits of meditation but is more vital to developing your psychic sense of clairvoyance. Awakening your inner sight requires you to practice exercises targeted at your mind's eye.

There are different visualization exercises you can use to sharpen your inner sight. You don't have to learn all these techniques. Just committing one or two to memory can make all the difference you want. Below are two exercises to train your psychic eye.

Exercise 1: Basic Visualization

This exercise is all about internal visualization. But then, all visualization techniques are somewhat internally generated. From the name, one may assume this basic method is easy to learn. But that depends on your work ethic. With consistency, it's easy to master. If you don't strive to be consistent, learning it may be challenging. Practice is the key to progress. So, even if it is just five minutes of your whole day, make sure you get this exercise done daily.

- Find a calm and friendly spot, close your eyes, and start breathing steadily. Focus on your breath as it goes in and comes out. Do this for at least 2 minutes.

- Picture a place in your head – this could be anywhere from your favorite hangout place to your school. Just picture a familiar place. Imagine yourself in that place and look around.

- Visualize the scene with more specific detail. Imagine people walking by, breeze blowing, or birds chirping in nearby trees. You may even attempt to communicate with someone with you.

- Once you successfully interact within that scene, imagine yourself walking away from the place into the room where you are currently doing your visualization exercise.

- Further, imagine yourself sitting down to the exact place you are now seated. It should feel like you have just merged your real self and your imagined self.

Don't use the same scene for your daily practice. Otherwise, your mind will become used to that scene. When this happens, it means that your mind no longer actively participates in the process due to familiarity. That defeats the purpose you are visualizing. So, try different scenes every day. As you become better at visualization, try to include more details in the process. It will further strengthen your inner eye.

Exercise 2: Third Eye Visualization

This exercise aims at opening your inner clairvoyant. This is also basic because it is primarily for new practitioners. For this technique, be sure to sit or lie down. If you tend to go off to sleep easily, sit instead of lying down.

- Relax your body by doing your essential breathing exercise.

- Once you feel relaxed physically and mentally, bring your focus to your breathing. Imagine your breath getting lighter with each inhale and exhale. Visualize all the tension leaving your body as you exhale.

- After a few seconds, move your attention to the spot between your eyebrows. That is the home of your third eye. Remember to keep your physical eyes closed. Use your mind's eye to focus on that spot.

- Visualize a ball of glowing purple light around your head. Imagine the purple light growing bigger and bigger.

- Picture your pineal gland as a glowing little space in the middle of your head.

- Imagine a sparkling white light flowing out of your pineal gland. You should start feeling a warm, tingling sensation in the area around the center of your head. It means that your third eye is awakening.

- Once you feel ready to complete your meditation, slowly twitch or wiggle your toes and fingers. Then, gently open your eyes and take a couple of relaxing breaths.

Note: If your third eye spot suddenly feels too uncomfortable or overheated, pause the exercise immediately. You may also put a wet cloth over that area and breathe in your favorite essential oil.

Journaling

Journaling is one thing that new intuits ignore because they don't understand its importance. Yet, it is an essential part of any psychic journey. An individual's psychic awakening is not complete without it. It helps you achieve clarity, enhance your intuition, and mentally declutter as you progress in your path. These are just some of the most common benefits.

Before you engage in actual mediumship activities such as channeling spirits or ghosts, purchase a journal and pens. It might sound like an unimportant step, but I assure you it is not something to take lightly.

Don't just buy any journal. Get one that speaks to you. Connecting with your journal makes you want to open it and write things down every day. Your journal is unique to you and is a means of sharing your experiences with the spirit world, which means it should reflect your taste and personality. I recommend getting a celestial journal.

I should note you need not get a physical journal. You can also write on your phone or computer. But writing in a spiritual journal is much more personal. And it gives less room for distractions. There should be nothing to pull your mind away when recording your psychic experiences with the spirit world.

An important thing to note is that journaling must come naturally. Do not force the process. It is okay to feel stuck when you just get started. If that happens to you, don't push yourself. Growing up, we learn to filter our words before we speak or write. Due to this, we find it difficult to express ourselves through unfiltered words. Well, when it comes to psychic journaling, getting rid of your filters is essential. No-filter is what you need.

You have to allow yourself to get into the flow. If you can't get into the flow, pause your writing until you can. Pour out your thoughts exactly as they surface. Do not censor or stop a particular thought because it doesn't fit your expectation. Being a beginner, consider buying a journal that comes with writing prompts. It will ensure you don't feel stuck every time you have to write.

Meditating before writing works for so many people. So, consider updating your journal after your daily psychic practices. Doing this is also a way to make sure you have relevant information to add to the journal.

A psychic journal is for you to record every step (and misstep) of your mediumship journey. By writing your experiences down, you can measure your progress. More importantly, it makes for easy analysis of the spiritual messages you receive.

As you get started on your mediumship journey, you may need extra help to boost your abilities. In that case, think about using pendulums, crystals, tarot cards, gemstones, or a Ouija board in your practices. These are all psychic tools that can amplify your psychic abilities and help you tune into them more quickly.

Chapter Four: Understanding Your Spiritual Body

"You don't have a soul. You are a Soul. You have a body."

−C. S. Lewis

In the last few chapters, I mentioned something called the "energy field." Well, this chapter is all about this field and the spiritual body. In spiritual settings, an energy field is called an aura.

Every individual and object in the universe emits energy. An aura is an electromagnetic field through which you channel spiritual energy, surrounding every living and non-living thing. Your aura is an invisible projection of your life force. Contrary to what many people think, it is not a single entity.

The aura comprises seven separate layers, all of which are interconnected. Together, these layers form a somewhat cohesive body. Thus, it might look like a less refined form of their physical body when you see the aura around someone. Each layer reflects one aspect of a person's life.

A person's aura is a sign of their energy. It has a lot of impact on their ability to connect with others. Typically, it extends about two to three feet from the body, but those who have experienced tragedy and trauma often have much broader auras, meaning that theirs may extend over three feet from their body.

The energy field is invisible, so most people don't see it around others. But those with the gift of clairvoyance can see, read, and interpret the aura. Being clairvoyant means you can see people's energy patterns, scenes, and blockages when looking at their aura.

When you meet a person, and you sense their "vibe," it is the emission of their personal energy you perceive. The aura is the channel through which you get specific information about people you don't know. It is the reason you can tell if someone is trustworthy or not. How you react to someone depends on the energy they radiate around you.

At this point, you are likely wondering what this has to do with your journey to mediumship. As I said, an aura is a projection or manifestation of a person's spiritual energy. You can tell a person's mental, emotional, spiritual, and even physical standing by reading their aura's colors. From the shape to the color and color shade, all aspects of the life force energy field are there for you to understand a person better.

As a medium, when you clairvoyantly see a ghost, you can also see its aura. Through this, you can detect valuable information about the spirit.

One of the auric field layers is the astral layer which you may call the spiritual layer. This layer is home to your celestial body, or if you prefer, your spiritual body. You cannot go to spiritual dimensions in your physical form because it is made of entirely different elements. To visit nonphysical dimensions, you need your astral body. Some people also call the astral form *the soul.*

When you start developing your mediumship ability, there will be plenty of situations when you need to go into a spiritual dimension yourself. It might be because you need to talk to a spirit, your spirit guide, or another higher-dimensional being. Regardless of the reason, you can only astral travel in your spiritual form. Therefore, understanding the aura's operations and the spiritual body can make all the difference for you.

Back to the layers of the aura, there are seven, as I said. Each layer has one solid color, which carries a lot of meaning, but it goes beyond that. Every layer is also connected to your seven energy centers, which are also known as the Chakras.

Individually, the auric layers vary in size and depth, and this is determined by an individual and the point they are in life. In a healthy individual, the aura usually has very bright colors. In contrast, dull colors are found in an unhealthy and weak aura. The size may also become small or large, depending on a person's quality of health. This means that no two people have the same auras.

The seven layers of your aura pulsate from your body. The first layer is the closest to your material form, while the 7th layer is the furthest. In retrospect, the seventh layer is the closest to your higher awareness. It has the highest vibrations because the further away a layer is from the physical body, the more vibration increases.

Some layers can be odd-numbered, while others are even-numbered. The odd-numbered layers have a defined structure, and they carry yang energy. In contrast, the even-numbered layers are more fluid, and they carry yin energy. Together, they culminate in a balanced and harmonization of your energy field.

The Seven Auric Layers

1. Etheric Layer: This layer is the closest to your material body. It is directly connected to the root chakra. With a bluish-grey color, you can easily see the etheric layer with your physical eyes.

2. Emotional Layer: After the subtle etheric body, the next is the emotional layer. It is the home of emotions and feelings. It is directly connected to the sacral chakra. In most people, this layer has all the colors of the rainbow. When you go through emotional stress, the colors turn murky and dark. You can tell someone's emotional state from reading this layer. It can also provide information on the state of the chakras.

3. Mental Layer: The mental layer is the third subtle energy body of the aura. It is linked to your solar plexus chakra. It indicates your cognitive processes and mental state, which makes it the seat of your thoughts. The standard color of this layer is bright yellow.

4. Astral Layer: When you hear of a spiritual cord connected to everything in the universe, the astral layer is the first thing that should come to mind. It is where you form the thread that connects you with every other being. This subtle body usually is bright pink with a rosy tint. And is connected to your heart chakra. You can get information about interpersonal relationships by reading the astral layer colors.

5. Etheric Template: An etheric template is a nonphysical form of your body. It contains the blueprint of your material body on the physical plane. Everything that happens on the physical level is recorded in your etheric template. The color may vary from person to person. The throat chakra is associated with this layer.

6. Celestial Layer: This is the sixth layer away from your physical body. It is linked to the third eye chakra. The celestial layer carries powerful vibrations, so the third eye is the seat of intuition. It is your connection to the Divine and all other higher-dimensional beings. This layer typically has a pearly white color.

7. Ketheric Template: The Ketheric template is about 3 feet from the body. It is the layer where you can become one with the universe. It contains every information about your previous lifetimes. Of all the auric layers, this one has the most potent and most powerful vibrations. It is connected to the crown chakra, with a golden color.

Your aura can change, depending on the events of your life. Still, most people always have two primary colors around them. Sometimes, an inauthentic color may even appear around a person's aura. That happens because of environmental issues or programming. For instance, being in a stressful relationship can add another color to your aura for the relationship duration.

Also, your emotional and physical experiences impact the colors in your aura. Suppose you have a severe case of acute pain. There, your aura's colors may change to reflect that. Having a hangover can also change your auric colors.

Despite all these, some colors usually are part of everyone's aura. These colors represent different things in different people, particularly when they appear with other colors. Interestingly, their meanings also change based on their tone and shade. A bright orange color in the auric field has a different interpretation from a dark orange color.

You must keep this information in mind when reading your aura or that of another person. Here are the most common colors in the aura and their respective meanings. Note these colors aren't in order, and they can appear in any of the seven subtle energy bodies.

- **Yellow**

Yellow means creativity, friendliness, and relaxation. You can find this in the aura of an individual who is curious and highly interesting. A yellow aura represents a busy mind. Someone with this aura color always has something going on in their head. To deal with this, you will find them immersing themselves in things such as baking, sewing, interior design, painting, and other practical forms of art. This color concentrates strongly on joy and is typically found around intelligent people.

- **Green**

Green in a person's aura indicates compassion, healing energy, divine wisdom, and a natural connection to Mother Earth. It is the color you find around the auras of energy healers. People of this color are innovative, logical, and visionary. They tend to live in their reality. They have a knack for solo activities due to their lone-wolf nature. A green aura means that the person is nurturing, social, and a great communicator.

- **Red**

Red in an aura symbolizes materialism. It is a color centered upon the material realm. Individuals with red in their auras like to think and do. They are strong and assertive, making them suitable for leadership positions. They are also risk-takers and are intrinsically motivated in life. They love to win, which is why this color is common among professional athletes and CEOs. Red-aura people also love intense activities.

- **Purple**

Conversely, auric purple represents intuition, creativity, and emotions. That explains why purple is the color of the third eye chakra, the intuition seat in the energy system. If you find purple in your aura, it means you take spiritual evolution seriously. It also indicates that you are gentle and spiritually enlightened.

• Blue

A blue aura can be called the complete opposite of a red aura. Just like red, blue represents compassion. But it also represents a tendency to shy away from the spotlight. People with this color in their aura are selfless by nature, which explains why it is common among teachers, nurses, caregivers, etc. Empaths typically have blue auras.

The above are the most common colors you would typically find in people's auras. Some people have more peachy colors, such as pink, orange, peach, in their field. Colors like these symbolize a sort of creativity quite peculiar. They also focus significantly on relationships, fun, and companionship. To people with peachy auras, family and friends are everything.

Knowing the meanings of the aura colors is not quite as important as seeing the aura itself. To read your aura, you need to learn how to see it first. Now, you can either perceive the aura through your clairvoyance or intuition.

For you or anyone else to sense or perceive the aura, some level of self-awareness is necessary. You must be perceptive enough to understand the end of the self and the beginning of another. Otherwise, your perception and interpretation of someone's aura may be your perception of them.

Put simply; you must develop the ability to see through yourself to see someone else's energy field. You have your energy field, meaning you perceive yours first before seeing other people's. If you don't learn to make a discernment, you may read your aura as that of another person.

If this happens, it can lead to you forming a wrong perception of the said person. Spiritual mediums take time to master the skill of bilocation (the ability to leave one's own body while remaining close to monitoring or perceiving the environment). With this skill, you can be adept at providing accurate aura interpretations.

How to See the Aura

Seeing your aura (or *any* aura) requires you to be in the right environment. Beginners need to have the right setting. Otherwise, you may keep practicing . . . achieving nothing tangible. A suitable background can make or mar your practice.

A plain-colored background is needed to see the vibrant colors of your energy field. So, try it in a room with a white wall or background. You may also use a backdrop. If you are trying to see your aura, you will need a mirror. In case you don't have one, you can try seeing the aura around your hand by placing it on a white piece of paper.

The environment you use should be quiet and comfortable. It should be a place where you can focus on the aura without being distracted or interrupted. Assuming you already have a part of your house designated for psychic exercises and practice, that room would be the perfect place to practice.

Furthermore, your location needs proper lighting. Low lighting can hinder your ability to perceive the energy field. The light in your room should be soft, without being too dark or too light. It should be the right amount. To avoid being strained or stressed, your eyes should be comfortable with the level of light. Natural light is ideal for aura practice, but you may use lamps or candles. Just make sure that you have the right concentration of light.

Once the environment is set for practice, you can go ahead by following the instructions below.

Seeing Someone Else's Aura

- Ask your subject to stand in front of a white wall. Make sure the individual already knows the details of what you will be doing. The subject should wear clothes that have no patterns because they can be distracting.

- Look directly at your subject. As you gaze, relax your sight. Stare at a specific spot for about 30 to 60 seconds. Focus on the spots in your peripheral vision, but make sure your eyes are a little out of focus. A hazy outline may appear to you around the edges. It should look transparent or look like white light. In a few minutes, this color may change to the aura's color.

It is best to practice by focusing on a small area. When trying to see someone else's aura, pick a specific part of their body, such as their head, to be your focal point. Suppose colors appear to you on your first try. There, try to determine the colors you see. Remember that the colors may be clear and bright, dark, cloudy, and muddy.

Note: you may follow the same steps to see your own aura. But stand in front of your mirror rather than against a white wall. Also, consider starting with just your hand when trying to see your aura. It makes the process easier for you.

Most beginners don't see more than one color on their first try. But in exceptional cases, some see several colors at once. The more you practice seeing auras, the more color variations you can see. It, of course, takes consistent practice.

You must be aware of after images when you try aura reading. After-images are usually the result of staring at one spot for a long time. They are the direct inverse of the object you are staring at, and they are not auras.

The difference is clear - after images tend to appear briefly in front of your eyes, regardless of where you look. The colors also appear in pairs – black and white, orange and blue, green and pink, yellow and violet.

Don't forget to record whatever you see in your journal. You can even draw instead of writing down. So, sketch out an outline and shade with the colors you see, using this for later analysis. You may show the drawing to your subject to let them know their aura's look.

The aura sometimes shows colors that are hard to reimagine or recreate artistically. If you see colors like that, try your best to get a close representation. Then, you can verbally describe whatever differences there are between your drawing and what you saw.

Cleansing Your Aura

Sometimes, the aura becomes toxic and murky because of the energy it picks up around. When this happens, the consequence is usually a disruption in the smooth running of the energy field. You must make sure your energy field is in optimal condition at all times. The best way to make sure this is to cleanse it regularly. Aura cleansing is a vital ritual that should be a part of your daily or weekly routine. A few useful techniques for cleansing the aura include:

- Meditation
- Visualization
- Positive affirmations
- Smudging, also known as burning sage,
- Energy healing
- Crystal healing

The exercises discussed in Chapter 3 can help with cleansing and balancing your aura.

Your spiritual body is just as important as your physical body. Taking care of your aura is your way of ensuring that your spiritual journey into mediumship progresses without hiccups getting in the way. Understanding your aura and developing awareness of other people's auras can take time. But if you dedicate yourself to the process, you will reap the benefits in time.

Perhaps the most critical thing with aura reading is that your ability to see an aura depends on your dominant psychic sense. If you are clairvoyant, you are more likely to see the aura with your physical eyes. Otherwise, you may sense or perceive it through intuition; how you see the aura does not matter. What matters is your interpretation of what you see.

Chapter Five: Preparation, Protection, and Intention

"Spirit can only communicate with us on our current level of understanding. Our spiritual habits determine what that level will be."

—Anthon St. Maarten

One of the most important things to remember when starting your mediumship journey is protection. Perhaps it is more important than any other thing. Going on a spiritual journey is no easy task, particularly for beginners. You don't know what to expect. The spiritual dimensions are not like the ones familiar to you already.

Connecting with spirit requires you to let go of control and submit yourself to your feelings to a reasonable extent. It is difficult for many. Plus, if you don't do it the right way, it might backfire. Whether you want to visit a spirit realm or channel a spirit to the material realm, preparing yourself for the experience is necessary.

Good preparation isn't just physical; you must also prepare spiritually. Meditating is one way you can prepare for the spiritual journey, but it is just a basic ritual. You have to do much more than meditating. Whether you are working by yourself or helped by a spirit guide or any other person, conducting a ritual cleansing is the first thing you do to prepare yourself.

Ritual cleansing is a symbolic way of getting rid of old and toxic energy to set an intention for your spiritual journey. Every day, you encounter negativity in the form of gossip, work stress, relationship breakups, and other things. All of these can cumulatively result in spiritual energy blockage if you allow them to gather power. Going on a spiritual journey with so many energy blockages can hinder you from achieving your goals.

The purpose of spiritual cleansing is to eliminate all the negativity from your spiritual body so you can be at the highest vibration possible. It is a way of reclaiming your power and preparing for what is to come.

To prepare yourself for spiritual cleansing, you need to take a bath. A bath, in this context, does not refer to your regular cleaning routine. You need to add bath salts to your bathwater. Salt is regarded as a traditional cleansing element. It is believed that one can use it to get rid of negative spirits and energy. Your bath water should be hot and steamy.

As you bath in the water, think of certain areas in your life that need to be rid of toxicity and negativity. Meditate on the things that seem to keep your energy stuck. Reflect on everything that needs to be released so you can clear your spirit.

Consider writing down everything that comes to mind. Put it all in a list. Then, visualize the negativity disappearing from your life in the form of clouds of dust going with the wind. In the process, chant a mantra that represents what you want to do. An example of a good mantra is "I release negative energy from my life and body. I release its hold over me. I reclaim my power. I reclaim the strength of my spirit."

After this, burn the paper on which you have the list. You may use a match, lighter, or candle to ignite the fire. Make sure to do it in a spot where you are unlikely to start a fire. A good place is in the bathroom, over your sink or bathtub. Put a plate beneath so you can get the ashes. Then, scatter them outside.

Recite "I am cleansed and freed by the flame. My spirit is purified" as the paper burns, and you scatter the ashes outside. As you recite, envision the negativity vaporizing from your spirit.

Once you have performed the ritual bath and cleansed yourself to prepare for your connection to the spiritual dimension, the next thing is to set your intention.

Many people underestimate the importance of intention setting in spiritual endeavors. They don't understand that it can make all the difference in their journey. Perhaps the reason is that most people confuse intention for goals. Setting an intention differs from setting goals for the spiritual connection you want to establish.

Some people think that letting go of control equals having no established objective for what you are doing. That is wrong. Having an intention is the key to staying grounded when you feel confused. It is like a raft – something you can hold on to while connected to the spiritual dimension.

It is normal to experience fleeting moments of confusion during a spiritual journey. You can't always navigate everything mentally. Trying to process it intellectually might make your head explode. But when you have an intention, you have no reason to worry because your mind will remain in the right place.

The question is, how do you set a definite intention that can act as your raft in the spiritual realm? Remember that the intention also has to be open-ended enough to encompass any kind of experience you have in the spiritual realm.

For one, you have to distinguish between your intentions and goals. Understand that they are two different things. From personal experience, I can affirm that using an intention is much better for enabling spiritual growth. Goals are fixated on particular outcomes you want to achieve before a specific period. They are typically black or white – it is either this or that. There is no in-between, but when you consider that you are dabbling in waters you have never been before, you will see why it is more reasonable to set an intention instead of setting goals.

Set the Intention

Setting the intention may appear like an easy task, but it requires you to put in work. First, you need to answer the question of what you want to know. What knowledge do you seek from the spirit world? You may need time to think about this to develop the best answer possible. You must be transparent when determining your intention.

Once you know your intention, you must work on being your best self for the trip ahead. One way I recommend is to incorporate a lot of spiritual activities into your daily routine. Start and end your day with meditation. Try inviting happy spirits from the other side through visualization. Make it a deliberate point to invite happy spirits when you make your intention. Also, work on improving your awareness by grounding yourself in the present regularly.

Some tips to help you set an excellent intention are:

- Word it as something you control.

- Put it in the present tense.

- Focus on the vibe you get from the intention. It should resonate and feel inspiring.

- Consider writing it down in your journal.

- Remember to keep it to yourself only.

While setting the intention, you must also raise your vibration. It is an integral part of your preparation. Of course, you already know that meditation is the best way to raise your vibrational level. But it is not the only way – spending time in nature, lighting scented candles, and decluttering are other ways you can do that. Listening to high vibrational music also helps. The essential thing is to do things that light you up on the inside. These things are different for everyone, so find what works for you.

Raising your vibration requires a lot of energy. But it is a crucial part of your preparation, so you cannot pass it up. As I mentioned before, spirits on the other side also have to reduce their vibration so you can communicate with them. Anything to the contrary will cause an imbalance.

Protecting Yourself

The spiritual realm is unpredictable, meaning that anything can happen to a medium while they are there. Not all spirits are festive. Some are malicious and toxic. Protecting yourself before you establish a connection with the spiritual realm is a must. No protection means leaving yourself vulnerable to unwanted entities.

Protecting yourself begins with having a strong assurance in yourself. The intention you set determines the efficacy of your protection. The time you use to create your protection should match your needs or goals.

Below, I have an exercise you can do once a day to build confidence and prepare for the spiritual dimension. The exercise involves creating a sort of protective shield around yourself. The purpose of this is to prevent yourself from attacking negative spirits or energies.

Visualization Exercise for Protection

- Envision a stream of pure white light entering your head from above. Let it fill your body until every part is covered. Imagine every grey-colored force in your system being transformed into white when the stream of light touches them.

- Once your entire body is filled with white light, allow it to radiate through your body and about 1 meter from your body. If done the right way, others can see the white light force around you in the shape of a nebula.

- Conclusively, picture a protective sphere-forming around the nebula to create a sort of protective envelope around your energy field.

If you could see the protection, it would look similar to an egg. You may even sense it physically surrounding you. The more you can sense it, the stronger it is, so its chances of being penetrated are meager.

I recommend doing this exercise every morning and evening to enter your force completely.

Naturally, there are plenty of other things that can help you prepare effectively for your spiritual voyage. For a start, consider using appropriate trigger items to engage the spirit you are channeling. That means you have to do some research on the spirit before the D-day. Using items associated with spirits while they were alive is suitable to invoke responses and interactions. If you have anything linking you to the spirit, talk about it out loud. It will help pique the spirit's interest so he or she can interact with you.

Acting the role of an ally or caring observer can help you form a closer connection with spirits, resulting in a more wholesome experience. But this requires you to protect yourself. Otherwise, you might end up with an undesired attachment. Bringing forth a spirit is one thing but being haunted or stalked by ghosts is a different ball game entirely. You have to be careful.

Once you can sense, hear, or see a spirit or another otherworldly entity, communicate with respect and empathy. It does not matter whether the spirit is talking to you or through you. Mutual respect is necessary. If you don't understand a message, you have the option of requesting clarity.

Do nothing that could feel like a threat or provocation to the spirit. Ghost hunters typically use provocative methods, but as a medium, you shouldn't. You might end up with a hurt or angry spirit seeking revenge. Be firm and polite in your interactions.

Again, trust your instincts. If your instincts tell you that a situation cannot be handled or contained, then leave. That is another reason protection is essential. There are lots of ways besides the protection technique explained earlier. You can carry protective crystals and gemstones, wear a pentagram or crucifix, and do a ritual before you leave.

A stated earlier, some messages may not be clear to you but always trust what you hear. If you hear nothing, then ask the spirit to clarify. Doubt scares spirits away; it's good to keep any manifestation of doubt away. Judge properly.

Before trying to channel a real spirit, try testing yourself first. Do this alone or with friends. Get a mirror, meditate in front of the mirror, and try to induce a trance. Fortunately, this is something you can do anywhere. It is an excellent way of teaching yourself to be open to spirit.

Go for a place where you sense intense spiritual energies. Observe any messages, sensations, or impressions. Afterward, research and crosscheck the accuracy of your channeling and reading session. Remember that the results of your test may differ from the actual thing. After all, a lived experience differs significantly from an imagined or imitated one.

Other ways to prepare for your spiritual trance include:

- **Don't Smudge**: Smudging means burning sage – an ancient herb for cleansing rituals. It is typically the foundation of rituals and spells, but it is not for spirits. The purpose of sage is to keep ghosts and spirits away, whether bad or good. Using sage before a session is your way of telling ghosts to stay away from you. If you smudge before attempting the communication, the spirit would likely be cranky and ill-mannered.

- **Set Up Multiple Conduits**: The point of conduits is to help the ghosts deliver messages. Spirits need conductors sometimes. As you prepare to contact the dead, set up different conduits within the venue. Throughout history, spirits have been recorded as communicating through a liquid, candle flames, and scent. You may also set up audio-visual recording devices since they are known to be useful as well.

- **Embrace Death**: Embracing death is a way of celebrating life. Remember that I said there is nothing like death. We grow up with a fear of ghosts thanks to the horror movies we watched. In reality, you will see that your fear of ghosts reflects your relationship with mortality. Accepting the actuality of death is difficult – the experience is scary, painful, and heartbreaking. Connecting with the spiritual realm is an opportunity for you to explore your own physical realm's impertinence. In the end, you will realize that a robust and beautiful soul results from "death."

I want to conclude this chapter by emphasizing that creating a bridge between the physical and spirit realms requires you to develop a language between spirit and yourself. It will be your way of "talking" to spirit. Doing this means paying attention to the signs around you.

That brings me to the three clairs most important to psychics: clairvoyance, clairsentience, and clairaudience. These allow you to see, hear and feel when forming your connection with the other side. They are the most common channels through which spirit initiates communication with humans. As you work on developing a shared language with spirit, you will experience more and more signs. Pay attention to them all!

The next three chapters focus on the three clairs as stated above. Discover more about their pivotal importance in your spiritual mediumship development.

Chapter Six: Psychic Abilities I: Clairsentience

"People high in the psychic gift of clairsentience are some of the sweetest people you will ever meet."

—Catherine Corrigan

Clairsentience is a prominent psychic ability that mediums tend to have. As defined in an earlier chapter, it is the gift of "clear feeling." It is the ability to feel and experience people's emotions precisely as if they were yours. Interestingly, clairsentience is not a widely known ability. You don't see it portrayed in movies and TV shows like other psychic senses.

When people think about psychic abilities, they think more about clairvoyance and clairaudience. As a result, most people don't even realize when having psychic experiences connected with their clairsentience ability.

A clairsentient psychic can receive psychic information, messages, and impressions via emotions, feelings, and physical sensations. To put it simply, perhaps it is about receiving intuitive hits through sensing. Being a clairsentient psychic means you get gut feelings about people and objects alike, *even places.* You can receive intuitive impressions from anything that emits energy.

An example of clairsentience is if you pass by a homeless shelter and feel pangs of hunger. Or if you hug your friend and feel incredibly happy or sad, depending on their emotion. Your clairsentience may even reflect when watching movies or news stories. Seeing reports on violent crimes may move you to tears. If you can relate to one or more of these examples, you may just be clairsentient.

Here are other signs that can help you discover whether clairsentience is your dominant psychic ability.

- You can feel someone else's physical or emotional pain.

- You cannot withstand being in crowds due to the influx of feelings.

- You get physically and emotionally drained when you spend time with people.

- Your instincts about people, places, and situations are usually correct.

- You can't stand cluttered or messy home or workspace because it makes you feel stressed.

- You get waves of emotions from nowhere

These are some of the most common signs experienced by clairsentient psychics. Check if any of these apply to you. If your friends have always said you are emotional or too sentimental, that could be another indication.

I stated earlier that everyone has all psychic abilities, but we all tend to tilt toward one or more abilities more than the others. Mediums tilt toward clairsentience, clairvoyance, and clairaudience because they are the senses through which spirits communicate. It does not mean they do not or cannot communicate through the other psychic senses; they prefer these three over the other.

Developing your clairsentience is vital to be in-tune with your intuition. Before I get there, you may wonder how constantly soaking in feelings, emotions, and energies feels.

Yes, being clairsentient is akin to being a sponge. But that is if you don't learn to control your ability. Learning to manage your ability is necessary. If you don't, you will always find yourself stuck with unwanted emotions and energies. You must also know how to respond to the intuitive hits you get.

The only way to do this is to practice knowing when you have a clairsentient hit and, more important, managing your psychic senses. Once you master this, you won't feel drained of energy. And you can use your ability to further your interest in mediumship. Quickly at all, you will start accessing clear and prompt psychic messages.

Now that you understand that clairsentience isn't a bad thing if you manage it in the right way, here's what a clairsentience experience might feel like to you.

- **Emotional Feelings:** Clairsentient psychics often receive messages through emotions. For example, you may mirror your partner's anxiety over a scheduled visit to the doctor.

- **Physical Sensations**: Another way you may get clairsentient experiences is through sensations in the physical body. A good example is feeling pangs of hunger when you pass by a homeless shelter.

When you mirror the sensation, it does not mean you are hungry as well. It usually doesn't last beyond a few minutes. It often happens when you connect with spirits. If the spirit passed from a physical condition, you might get a tingling sensation in that part of your body as well. It is usually brief, and it is not scary.

Managing clairsentience is essential, yet it seems hard. With nothing to guide their way, people stay indoors because they fear getting drained when they spend time among people. Feeling the energy from people, places, and objects gets draining, which makes control necessary.

If you can't manage clairsentience, you may learn to shy away from parties or become a social recluse in the worst scenario. That does not have to happen. As I said, you can learn to manage your clairsentient hits. Only those who haven't mastered their gift experience overwhelming feelings from others.

However, there are ways you can develop and master your clairsentience ability. Don't forget that mastering it is the key to managing it.

Focus on Your Environment

Clairsentient psychics are extra conscious and super sensitive to their immediate environment. They simply can't miss a thing. They will notice if someone moves their favorite flower vase an inch. That is how incredibly aware they are. It is one thing you can use to your advantage. You can develop your clairsentience by focusing on your surroundings.

How does your environment look? Is the space cluttered? Do the dirty dishes make you feel anxious? Well, clutter in your home can invoke a lot of feelings. But that is not the point. You have to create a specific space in your home that isn't like the others. This space will be your psychic development area. It should be clean and fresh with a sacred ambiance. More than once, I have mentioned the importance of having space solely for psychic reasons.

Choose a spot like the corner of your room or, if you can, a whole room you can use for psychic things. Add everything, such as your meditation mat or chair, journal, blanket, crystals, and other psychic tools, in that space. Put anything else that makes you happy and is crucial to your psychic journey into this space. Add nothing that could be needlessly distracting from the purpose of the sacred space.

Clairsentience heightens sensitivity, so it helps to design your psychic space, making sensitivity feel good. The key to this is to go green. Greenery makes you feel calm, which is how you should always feel when you are in psychic mode. It makes you feel grounded and connected to nature. Besides having a green scenery, consider using organic cleaning products made from plants and essential oils. They are amazing.

Use sage to clear up space. Yes, sage is used to tell spirits to stay away, but that only if you burn it right before going into a trance. Here, you have to set an intention for the sage to keep negativity and darkness away. Set an intention for love and light to fill up your space before smudging.

Doing all the above can make a significant difference in how clairsentience affects you and how you respond to it. Now that you have set up the right space for clairsentience (and other psychic practices), get to the actual exercises for developing your ability.

Use Photos to Develop Clairsentience

The photo technique is a fun exercise I love doing. The best thing about it is that you might do even better than you expect. Just make sure you feel free and relaxed before you try it. You need a photo of someone you have no information about. You should have never met that person before. Don't use the picture of your favorite celebrity even if you have never met them. Celebrities have enough information about their lives on the internet. Instead, you can ask your friend to show you a photo of a family member you don't know. Your friend should know the person well so they can help corroborate the information you get.

- Hold the photo in your two hands. Look at the person's face and focus specifically on their eyes. Envision their feelings from the picture. How did they feel when the picture was taken? Happy? Sad? Anxious? Enthusiastic? Do they seem trustworthy? Allow yourself to imagine and go with the flow.

- Focus for a few minutes until you have the information you want. When you are done, deliberate on it for a few more minutes, then relay it to your friend. Ask them for feedback.

Repeat this clairsentient exercise at least twice every week with different photos all the time. Consistency will allow you to build your clairsentience and confidence.

Try Psychometry

Psychometry is the practice of reading the energy of an object. When you touch something, you leave an energetic imprint on that item. Your favorite sweatshirt, toy, and necklace all hold an imprint of your energy. We all unknowingly transfer energy to objects, usually those that we own. The more you use or love the item, the more energy you leave on it. Before you know it, you have accumulated energy. That is precisely why psychometry is useful for developing clairsentience.

By reading the energy of an object, you can get enough information about the object's owner. It is best to practice psychometry on an object you do not own. You already know everything about yourself, so there is no point in that. Ask your best friend to come over with a piece of jewelry owned by someone in their family or anything else that is a family heirloom. Jewelry is the best because metal retains energy better than other elements. Again, the owner of the item should be someone you don't know.

- Rub your palms together for a few seconds. Do a quick breathing exercise, then hold the object in your hand. Don't do anything for a couple of minutes. Just hold on to the object.

- Sense the energy radiating from the object. Is it negative or positive? Determine what kind of energy it is.

- Feel the owner's energy. What can you sense? Try to get as much information as you can from the energy you sense. Several sensations can come to you about the history of the item and its owner.

As usual, let your friend corroborate whatever information you receive from the item. When you practice psychometry consistently, you can read an object's energy without touching or holding it.

Form a Crystal Grid

Crystals enhance psychic abilities, which makes having them around a great thing for mediums. My favorite thing about using crystals for psychic development is that they require little to no effort. Crystals such as amethyst and fluorite support all psychic abilities, but they are great for clairsentience in particular. You can make crystal grids effortlessly. They take just a few minutes, and the possibilities of mistakes are nonexistent.

- Buy 12 crystals. Choose crystals that feel connected to you. You can get more than 12. You may buy 12 of one crystal or mix them up. I recommend buying a mix of amethyst and fluorite.
- Place a crystal in the center and arrange the remaining around it to form a circle.
- While setting the crystals in place, set the intention to enhance your clairsentience ability. Make it Clair, or clear, that you want to receive psychic messages through clairsentient hits.
- Place the crystal grid in your sacred psychic space or under your bed.
- That's all!

To boost your crystals' powers, you may rub essential oils on them before you form the grid.

Don't forget that meditation is essential in all you do, psychic-wise. Make meditation a part of your clairsentience development exercises. Follow the instructions for traditional meditation but set the intention to connect with your intuitive ability.

You can develop clairsentience. Anyone can develop clairsentience. Follow all the tips in this chapter, and you will master your gift in time. Remember that you learn at your own pace, so don't be too anxious to learn in no time.

Chapter Seven: Psychic Abilities II: Clairaudience

"Intuition goes before you, showing you the way. Emotion follows behind to let you know when you go astray. Listen to your inner voice. It is the calling of your inner voice. It is the calling of your spiritual GPS seeking to keep you on track towards your true destiny."

−Anthon St. Maarten

Clairaudience is another psychic ability dominant in mediums. It is possibly the second most-known ability after clairvoyance. As you already know, it is the gift of psychic hearing. When you start your psychic development journey, you will find that some skills are more comfortable to master than others. Fortunately, clairaudience is one of those that is easiest to develop. But what is clairaudience?

It is a psychic ability or sense that allows you to receive psychic impressions, messages, and information via hearing. You might get them in the form of voices, words, sounds, or music. The good thing is the experience is neither creepy nor scary. You hear everything in your head as if you were thinking out aloud. Sometimes, you might even hear with your physical ears. But remember, spirits on the other side are no longer in a material form – therefore, they need not communicate with a physical voice.

Clairaudient psychics usually receive intuitive messages in five different ways. You may have experienced some of these before.

The first way is to hear your voice aloud in your head. The voice is usually soft and subtle, and it may sound like you have an internal monologue. If you are doing a mediumship reading and the connected spirit communicates via clairaudience, you won't hear the voice they had when they were on Earth. Instead, you hear the spirit in your voice, inside your head. It is like communicating telepathically. As you develop your ability, you will learn to differentiate between your voice and spirit.

A second way that clairaudient messages may be received is via sounds. These sounds always have a symbolic or literal meaning you can interpret. If a spirit wants to tell you something, it might communicate via music. For example, you might hear a birthday-themed song if they recently had their birthday.

On relatively rare occasions, spirits communicate via physical sounds from your normal hearing. This rarely happens. You might hear sounds, words, or music without a recognized source. The sound is usually ethereal and beautiful. It may leave you feeling enchanted.

Another way spirits communicate is via their ethereal voice. Established mediums can hear the voice of the spirit telepathically. When this happens, you will hear the voice precisely as it was when they were alive. It tends to happen with spirits you are already familiar with—for example, the spirit of your grandfather or deceased uncle.

Last, spirits communicate via distress warnings. Experiences like this may be scary, which is why spirits only use this method when it is incredibly urgent. Clairaudient warnings often sound out loudly in your head. For example, you might hear a sudden "STOP" in your head as you are about to drive onto the highway. You might be startled, but it often turns out to be for a good cause.

Clairaudient experiences are easy to pass off as "It's all in your head," which many people do when they can't explain the voice source in their head. Understanding what clairaudient messages come from and how it feels to have the experience can provide insight into the events you have dismissed as "just in my head" in the past.

No psychic can deny this psychic ability has a dramatic flair, but it is not as dramatic as many believe. It is often very subtle – enough to dismiss without a second thought. How do you know when you have a clairaudient experience instead of regular thinking?

Knowing what to look for is vital. When you think of clairaudience, think of telepathy because it revolves around that. After all, telepathy is mind-to-mind communication that takes place without the use of any known sensory channels. When spirit drops a message in your head, they are communicating telepathically.

Clairaudience is like receiving a call from your cellphone without actually picking it up. Here are some things to help you recognize the experience:

- It sounds like you are reading or thinking to yourself. It is like when reading alone by yourself. You can "hear" what you are reading in your head.
- The hearing is always internal but may be external on the rarest occasions.
- It is always for a good reason.
- It does not take away your free will. You can make your own choice.
- Sometimes appear like auditory impressions. Thoughts may "pop" into your head out of nowhere.
- Typically, brief and straight to the point.

Clairaudient messages come from the Divine, your spiritual team, and spirits on the other side. At first, you may not be able to tell the source of the psychic messages you receive. But, in time, you will start to get an idea or sense of who the message's sender is and why.

If the gift of clairaudience is your dominant psychic ability, then spirits will send you messages via clairaudient channels most times. However, how can you tell if you are a clairaudient psychic? There are many signs to observe.

- You often hear your name when no one is around you. If this happens to you regularly, it is an indicator you have the ability. Psychic hearing allows you to hear things that other people don't.

- Sensitivity to noise is a good sign of clairaudience. You may feel irritable, tired, or stressed when you are in an environment with too much noise. It is even more frustrating when people around you can't understand your sensitivity. So, you seek quiet and solitude. Consider getting headphones with noise-canceling technology to manage this sensitivity.

- Talking to yourself is another sign. Clairaudience pushes you to have conversations in your head most or all the time. You may find you are customarily distracted from interactions because you are immersed in your head.

- You enjoy music because it connects you to your soul. Clairaudient people often find music uplifting. Listening to music is an excellent way to raise your vibration and reconnect to your spirit. You may even have a music talent.

There are many other signs, but most clairaudient psychics often experience some or all the signs above. Think back on which of these you are familiar with and use your answer to determine if a psychic hearing is your prominent ability.

Whether you can relate to most of the signs discussed or not, psychic hearing is crucial to your mediumship journey. Therefore, you must learn to develop it regardless. The good thing is clairaudience is relatively easy to develop. All you need is practice and a genuine desire to learn.

Think about your car or home radio. It has inbuilt stations, right? Any time you want to hear a station, you just have to tune in clearly, and you will hear everything they have. Clairaudience is just the same, with an almost imperceptible difference. The difference is in the subtlety of hearing. In this case, you are the radio. To develop psychic hearing, you have to tune into yourself. Developing psychic hearing is practically about learning how to tune inside and always receive clear messages.

Let's discuss ways you can develop your psychic hearing skills.

Train Yourself to Pick up Astral Sounds

For starters, you need to practice the sensitization of your hearing. It is simple yet effective. It works because training your regular hearing makes it easier to pick up nonphysical sounds from the spirit world.

A physical plane is generally a noisy place that has trained us to filter noise before it can alert our consciousness. But you can use the noisy environment to your advantage. That is where sensitization comes in. Here is an exercise to this effect.

- Find a safe space for this exercise. Take some deep breaths to ground yourself.

- Set an intention you want to enhance your gift of psychic hearing.

- Relax and focus on your hearing. At that moment, let it be your dominant sense.

- Gently allow yourself to tune into your environment. Focus on sounds that you rarely give attention to. Identify what you can hear. Perhaps a wind traveling through the trees behind your house or birds chirping.

Do this exercise every day but use different locations for each practice. See how much you can hear with each try. As you progress, put in more effort by stretching yourself in different directions with a different focus.

Musical Exercise

The point of this exercise is to help you detect and differentiate between subtle sounds. Practicing it can train you to discern between your thoughts and clairaudient messages. This exercise is quite an interesting one, so you might even have fun while at it. Try using music with heavy instrumentals. It helps to use band music. But classical music is also an excellent choice for training.

- Play your chosen band music and get into the groove. Submit to the jam.

- Now, focus on one instrument you can hear in the music. Yes, they are playing in harmony simultaneously, but you can single one out and focus on it. Isolate its sound from the remaining instruments.

One by one, isolate all the playing instruments' sounds until you have covered them all. With practice, you will get to that stage where you can cut off one of the sounds away until you can't hear the rest. Try this exercise two to three times weekly with different music.

"Visualize" Sound

Visualization is a visual technique, so how can you possibly "visualize" sound? Well, this exercise does not involve envisioning. The purpose is to improve your ability to hear messages communicated telepathically.

Can you imagine music playing in your head, almost as if you were using an actual music player? You need to do that alone in a still and quiet room where there are no other sounds. It is a beautiful way to develop clairaudience overall. Don't just stop at music. Try to imagine other sounds.

Envision all the sounds you were familiar with while growing up. Imagining sounds in your mind is a straightforward method to enhance your psychic hearing. Visualize your favorite artiste singing out in your mind as if you were in their concert.

Request for Spirit Messages

This trains you to have two-way conversations with spirit. It is a foolproof method for building confidence in your psychic hearing abilities. You can ask spirit for information – they need not come to you first. Practice requesting and receiving messages from higher-dimensional beings. In this context, spirit refers to your spiritual guides, not those on the other side. It also refers to Ascended Masters and your Higher Self.

Before you make any decision, ask your spirit guides for guidance. Then, wait for an answer to come. The answer can come in any form. Having two-way conversations with your spiritual team can advance your spiritual journey by a whole lot, particularly as an intending medium. It will also help you master the art of detecting spirit subtlety.

The most important thing with all your clairaudience exercises is to have fun while you are practicing them. That is important. Don't make it feel like a job or a task that you have to complete at a specific time. Have fun and allow yourself to go with the flow.

Note: Sometimes, clairaudience may be hard to develop. You might practice and practice without making headway in your development goals. If this happens, it could mean that your throat chakra is blocked. The psychic portal for clairaudience is directly connected to the throat chakra. Thus, blockage there hinders your ability to tune into your psychic hearing. If this happens to you, use your crystal grid to unblock it and get back in action.

Chapter Eight: Psychic Abilities III: Clairvoyance

"After years in utter darkness, I force my eyes into the light. For I must retain my sight, that I might view the wholeness of the void, objectively."

−Justin K. McFarlane Beau

Clairvoyance is the most known psychic ability. It is no wonder why some people use it synonymously with the word "psychic." It is widely portrayed in movies and TV shows as an over-the-top ability. Dramatic exaggeration is one reason it is widely misconceived. The extent of misconception is due to familiarity.

As you have learned, clairvoyance translates to "clear seeing." It is the ability to receive psychic or intuitive information via images, symbols, and visions. The "seeing" in clairvoyance happens in your mind's eye, which you already know as the third eye. So, don't expect to physically see a spirit lounging around in your home, waiting for you to get back from work. That is not how this gift works.

Suppose you are clairvoyant. In that case, you have likely noticed:

- Flashes of light and color around the corner of your eyes.

- Random images that disappear as fast as they appear, almost like a "flash."

- Movement out of your peripheral vision even when there is nobody else in a room with you.

- Vivid dreams that feel real enough.

Let's discuss these signs briefly so you can understand how they appear to you.

- **Visual Psychic Flashes**: Being clairvoyant means that you get flashes of light and color vision. It may be your spiritual team trying to get your attention or tell you something. For instance, you may see floating orbs of light, auras, glittering lights, twinkling lights, and shadows around the corner of your eyes.

- **Daydreams**: Psychic seeing concerns sight; therefore, visualization is a significant part of the ability. If you are clairvoyant, envisioning will come quickly to you. You can easily picture something in your mind because you see how it should all fit together.

- **Good with Direction**: Have you ever been to a location once, and it becomes imprinted in your mind? Do people describe you as a human GPS tracker? If you can relate to these, you are likely a clairvoyant psychic. It also means you are proficient at solving puzzles, reading maps, and completing mazes.

- **Vivid Imagination**: This links back with the previous sign. If you've been told that you have a very vivid imagination, it could be a manifestation of your psychic ability.

Without realizing it, you have probably experienced signs of clairvoyance all your life. The good thing is that you can pay more attention to clairvoyant signs once you know what to look for in yourself.

Even if you are already self-aware of your abilities, sometimes, feelings of doubt set in. Doubt is a recurring emotion when you begin your psychic journey. We all experience doubt at first.

One day, you are confident that everything you are experiencing is real. You feel attuned to your soul. You are amazed by the things you can do, and you enjoy sending love and light out to the universe. Another day, you feel doubt. "Do I have this ability?" "Can I communicate with spirits? Maybe it is all in my head." Or "I don't think I am made for this."

Questions like these are bound to arise, but it is up to you not to give in to them. Being a clairvoyant is tough, especially when everyone around you thinks it is a fluke and you are just wasting your time. You must avoid giving in to the feelings of doubt you experience by learning to trust your experience.

First, you must have faith in your personal experiences. Negative self-talk does not help. It causes blockage in your spiritual system. Then, you must turn to your spirit guides for signs. Even if you have never connected with any member of your spiritual team, they are waiting for you to seek their guidance. You can ask for signs at any time because they serve as reassurance.

Sometimes, you might receive messages that seem outrightly weird. It might push you to doubt your guides, but don't do it. Having trust in your spirit guides is not an option; it is a must. Your guides always send the right messages. It is up to you to interpret in the right way. Interpreting messages from spirit guides does take some practice. Symbols and metaphors are notably harder to interpret. Understand that you are taking baby steps. Don't judge yourself or feel bad about it.

In the movies, clairvoyant psychics often see the future precisely as it is going to happen. Most of the time, they get a frightening caption attached to it. But in reality, clairvoyant hits are less dramatic and more subtle. Spirits love subtlety, meaning you should learn to expect subtle messages.

Below are the ways that you might receive clairvoyant messages:

- **Third Eye:** Clairvoyant messages are not physically visible - if you have the ability, you can only "see" with your mind's eye. The third eye chakra makes this possible. It is the channel through which messages from the spiritual dimensions are sent to this plane.

- **Images and Movies:** Another way clairvoyant messages appear is in an image snapshot or a movie scene. You might feel like there is a TV screen open in your mind where a movie is playing. All of these, of course, happen in your head. Some also appear as visions. For example, you might receive a vision of one symbol representing something you are familiar with - like a ring to symbolize "marriage."

- **Symbols:** It is vital to talk about symbols separately because they are critical to psychic messages. There are lots of times when you receive symbols instead of something you can easily interpret. Spirit guides send symbols so you can work on interpretation. For instance, you may see images of a baby crib in your trance. It could mean that your subject is about to experience the birth of a child. If you cannot decipher the symbols immediately, don't fret. Just take your time until you crack them. Over time, you can even work with your spirit guides to decipher the literal meanings of received symbols.

Developing clairvoyance is easily one of the most fun things to do. Like everything else discussed so far, you only need to be dedicated to the practice. The learning process can be exciting. But don't forget to be kind to yourself. Even if you see no progress, ensure you keep practicing till you get it right. You will eventually get the hang out of it.

Numbers Visualization

As a clairvoyant, visualization is your stronghold. You can train yourself to become a super visualizer in time. The more you hone the skill, the more comfortable you will find using it. Remember that your third eye is responsible for psychic seeing. Therefore, these exercises are centered upon the third eye. That means you will practice seeing the pictures, symbols, and visions in your head.

Keeping your third eye chakra open is the key to receiving clairvoyant messages. That is why you must open your third eye first. Understand that the third eye chakra cannot be opened on the first try. Naturally, it requires you to put in several sessions. A few minutes of visualization practice every day can jumpstart your psychic seeing ability.

To visualize with numbers:

- Close your eyes. Perform a quick breathing exercise.

- Picture the number one in your head. Hold on to the picture for at least 10 seconds.

- If you can successfully do that, move on to the next number, which is two.

- Keep imagining until you get all the way to number ten.

Try this exercise for five to ten minutes every day—the more consistent, the better.

Clairvoyance Game

This game is played with a pack of Zener cards. These cards have different shapes, ranging from stars to circles and squares. They are fun for practicing clairvoyance, usually with a partner. You can order a pack on Amazon or check your local store. You can also make these cards on your own. Just get some index cards and draw different shapes on them. The shapes should include a circle, wavy lines, a star, a square, and a plus sign.

- Sit across from your partner or in separate chairs with your backs to each other.

- Grab one card, but don't let your partner see it. Let's assume you chose the circle card.

- Concentrate on seeing the circle with your third eye. Once the image has formed in your head, send it to your game partner telepathically.

- Next, let your partner know that you have sent the image, then ask them to reveal the image they received.

- Switch places with your partner - become the receiver while they send.

- Repeat the first few steps as explained

You can keep switching places for as long as you want. To make it more fun, try doing this exercise over the phone.

Crystals

As mentioned in the chapter about clairsentience, crystals are super incredible for developing psychic abilities. They are great for opening the third eye chakra. You can keep them in your psychic space or put them under your pillow when you go to bed. They are portable, which is why you can also carry them around with you. I recommend carrying them around because it is a constant reminder of your intention to work on your psychic abilities every day. Plus, they are pretty. Amethyst and fluorite help to open the third eye just as they can increase your psychic ability.

Dream Journal

Remember I said that vivid dreams are signs of clairvoyance. When you have vivid dreams, you shouldn't just let them go. Recording the dreams is essential. Sometimes, spirits send messages through the dream portal. Writing down your dreams and analyzing them can help you decipher such messages. When you sleep, your subconscious mind is the one in full charge of your body. That allows you to accept spiritual guidance more freely without your logical mind interfering. Your logical mind is why you would usually overlook or ignore psychic messages.

Sleep with your journal by your side. That way, you can write down your dreams when you are awake. After some days, weeks, or months, you may notice symbols and patterns that hold meaning. These symbols can remind you of an experience or something about another person.

Perhaps the best reason you should keep a dream journal is to help you understand how your ability is evolving. There is nothing more inspiring and motivating than seeing your progress. It helps you appreciate the effort you put in more.

Meditation to Open the Third Eye

Traditional meditation can help develop your psychic seeing ability. However, some meditations are specifically targeted at the third eye. They are much more effective and faster for someone on a psychic development path. The third eye can help you see mental blockages, energies, and other experiences in its full force and capacity.

As I said, you may be wondering why the third eye is not already opened. The third eye mostly stays closed and dormant. Unless you work actively toward opening it, it might never open – which explains why many people are not aware of their abilities. While third eye opening can help, learning to open and close your third eye at will is crucial. Otherwise, you will leave your psychic portal open to all kinds of intuitive hits. Not regulating when, how, and where you receive psychic hits can disrupt your life to an alarming extent.

Like other meditation types, third eye meditation should be done in a quiet and calm environment to benefit from the soothing vibes.

- Sit comfortably on the floor or a chair. Keep your spine upright, shoulders relaxed, and palms on your knees. Release the tension from your stomach, jaw, and face. Every part of your body should feel relaxed and be open to the incoming energy.

- Join your thumb and index fingers together as you close your eyes gently. Breathe in slowly and breathe out through your nose. With your physical eyes still closed, look up at the location of your third eye. You may also use your fingers to pinpoint the exact location.

- Allow your gaze to relax as you focus on your third eye. Keep breathing slowly until a white light appears. Let the white light spread and surround you.

- Enter a transcendental state of energy healing as the light surrounds you. Your focus will be at the highest and most powerful level.

- Release every lousy thought, feeling, and energy from your field. Just concentrate on improving the potentials of your third eye chakra.

Remain in this position for up to 20 minutes at a stretch. Playing relaxing music in the background can further help improve your focus. After 20 minutes, end the meditative session by bringing your palms to your heart and rubbing them together. After opening your eyes, sit for some minutes before you stand and get back to your routine.

This meditation exercise can be repeated every day until you are confident that your third eye is sufficiently open.

Below is another simple exercise for the third eye:

- Sit in the usual position

- Set the intention to open your third eye and improve your clairvoyant abilities

- Focus on the area where your third eye is located

- Visualize the chakra in a beautiful purple color, majestically spinning as it opens wider and wider

You may experience tingling between your eyebrows when you perform these exercises. It means that your third eye is opening. Be happy because it is a sign you will flourish with your clairvoyant gifts.

Now that you know how to master the three psychic abilities that will define your journey as a medium, let's contact the spirit world. It promises to be fun!

Chapter Nine: Contacting the Spirit World

"Think the thought,

> *See the image,*

> *Develop a feeling,*

> *Respond with the body,*

> *Produce the results."*

—James E. Melton

The time to contact the spirit world has come. The question is, how do you go about it? Everything you have been learning so far is a buildup to this. If you follow everything you have learned throughout the book correctly, contacting the spirit world will be like calling briefly at your best friend's house.

Forget everything you believe you know. Even if you have seen an otherworldly being before, this is different. Channeling spirits or establishing communication with the spirit world feels more real and intense when you are in the middle of it. Feeling spirits is fleeting and spontaneous. However, this is a deliberate action, which requires you to be in the best possible state.

I have explained the process of preparation for contacting the spirit world. As explained, you have to set the intention and protect yourself against unseen forces and spirits. Before you establish the connection, double-check to ensure that your protection is intact and functional. Set the intention firmly and clearly.

Here is a rundown of the steps involved in preparing yourself:

- Meditate to clear your mind and raise your vibration
- Do the protection exercise to form a protective shell around yourself
- Set the intention

Your intuition must be at the highest level possible, while your spiritual energy must be robust. Since this would likely be your first time contacting a spirit, consider calling a familiar spirit. An example is a family member or friend who has passed on to the other side. In time, you may contact spirits not directly linked or connected to you.

In a spiritual setting, the process of establishing communication with an otherworldly being is often called a séance. However, going by the literal meaning of a séance, it must be done by at least eight people. Also, a séance entails the invoked spirit using the medium as a vehicle.

Do not allow yourself to be possessed by any spirit – familiar or not – on your first practice. Besides the fact that it takes a lot of vital energy, it is also potentially dangerous. This chapter will explain two useful techniques for contacting the spiritual realm. The first is a formal technique for connecting with spirit, while the second is a method called mirror gazing.

There are so many rules to remember if you want your séance to succeed. These rules may seem too much, but they are vital for your safety. Following the correct framework is the key to getting it right. Understandably, you may miss a few things the first time. But, in time, the rules and steps will become second nature. When you get to that point, you will have a relatively smooth experience than you did your first time.

Here are the rules:

- Do not be skeptical about the experience you are about to have. Skepticism attracts negative energy, which frightens spirits away. Even when the spirit appears, it can block and affect communication. Have faith in yourself and your ability.

- Leave the invoked spirit alone if they don't initiate contact. If they show any sign of resistance, allow them to return. Do not bother spirit. They will inform you if they do have any message for you.

- Avoid channeling spirits just for curiosity. Do not do this for fun – it is not meant for your entertainment or amusement. Initiate contact only if you have questions to ask. Prepare your questions before connecting them. Be constructive with the questions.

- Accept the answers you receive without questioning the spirit. Even when it does not make sense to you at first, you will later decipher the meaning. Meanwhile, receive the answers.

- Spirits form attachments quickly. Do not be frightened if the spirit tries to touch or talk to you. But never should you touch the entity first – not unless they signal it is okay.

- Do not fabricate or stretching the information you receive. As people say on Twitter, don't "reach." In this context, reaching means going to an outrageous degree to force a specific meaning out of the situation. Avoid making personal observations, no matter how tempting.

- Do not lead people on with the information you receive. Avoid relying on incomplete information that can be interpreted in different ways. If you need to, ask the apparition to be specific with the message.

- There are several doorways in the spiritual realm. Be careful of the ones you open.

Read through all the rules again and again until they are resounding in your head. Do not try to contact the spiritual realm until you are confident you have mastered these rules. It is key to doing your mediumship the right way. A well-coordinated preparation isn't complete until you have double-checked the rule. Learning the rule is one thing, but compliance is another thing entirely. Follow everything discussed.

Technique 1: Formal Contact with Spirit

You have learned how to prepare for the spirit world spiritually. Physical preparation is also a must. There are specific considerations you must put in place for a comfortable environment. The venue must be cohesive and user-friendly. That does not mean you must be overly concerned with all the minor details. But naturally, there are things you should do.

- Consider contacting the spirit world in the evening – 8:00 is an excellent time for the session.

- Write down your questions for the spirit.

- Select the spirit to be contacted.

- Choose a quiet room with a table in the center.

- Disconnect all the radios, televisions, telephones, and stereos in your building.

- Tape a "Do Not Disturb" note to the door of your practice room.

- Dim the lights in the room. Turn them off if they can't be dimmed. Light two scented candles so you can have enough illumination in the room.

- You may add a bowl of flowers to the table if the spirit wants one.

- Place a bowl of water on the table – spirits sometimes communicate through the water.

- Add a bowl of hard candy to the table – they are great for accessing instant energy.

Now, you are at the point of summoning a spirit from the otherworldly realm. The most advanced mediums have used these steps for years. If you follow them as laid out, they will undoubtedly work for you. Never forget that intention is key to successful contact.

1. Sit in front of the table. Put yourself in a relaxed and calm state by focusing on stimulating thoughts.

2. Focus on breathing exercises for at least 10 minutes. Breathe as deeply as you can until you are confident you are in the right mental state to begin.

3. Place your palms down on the table. Spread your fingers out flatly to channel energy through your hands.

4. Now, recite your protection oath to form to reinforce the protective shell around you. Repeat the oat three times as you raise your vibration to induce a trance. Ensure your eyes are closed.

5. Once you are in a trance, call on your spirit guide to be part of the session. Some sensations you will get when your guide arrives include tingling, face stroking, ringing in your ears, and whispers around the room. You may even receive a vision at that moment.

6. Call out to the spirit you seek communication within a firm but calm tone. "Dearly departed, do you come with a message for me?" "Please come through to me." "I am ready for you." "May I ask questions?"

Sometimes, you may need to repeat your questions a couple of times. Don't start talking until you receive a mental image showing that the spirit is pleased to be in your presence. You may talk when the spirit initiates communication.

It is best not to be impatient. If the contact isn't immediate, don't force it. You cannot force the flow. Even as the spirit is in your presence, keep raising your vibrational level. Doing that will prevent an abrupt disconnection from the spirit world or the ghost with you.

When you feel like you have achieved your goal, you can conclude the session using the oath of conclusion.

"I thank you for the knowledge you have given. Thank you"

If the spirit refuses to leave:

"Thank you for joining me, but it is time to leave. Go with my love as your life is over. Leave me with my life. Go with love and light."

That's it – you have successfully contacted and communicated with an entity from the spirit world.

Remember two vital things: there are spirits and ghosts everywhere in the spiritual planes (parallel dimension), and the reality you create for spirits in this dimension is the only one they have. By raising the intensity of your vibrational level and your faith, you can attract any spirit you want to this dimension.

Why do you need the presence of your spirit guide before contacting the spirit world?

As a beginner, you may need extra help to strengthen your connection to the cosmic dimensions. Through your mind, ask your guide to assist in contacting the departed soul you want. When you do this, your guide will go to where that spirit is and ask them if they are interested in meeting you. If the spirit agrees, he comes through the opening you created. Otherwise, you may experience some back and forth until they agree.

Understand that departed souls owe you nothing; therefore, they can choose not to come when you summon them. The ghost you want may have no desire to establish contact with this plane. Suppose that happens. There, you have to respect their wishes. Do not persist if you don't want to be viewed as a problem.

Technique 2: Mirror Gazing

The mirror-gazing method is also called Psychomanteum. The modern techniques I explain here draw on the original method, which started in ancient Greece. Many people have successfully used mirror-gazing to have contact with spirits. The original method from Greece is complicated and is for advanced mediums. It is a more simplified version just as effective for spirit communication.

This technique was conceptualized by Dr. Raymond Moody, a psychologist and philosopher who created the term "near-death experience." To practice his mirror-gazing technique, all you need is a mirror, nothing else. In the past, the ancient Greeks needed animal sacrifice to summon their dead ones. Psychomanteum is similar to the practice of scrying. The only difference between both is that scrying is done with the use of a crystal ball.

Several steps are involved in performing a successful mirror-gazing session to invoke a spirit or contact the spirit world. They include:

- **Food:** Consume no caffeine or dairy a day before your session. Fruit and vegetables will help put you in a peaceful state of mind.

- **Location:** Choose a quiet location for the session. If you have already set up the sacred psychic space, then that is perfect. Use that location.

- **Clothing:** Remove all jewelry from your body. Put on loose, comfortable clothing.

- **Mirror**: Place a full-length mirror in front of a comfortable chair. Set it so you can look at it without straining your eyes. Make sure you cannot see your reflection.

- **Chair:** Sit in the chair while giving your head support.

- **Posture:** Release the tension from your body and relax your posture.

- **Awareness:** Increase your awareness to ease into the transition.

- **Music:** Calm and soothe your spirit by listening to beautiful music for about 15 minutes. Doing this further stimulates awareness.

- **Memories:** Select one or more personal items of the departed you wish to contact. Hold them in your hands and let memories flood into your mind. Pictures, videos, and anything else associated with the spirit can help.

- **Candle:** Light a candle behind you. Dim the light in the room to the ideal level. Twilight is the best time to practice, so adjust the light accordingly.

After executing all the steps above in order, your arms may start to feel heavy, with your fingers experiencing intense tingling sensations. You will feel yourself slipping into a trance-like, meditative state. The mirror might take on a cloudy appearance as if you were looking at a cloudy sky. Remain passive at that moment. Doing anything to the contrary can jar you from your hypnagogic state and interfere with the connection you are establishing.

The experience may not last for more than one minute since you are a beginner. Advanced practitioners often have far longer experiences. Some experiences you can have through a mirror-gazing session include seeing departed spirits and possibly future events. Proper preparation is vital for successful mirror-gazing – ensure you follow all the instructions given.

As always, record the events of your mirror-gazing sessions. Practice at least once a week to improve your skills and communicate with different entities from the spiritual dimensions.

Chapter Ten: Finding Your Spirit Guides

"The thought that the world will go on without you, that you will become nothing, is very hard to take in."

−Thomas Nagel

Everyone has a spiritual team, regardless of personality or background. Spirit guides exist to help and assist you along your way to fulfilling your destiny. No matter where you are in life currently, spirit guides must send helpful messages. They are filled with infinite wisdom that can never run dry. These souls have lived multiple lifetimes in the past; therefore, they understand just how it feels to experience life.

Spirit guides can help you with anything you want. If something is important to you, then it is essential to them. They are your guides because they are filled with positive energy while alive, and even now, they are higher-dimensional beings. Should you be wondering how you can find your unique guides so you can drink in the fountain of their wisdom and communicate with them at will, I have an explanation for you.

There are different types of spirit guides. Some had existed as your guides long before you were born into this plane. Others joined your team as the need for them manifested in your life at different points. You also can add more guides to your team if you so wish. After all, they are your spiritual squad.

I mentioned previously that every human typically has a spiritual team that holds up to six guides. Each guide performs different duties and obligations. Here are the types of guides that make up your spiritual team.

- **Archangels**

Archangels lead the plane where angels reside. They are mighty beings with a vast energy signature. You can instantly feel their impact wherever they appear or visit. If an archangel appears in your presence, you are bound to feel a literal energy shift in the environment. Archangels typically specialize in something. Your archangel might have a specialty in healing. Archangel Raphael is generally recognized as the angel of healing, with the power to attend to countless people at a time.

- **Guardian Angels**

Unlike archangels, guardian angels are assigned exclusively to you. Everyone has at least three, all of which have dedicated their lives towards helping just you. Anytime you need immediate assistance, your guardian angels are the right guides to call upon. Their love for you is unconditional and everlasting. They will stand with you from beginning to end. Even when you make huge mistakes, they won't chastise you. Instead, they will find ways to work with you on rectifying the mistakes. Your guardian angels are nondenominational, meaning they work with you regardless of your spiritual beliefs or faith.

- **Spirit Animal**

Your spirit animal might be a pet that passed away and has now joined your spiritual team. A spirit animal will always be a part of your squad, even if you have never had a pet. What matters is that the animal has the wisdom to teach and guide you. A peacock in your spiritual team might teach you the beauty of your abilities, while a wolf may show you how to survive the world with them. Spirit animals may appear to you in a dream, on a coffee mug, or in your garden. You may call on them whenever you want comfort and company.

- **Ascended Masters**

Having an ascended master on your team is a great feeling. With the amount of wisdom and experience they gained while on the physical plane, they have the necessary facilities to help you advance spiritual growth and development. They can also help you build spiritual influence. Ascended masters are considered leaders in the spiritual dimensions and teachers to those in the physical dimension. All the masters work together to create harmony throughout the universe. Religion and culture do not define them.

- **Departed Loved Ones**

Loved ones that have passed away to the other side sometimes choose to be a part of one's spirit guides. Since they are now higher-dimensional beings, they can help you from the highest planes practically. They may send job opportunities and healthy relationships your way. A great grandmother that has long since passed on may be part of your spiritual team, whether you knew her in this life or not. Even spirits you don't know can join your team due to a desire to help you achieve greatness.

- **Helper Angels**

These are like freelancers you have on your team. They are just there to help you in tricky or specific situations. For example, they can help you find a new space for your business or help you make new friends.

It is a fact that spirit guides exist to help you through your journey in life. But one question I often get from inquisitive clients is, "Can spirit guides be wrong?"

The above question is a crucial and loaded one. Many people often wonder if spirit guides are indecisive. Can they tell you to go that way after telling you to go this way?

Don't ever believe for a minute that your spirit guides are indecisive or that they are confusing. Second, psychic development requires that you let your spirit guide you at all times. However, this is not as easy as it sounds. Every new psychic finds it challenging to trust the guidance from their intuition.

When you are not used to getting support from family or friends, trusting your guides can be challenging. If you feel overwhelmed and confused initially, remind yourself that you have other incredible helpers besides your spiritual squad.

For one, you have your Higher Self – also called your authentic self, inner being, or soul. When you seek spiritual guidance from your spirit team, your Higher Self is ever-present to inform your decisions. Your Higher Self is the wisest and most confident version of yourself.

Second, understand that your spirit guides will always work for your highest good. That is why they are part of your team. Therefore, they will never steer you in the wrong direction. But that does not mean they are entirely in charge of your life. You are still the ultimate controller of your life. The spirit guides are there to act as your supporting cast.

So, the answer to that question is no. Your guides will never point you in the right direction. But you might decide not to follow the path advised by your guides sometimes. That is also okay. Before you make any decision, remember that your spirit guides always work for your highest good. They want the best for you, and it reflects in their guidance.

Connect with Your Spirit Guides

There are practical strategies to connect with your guides. These are simple things you can integrate into your daily life. Connecting with your spiritual team is like learning how to use a new recipe. At first, you know nothing about what you are doing. But if you have the proper instructions and stick to them, you will master them in time. Here are some of the best and easiest ways to connect with your spiritual team.

1. Be More Mindful and Present

Receiving guidance from your spiritual team is impossible without mindfulness. Being present in your daily life is crucial to recognize the signs and messages sent from the higher planes. Most of the time, you miss the signs because you are too immersed in other activities or too worried about other things. Actively make time in your schedule and dedicate it to mindfulness practice. After meditation, use at least 15 minutes of your time to simply take in your environment and ground yourself on the Earth.

2. Watch Out for Signs

Whether you are taking the bus to work or driving down, always remind yourself that your guides have messages for you. Don't take your mind off it when you are taking your bath in the morning. The more you prepare yourself to receive signs, the faster you can recognize them when they arrive. It gets interesting – as your spiritual team senses you are more aware and watchful for their messages, more messages are sent to help you. Always pay attention when you have a big decision to make – the guidance increases in situations like that.

3. Keep a Spirit Guide Journal

The purpose of a spirit guide journal is to increase interactions between you and your guides. Do not use the journal for recording your progress for this purpose; get another journal. In your spirit guide journal, you can write letters to your team and ask for concrete spiritual assistance. Using your free will to seek guidance is powerful. You may also record signs from them in this remarkable journey.

Make it a weekly activity to write the guides a letter. Appreciate and show gratitude for their presence in your life. Think about anything they have helped with recently and send your thanks. Then, ask for help on a specific situation in the next few sentences. Throughout the rest of the week, look out for synchronicities regarding the situation for which you requested guidance.

4. Name Your Guides

Naming your guides, particularly your guardian angels, enhances your ability to connect with them. It makes them feel more real than they already are, plus names push you to connect more regularly. Giving them names makes you closer than ever to your guides. After working closely with them over time, you may even begin to unravel their personalities. Use intuition to decide on names for your guides, or simply allow yourself to be creative.

5. Use Psychic and Divination Tools

Tools such as tarot cards, pendulums, crystals, or Ouija boards can heighten your connection with the guides. For years, humans have been communicating with the spirit world through psychic tools. While I make it a rule to recommend no-tools training to new mediums, you can start using tools depending on where you are in your training. In the first few months of dedicated practice, staying away from divination tools is the best decision you could make. However, you may use them once you get the hang of mediumship and psychic development.

Other ways you can connect with your spirit guides include:

- Inviting them into your home
- Meeting them in dreams and daydreams
- Opening yourself up to unexpected visits
- Spirit guide meditation

- Walking in nature with them

- Creating artistic pieces with them or exercising with them

- Doing occasional questions and answers reading with the squad

Never forget to set the intention whenever you connect with a spirit guide. Seek their help, the intention, seek guidance, and trust in the answer you receive.

Did you know that you can go on dates with your spirit guide? Yes, you can. It is just like when you go on dates with someone you have just met to know them better.

Going on dates with your spirit guides is your way of building a relationship and bond with them. The key to forming a real connection with your guides is to treat your relationship with them like you treat all your other ones. This way, you can have fun while developing your psychic abilities.

Fifteen to thirty minutes is a reasonable time to spend with your guides. Since Mondays to Fridays are usually filled with work and other stuff, selecting Saturday for your weekly date with your psychic guides works well.

The first time you attempt doing this, the guide (s) might not appear to you. Instead, you might get a sense of energy around you. Another time, you might get a silhouette. Little by little, the guides will sooner or later reveal themselves to you.

Going on dates involves asking questions so you can get to know the person. Just as you would ask questions to know more about the person you have just met, you can also ask your guides questions. During your time with them, you may ask questions such as:

- What is your name?

- Can you reveal yourself to me?

- Did we spend a previous lifetime together?

- Why did you choose to be my guide?

- What information would you like to give me at this moment?

The more you know about the guides, the more comfortable you will connect and bond with them. Knowing and understanding your guides is a continuing process. Record the thoughts and impressions you receive from the guides on your "dates." You will likely have multiple guides, so set apart different sections for recording your interactions with each guide.

Below is a step-by-step instruction of how you can invite your spirit guide into your home and learn more about them.

• Set the Ambience

As with any psychic or spiritual ceremony, cleaning up your environment is the first step to inviting a spirit guide into your home. Your sacred space should be clean and well-organized, with no hint of clutter anywhere. Light one or two candles in the room, dim the light, and create a warm-looking space for your visitor. The mood in the room should be calm and peaceful. Add items that hold significant energy into the mix - they will help maintain a high vibration around you. More importantly, they will amplify the intention you set.

• Set the Intention

At this point, you must have realized that all spiritual endeavors require you to set a clear intention. The intention should specify whom you seek to connect with and your questions for them. With a clear focus, you can call in the most suited entities to inform you or answer the questions. If you desire self-healing, gentle, loving energy may be the right spirit to call. If you need profound spiritual teachings, calling an Ascended Master such as Buddha makes more sense. With a pure and straightforward directive, you can attract the pure energy of the most suited Guide to help you.

- **Practice Patience**

There is no rush in this process. It is easy and straightforward, yet some people try to hurry it. Do not be like this. Guides do not rush or hurry - they take their time in appearing and sending messages. Any information your guide has for you will wash over you as gently as a breeze. Avoid setting expectations. Start with patience and trust, and you will communicate with the spiritual forces around you.

- **Relax and Breathe**

Breathing is fundamental in psychic ceremonies and activities. It is the perfect way to get yourself in a mental state that resonates with the higher dimensional being you wish to connect. It is also the surest way to ground yourself into the present, which matters when connecting with guides. With every deep breath, your awareness deepens and becomes more relaxed. There is no strain nor stress. If you feel tense in your body, do a quick stretch to relieve the symptoms. Lying down also works, but you might go off to sleep if you get too comfortable. Opening the pathways to spirits requires you to achieve stillness of breath. In the spot where there is no mental chatter is where you will meet your guides.

- **Bless Yourself**

Blessing yourself and your space is a way of protecting yourself. As with any spiritual work, you have to seek protection when you meet your spirit guides. Imagine yourself in a stream of white light. Let the light wash away anything short of the highest good. When done, relaxed, and in the mental state to receive a higher being, request your guide to come forth.

- **Chant a Sacred Sound**

Chant "Om" to create an alignment between your energy and that of the Divine. The most sacred sound is your voice. Chanting a mantra is your way of reechoing the sounds of the cosmos. It raises your vibrations and attunes your spiritual energy to align with the most powerful energies in the universe. You will discover that chanting opens the gateway to your guides more quickly.

- ## Go Through the Doorway

As your sacred space is activated with deep breathing and "om" chanting, observe a shift in your energy and environment. This is the activation of your "light body," which will attract the guides to you. Your light body is the part of you that is made purely of spirit – focus on it. Imagine yourself walking into the spiritual dimension through an opened gateway. That is your entry to the location where you can meet your guides.

- ## Invite the Guides In

You can finally call in any of your spirit guides, be it your guardian angel or helper angel. Share your intention and permit them to join you if they wish. If you do not give explicit permission, the spirit will stay away until you have. Give a command or an express invitation. Otherwise, you will spend your time in the sacred space alone.

- ## Open to Subtle Frequencies

Their interactions with you may come as impressions, visions, thoughts, or smells. The messages may not always be explicitly clear. Pay attention to every feeling and thought you get during your time with them. That is their way of directly communicating with you.

- ## Ask Them to Show a Sign

To be sure that you are indeed in the company of your spirit guide, ask them to show you signs. Asking is not equal to telling them what to do. Instead, your way of getting assurance that your faith and trust in them can become even stronger. They will happily oblige anything you ask.

- **Ask for a Blessing**

On your first meeting or date, it is permissible to ask for a blessing or message. Remember that your spirit guides serve you, and as such, they can only assist in the ways you ask them. While you are still connected, ask for guidance, insight, or a sneak peek at what the future holds for you. You may ask the guide to activate your mediumship skills to accelerate your psychic development process.

- **Show Gratitude**

Everyone loves to be appreciated. It feels great to hear "thanks" from someone you have just helped. So, give thanks to your guide for taking their time to meet you and impart divine guidance. Expressing gratitude might seem like a small act, but it is the best way to incur their goodwill and ensure they show up on your next date.

- **Return**

Through the same doorway you came through, return to this dimension. Going back to the way you came in is extremely important. Wait for some minutes until you are fully back into your material form. Record the experience in your journal, and then take a nap. Open yourself up to receive the experience at every level of your physical being.

The sacred space where you have the first meeting is the same place you will go back to anytime you seek communication with your spirit guide. Don't just go when you need help – sometimes, visit so that you can spend time with your spiritual team.

Conclusively, do not attempt to call all your guides at once. Your energy vibration cannot handle it. The highest number of spirits to invite at once should be two. You may increase this number as you advance in your spiritual learning journey. In time, your ability to receive intuitive and psychic messages will develop beyond the ritual, and soon, you will begin to get messages all the time – ritual or no ritual.

Chapter Eleven: Working in Spirit Circles

"Death is an entrance to experience rather than an exit from it."

—Charles Lindbergh

Psychic development is not an easy journey. It is not something many people understand. Unless you were raised in a home with an inclination toward spirits, you might not have family members and friends to act as your spiritual support system. Still, it is essential to have people who share similar interests with you. Together, you can work on becoming the best version of yourself. But how do you find people like that? That is the work of a spirit circle.

A spirit circle is a spiritual development group consisting of 6 to 8 people with a collective aim to develop themselves mentally, emotionally, and spiritually. As a new medium, joining a spirit circle is candidly the best step you can take toward achieving your journey alone. Without like-minded spirits to inform and guide your ways, you may not know when doing something the wrong way.

Joining a circle helps you come together in spirit and further a common interest. But you can do more than just that. In a development group, you can talk and relay experiences about your spiritual journey. Getting insight from people who have been in the same situation you are now is one benefit of joining a spiritual development circle.

In the group, members can also practice every technique, method, and secret they have learned about mediumship and psychic development. Someone may teach you a new method you don't know about yet, or you may even be the one to help your spiritual partners with the information they don't have yet.

A circle is meant to be a transformational plane where you can create time and space for healing. There is usually an advanced medium who is more experienced than everyone else in a circle. The medium can help beginners with healing and guidance to make their journey more tolerable and enjoyable.

Another benefit is that a development circle is a place for members to teach in turn. You don't have to know a lot but just know enough. Teaching your partners is the key to informing yourself and learning more. When you teach a particular method to your group, you increase your knowledge of that method or topic in general.

Do not juxtapose a spirit circle with a class – they are different. A class is a place for you to learn from another person about their spiritual way. There is usually no discussion. But a circle involves weekly or monthly sessions where one or more persons teach the rest of the group. But ultimately, the decision-making lies with all or most members.

Being a new medium, you might not find an existing circle to join. Since spiritual circles must not have over eight members, you are unlikely to find a group with an opening for you. This means you must form your own circle or partner with another person to form the group. Your skills level does not matter. What matters is the companionship you will be offering other new psychics and mediums like you.

However, as a beginner, you cannot manage a spirit circle on your own. Until you get to a certain point in your journey, you will need to find an advanced medium. This medium should be a veteran interested in helping other people develop their gifts and move forward in their journey.

Think about the structure of your spirit circle before you form one. Some of these decisions must be made before the circle's first physical meeting. Meanwhile, you can discuss with other members on the internet. There are networking apps for psychics to connect and discuss spiritual development together. The right thing to do is link up with psychics and mediums around your local area and see who is interested in joining your development group.

Do not set up your first meeting until you have discussed and agreed on the group's structure. Too often, I have seen people set up spirit circles with no sense of direction. If you follow this path, your group may end up splitting up.

As the pioneer, be the one to figure the structure out. You already know that you shouldn't have over eight members. Think about other things, such as the number of hours you would like to invest every week. Consult with everyone and choose a day that works for you and everybody else. A typical circle lasts up to two hours, during which you can practice a variety of psychic skills. The group can even do a séance together.

What are the things to clarify when deciding the circle structure?

- How often will the circle meet, where, and how long?
- Who will be the facilitator or facilitators of the circle?
- What are the activities to engage in on a rotational basis?
- Will there be a fee? What will the money be used for?

- Who is in charge of sending reminders to participants?

- Will there be a prerequisite for the group?

- What level of commitment does the circle expect from members?

- Can members come late or leave early?

- How deep will the practices go?

There should be a format that details which skills will be practiced first and when. To prevent things from getting boring, consider rotating the skills each week. The format in most circles is usually categorized into two areas: personal development and spiritual development.

The personal development segment is all about sharpening your thinking, reasoning ability, and developing a more significant emotional understanding capacity. The spiritual development sessions aim to understand the nature of the universe and commit to your relationship with your Higher Self and the Divine.

Create and print out a circle format that all participants can easily understand in the group. Remember that the participants can be of any background, but it is best to be 18 years of age. The format should suit the level of understanding of all members. Most important, every practice must be geared towards balancing personal and spiritual development. Highlight that spiritual development is a unique and personal process and that, therefore, participants should improve their skills rather than try to be better than other members.

A standard spirit circle format should include:

- **Opening Prayer:** Recite this at the beginning to express gratitude to the Divine for your life experiences and physical/spiritual wellbeing. The prayer should involve everyone.

- **Meditation:** Participants must learn to still their minds in anticipation of spiritual experiences, which makes meditation a vital part of the process. There are many benefits of having a relaxed body and a still mind, as you have already learned.

- **Spiritual Readings:** Participants should do readings on one another to develop their ability to communicate with spirit.

- **Healing:** Members should channel healing energy between one another. It can help strengthen their hands-on healing ability.

- **Pendulum Reading:** Pendulums can channel and invoke spirits. Together, members can learn how to use it to communicate with their guides and other spirits.

- **Aura Reading:** Together, members can practice reading energy by working on one another's energy fields. You can create an outline or guideline of the steps involved in aura reading.

Furthermore, you can practice developing your psychic senses of clairvoyance, clairsentience, clairaudience, claircognizance, clairgustance, and clairalience. Psychic skills such as telepathy, psychometry, mediumship, etc., should also be on the roster for members to develop.

There are crucial elements to make your spiritual circle function as you wish.

The first thing is to clarify the purpose and method of the circle. That might seem like an obvious thing, but it helps to highlight it. No one wants to spend valuable time driving across from town to discover that their mediumship circle represents Druidry. Don't make people feel like the circle is a waste of time.

Second, there must be integrity and transparency in the setup of the group's structure. The power structure should be clear to members to facilitate a clear flow of power. Clarifying the structure to all is key to developing the circle members' bond. It also helps to prevent miscommunication and unnecessary conflicts. Conflicts are not avoidable, so you must have resolution guidelines set in place.

Members can leave at any time, so the group should be open to other people to come in. The structure should remain the same regardless of who goes and who joins. A formal power structure in place to encourage power-sharing will prevent misuse of power by power-holding members.

You will realize that each circle has its spirit. The more you meet, the stronger the spirit will become. Advise members to tap into the guiding force of the collective spirit to strengthen their energy.

A spirit circle's objective is to allow participants to develop their psychic, spiritual, and mediumship gifts continuously. Each week, work on different things with members. Members should also share their individual experiences in their journey to inspire and motivate other members to keep going.

You can learn to connect with your spirit guides and loved ones who have passed on to the other dimension with like-minded individuals.

An excellent app for meeting people who might want to join your spirit circle is the Amino for Witches and Pagans app, which is available to install on Google Playstore and Apple store. There are beginner groups on the app where you can connect with those who have just begun their mediumship journey like you. There are also advanced-members groups where you can meet established mediums and psychics. There, you may be able to find an advanced medium willing to be part of your spirit circle.

Chapter Twelve: Enhance Your Psychic Powers

"One of the most useful and important ways to be able to use your psychic gifts is to learn how to read what is happening in your own very body."

—Catherine Carrigan

You can enhance your psychic powers in a variety of ways. This chapter focuses on two things you can do to further your psychic powers - claircognizance and using essential oils.

Claircognizance is the gift of inner knowing. It enables you to intuitively know things in ways devoid of reason and logic. A claircognizant experience will leave you wondering, "Woah, how did I know that?"

Psychical knowing is a superb ability that can make a difference in your psychic journey. You have possibly had claircognizant experiences. Think about that time you decided not to take your usual route to work, only to discover there was a long traffic jam along that way. Or maybe you knew not to feed your new puppy a specific meal brand, only to discover they are allergic to one ingredient.

Claircognizance has likely manifested itself in your life through different channels. Let's dive into how it can help you further your psychic development and mediumship journey.

Often, people confuse claircognizance and clairsentience for each other. This happens because both psychic skills get presented as "gut feelings." Distinguishing between the two is essential. If you don't, it may confuse which one is your dominant psychic ability.

The psychic gift of inner feeling allows you to feel that someone might be dishonest, while inner knowing lets you know. Feeling differs from knowing. When convinced about someone or something, you can't shake your conviction; this is considered claircognizance. But clairsentience is when you feel strongly about something. The feelings may be fleeting, but they come to you.

Those who are claircognizant receive intuitive messages in three ways. The first way is via their gut feelings. The inner knowing sometimes comes from your guts. Unless you have experienced something like that before, describing it can be difficult. Those with the gift find it hard to describe or explain that they have no logical explanation. They opt to describe it as a "gut feeling" because that is a concept that most people can grasp, psychic or not. However, claircognizant messages may feel like they come from your guts because this psychic sense is linked to your solar plexus, which is around your guts.

Claircognizant messages sometimes come "out of the blue," meaning you don't know the source or origin. They just "pop" into people's heads from nowhere, leaving them surprised. They often come while you are engaged in an activity entirely unrelated and disrupts your thinking. You might be in the bathroom getting ready for work, and then the thought pops into your head, "Let me take another route to work today." Then when you discover that your usual route was blocked, you wonder why that thought popped into your head earlier.

The third way that claircognizant messages are received is in the sleep state. For example, you go to bed thinking about a business problem you have to solve. Suddenly, you awaken from your sleep with a brilliant solution in mind. "I wasn't even thinking. Where did this come from?" This particular experience has happened to me many times. You just wake up knowing things with no idea how they got to your mind or when.

Realistically, the idea of receiving messages that can't logically be explained to anyone is a little bit frightening. And it might even affect your social life. Imagine yelling "STOP" to your friend who is about to have a lousy drink unknowingly. Of course, they will regard you strangely even if they will thank you later.

Like all intuitive messages, claircognizant messages come from the spirit guides, your spiritual team, and your Higher Self. Once you are far developed in your psychic practice, you will understand the exact being responsible for the messages you receive. You may find yourself receiving messages you don't know how to deal with. There, the meanings will come to you over time.

Here are signs you may be claircognizant:

- You know when someone is insincere or fake

- You often awake with brilliant solutions to challenging problems

- You receive intuitive hits out of the blue, and they always end up being right

Even if claircognizance is not your primary psychic gift, you still have it in you. So, you can work on developing it regardless.

Claircognizance training can be done in many ways, but you can focus on two of the most effective methods. The first is to seek your spirit guides' help, while the second involves using visualization exercises to hone your skills. As a bonus, there is another method which you will find below.

Developing Claircognizance helped by your Spirit Guides

You have already learned how to contact your spirit guides, but how can you invite them to develop a specific psychic ability?

• Invite your spirit guide using the instructions in Chapter Ten.

• Set the intention you seek the help of your guide in developing your claircognizance gift.

• Call forth to your spirit guide.

• Ask them to give you guidance in honing your intuitive gifts.

• Thank them for honoring your invitation and obliging your request.

Use crystals and essential oils during the sessions with your spirit guides.

Claircognizance Visualization Exercise

This exercise should be combined with journaling to get the best results.

• Take out your journal and pen.

• Write about how you see yourself when you have fine-tuned and increased your claircognizance gift.

• Describe an aspect of your life where you would like to make a change and a positive impact.

• Visualize how your inner knowing gift will make you feel and how it can affect your daily life.

• Meditate on the day you just described for yourself. Then, picture it in wholesome details.

• Immerse yourself in the moment and visualize how you feel when you have a claircognizant experience.

Be specific with the meditation to increase your claircognizance.

Automatic Writing

Automatic writing or, if you prefer, freewriting is a productive and fun way of training your claircognizant sense. With this exercise, you can attune to your inner knowing gift. At the start of your psychic development journey, you will second-guess your gut feelings. Freewriting allows you to gain confidence in the messages you receive, and more importantly, get direct answers from your spirit guides and your Higher Self.

Here is how you can train with automatic writing:

- Grab your notebook and a pen. Before you write, ask your spirit guides a question.

- Place your pen on the paper and write down anything that comes to you. Just write and go with the flow, even if you think it is gibberish.

The writing may not make much sense to you immediately, so give it time. Over the next few days or weeks, the meaning will come to you gradually. On your first few tries, this automatic writing exercise might seem absurd to you. However, those first tries are to clear out your subconscious until it is ready to receive valuable information. Soon, your notes will be filled with things that make absolute sense to you. You will receive clear and concise claircognizant messages, and your psychic knowing skill will advance.

Essential Oils

Essential oils have several kinds of excellent benefits for upcoming and established psychic mediums. The right oil combinations can help you achieve many of your intuitive abilities. They are a must for anyone looking to train themselves in mediumships. Whether you apply them to your skin or rub on your crystals, there is more than one way to reap their benefits.

Here's the thing – you can't just apply essential oils and expect them to start enhancing your psychic powers. You have to set the intention. Intention setting is key to psychic rituals and ceremonies.

All essential oils have multiple functions, and they all work for psychic development. But the fact remains that some of these oils are more effective than others. Again, your intention must be clarified for you to reap the power-boosting benefits.

There are tons of oils, but how do you know which ones will be good for you? Before I go ahead, please understand that there are no perfect oils. Don't overwhelm yourself trying to choose perfect ones. Instead, let your intuition guide you toward the oils that will benefit you the most. Also, try the oils you feel connected to than others.

The following are the best oils for grounding and centering yourself while enhancing your intuition and sense of clarity. You have the liberty of changing the oils to use based on your mood, activity, and season.

1. Cedarwood: Mental decluttering is super vital in psychic training. This essential oil can help you get rid of mental clutter to gain the ultimate clarity your soul needs. Add it to your collection.

2. Rose Essential Oil: To strengthen your connection with your Higher Self while increasing harmony between all your six psychic senses, this is the oil for you. Rose oil can amplify your abilities to a considerable extent, and the effects are not temporary.

3. Lemon Oil: I am convinced that every psychic has lemon oil in their collection. Its benefits are simply too incredible for you to leave it out of your list. The vibrant citrus smell helps to promote an alert and present mind, which you need during psychic exercises training.

4. Chamomile: Drinking chamomile tea is good, but the oil is even better. Like the tea, chamomile has a powerful calming effect that can help release your mind from fears and open it to the truth. If you are doubtful or scared of your abilities, diffuse some chamomile into your bath water or rub it on your skin. The fear will be eradicated.

5. Peppermint Oil: Most psychic mediums add peppermint oil to their collection because of its great smell, but that is not the only reason. That smell is responsible for its immediate awakening of the mind to increase focus. It is so powerful that having it around can help you concentrate when communicating with spirits. The scent peppermint gives your home will just be an added benefit.

6. Lavender Oil: This oil is often recommended as a remedy for sleep due to its calmness-inducing properties. It can help you relax and let go of control when contacting your spirit guides. It is the right oil to diffuse during journaling or visualization practice.

7. Frankincense: The fantastic grounding properties in this oil is one reason it should be a part of your daily routine. Use it whenever you feel out of touch from your inner psychic.

8. Rosemary: This essential oil is a perfect alternative for sage. If you don't like the smell of burning sage, go for rosemary oil to keep harmful spirits and energies out of your life. Plus, you can use it to open your third eye and enhance clairvoyance.

9. Jasmine: Remember that psychic messages sometimes come in the dream state? Well, this is the perfect oil to help you receive more precise messages in your dreams and daydreams. Diffuse some jasmine oil before you go to bed every night to remember dream visits more clearly.

10. Sandalwood: This is one oil that has potent purifying properties. You can use sandalwood to release yourself from your past negativity – a crucial step to psychic awakening.

The best thing about essential oils is that you can apply them anytime you choose. Below is a simple exercise to use your essential oils safely and correctly.

- Sit in your sacred meditative spot.
- Get six drops of your chosen oil in your diffuser and concentrate internally.
- Do a simple meditation and set your intention.
- Try one of the psychic exercises you have learned in this book.
- Do some journaling or more meditation to commune with your spirit guides.

Some other ways you can use the essential oils include:

- Diffusing before you begin any activity.
- Dropping a little oil into your bathwater.
- Sprinkling on a fabric, then put under your pillow before you sleep.
- Add a little essential oil to a carrier oil and rub in the spots where you usually apply your perfume.

The psychic journey to mediumship is not something that you can master in one weekend. Give room for growth as you practice. Allow yourself to experiment, fail, and try again. Remember that psychic development can sometimes take years.

Conclusion

Mediumship is an interesting and awesome gift to master. The first few times you connect with the spirit world may leave you in awe. You may feel like you have no control over what you receive. Or maybe you don't feel a flow in your readings. No matter how you feel at the beginning, you will come to enjoy and appreciate your gift. That you can affect your life and the whole universe with your gift will keep you inspired as you go through the process of training.

Part 4 Pendulum

The Ultimate Guide to the Magic of Pendulums and How to Use Them for Divination, Dowsing, Tarot Reading, Healing, and Balancing Chakras

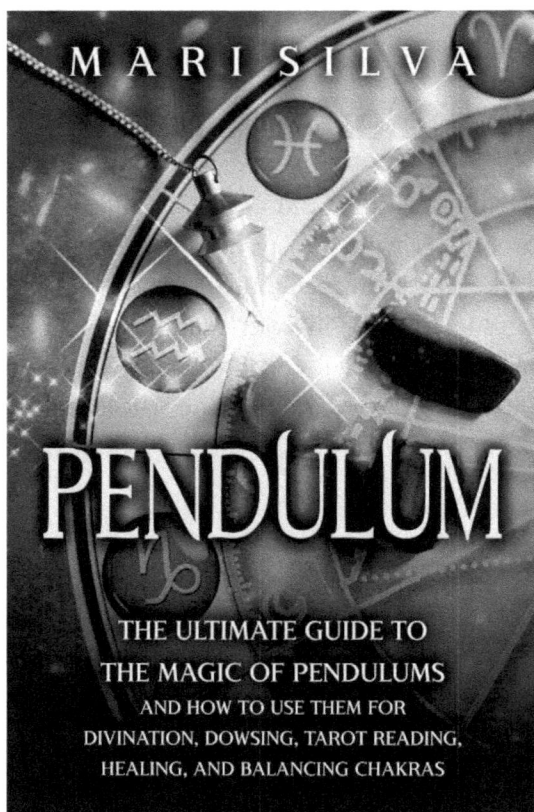

Introduction

Are you fascinated by the swaying magic of pendulums? Or are you just a little curious about this practice, which has suddenly gained popularity again? Whatever your reason, this book will help you to learn about pendulums and their uses in divination, tarot readings, dowsing, healing, and much more.

Once you grasp the pendulum's potential, you will gain control of your life and find fulfillment. The magic of pendulums can be used for a lot more than you might imagine. They are not just a part of those old grandfather clocks ticking away the time. With the right skills and a little practice, pendulums can be used in many magical ways.

A pendulum is a powerful tool that can help activate the left and right side of your brain and enable them to work in sync. It will enhance your intuitive abilities and help you pick up on energies from people, places, or objects around you. As you learn to use a pendulum, you will find it much easier to make decisions, and believe it or not, you'll see a reduction in your stress levels. You will also learn to find lost or hidden objects by using dowsing. As you discover the meaning behind your pendulum's movements, you can interpret what the pendulum is trying to tell you. This book will help you learn how to use pendulums for everything from dowsing to balancing chakras and much more.

In recent years, people have become more open to ancient practices that had slowly declined with the rise of scientific reasoning. Nowadays, alternative healing methods such as Reiki and acupuncture have gained popularity again. Many medical professionals have been adding these healing methods to their practices or suggesting them to their patients. Like alternative medicines, pendulum healing cannot replace conventional medicine; it works more like a complementary tool. With pendulums, you will be able to diagnose illness or imbalances in the energy system of the body. For an individual to completely heal, every aspect of their mental, emotional, physical, and spiritual being must be healed. With pendulums, you will be able to focus on more than the physical aspect of healing. As you read this book, you will explore the various uses of pendulums to diagnose an ailment in the body and restore balance to the chakra system.

If you are ready to unlock the potential of pendulums in your life, start reading. Pick a pendulum for yourself using the tips given here and trust in it to act as a guide that will enhance your life in many different ways.

Chapter 1: Introduction to Pendulums

What Is a Pendulum?

If you are interested in divination and magic, pendulums will open a whole new world for you. Pendulums are used for a type of metaphysical practice that is simple and yet extremely effective. Pendulums are also called dowsers, and they have been used for thousands of years. You can learn to use pendulums for personal self-improvement or as a tool that connects you to higher powers. Your purpose may vary from that of others, but the practice has been carried out since ancient times. If you want to try pendulum divination, this is where you get started.

What is a pendulum? It is essentially a simple weight that is suspended from a string so that it can swing freely on that string. In divination, a pendulum is used for channeling energy from a higher power, someone else, or even yourself. Pendulum dowsing is just one of many types of dowsing. Dowsing has been practiced for hundreds of years for many reasons.

Pendulums Are Not Just Used for Dowsing

A lot of people are confused about what dowsing entails. Just because you use a pendulum for something does not mean it is dowsing. If you ask questions and use a pendulum to get answers, it is dowsing. If you are using the pendulum to transform energy or for healing, it is not dowsing. The latter involves the act of intentionally making energetic changes. It is important that you know the meaning of dowsing and differentiate it from other pendulum uses. When you heal with a pendulum, it can be called pendulum healing. There is no complex or specific term for this, but it is not what you should consider dowsing.

An Introduction to Dowsing

Pendulums are generally used for dowsing in occultism. Dowsing is the practice of using pendulums, willow wood, rowan, or any y-shaped metal rod to look for hidden substances such as treasure, water, ancient ruins, and gravesites. The practice of dowsing started becoming popular around the Middle Ages in Europe. This practice is also called water dowsing, divining, or doodle bugging.

When you practice dowsing with a pendulum, you will be holding the string or thread from which the pendulum is hanging and proceed with your search. When the pendulum receives transmissions from any hidden objects, it will start moving to indicate the location. Some dowsers have been able to find hidden objects simply by using dowsing over maps indicating the area where the hidden objects may be.

In the olden days, dowsing was mostly used while searching for water, and therefore the practice is usually called water witching or water dowsing. But it was soon used while looking for other lost objects, divination, healing, and even to search for lost people or pets. This fascinating practice is still carried out by a lot of people around the world. As you read this book, you will learn simple ways in which you can start using pendulum dowsing as well.

History of Dowsing

One of the oldest cave drawings recording a man practicing dowsing has been dated back to 6000 BC. It was discovered in Algeria and depicted a man with a forked stick, probably dowsing for water. The Chinese also practiced dowsing. A statue of a Chinese emperor with a dowser was discovered, dating back to 2200 BC. There are dowsing depictions on many Egyptian papyri and paintings too. Emperor Yu used dowsing to locate geo-pathic stress zones. He left decrees that forbade the construction of homes in such locations. This same method is still used in Feng Shui.

The Old Testament mentions Moses and Aaron finding water using a rod. King Solomon also used dowsing to choose women for his harem. The earliest illustration known is of a dowser by Georgius Agricola in *De Re Metallica* (1556). It showed a man looking for mineral veins using a forked twig.

There is a lot of information on dowsing in French history as well. Around 1326, the Church condemned the use of dowsing for divination. Despite this, dowsing was mentioned in the works of priests like Abbe de Vallmont. In 1518, Martin Luther labeled dowsing as occultism.

The practice of dowsing as we know it now may have originated from 16th century Germany, where it was used for metal ore searches. In England, dowsing was used for calamine searches in the royal mines. Queen Elizabeth I introduced this practice when she saw the success it led to in Germany.

A Jesuit by the name of Gaspar Scott declared dowsing as a satanic and superstitious practice in 1662. In the 17th century, dowsing was used for searching for criminals in the South of France. The abuse of this practice in 1701 led to the decree of the inquisition, and it was then forbidden.

In the late 19th century, dowsing was used in South Dakota to help locate water on the land of farmers, ranchers, and homesteaders. During the Vietnam War, it was also used to look for tunnels and weapons.

Dowsing was considered a natural art until Victorian times. After the Industrial Revolution, it was categorized under other practices like herbal medicine. People started questioning or doubting the validity of this practice more since it wasn't exactly scientific but, in recent years, people have started realizing the importance of such practices again and acknowledging that not everything can be proven in a laboratory.

The practice of dowsing got carried down through the centuries. Many people still use it for different purposes, and this art is likely to survive for the foreseeable future.

Tools Used for Dowsing

While this book will primarily focus on using pendulums, dowsing can be done with a few different tools.

Y-Rods

If you watch movies, you will see that dowsing is done with a Y-shaped stick. This type of dowsing rod is a forked stick that can be anywhere between 12 and 24 inches long. Traditionally, these dowsing tools were made from wood, but people now prefer metal or plastic Y-rods since they are much easier to hold. This tool was primarily used for obtaining a "yes" answer during dowsing.

L-Rods

L-rods are more popular than Y-rods. You have to use two rods that are L-shaped while dowsing with this tool. Hold one rod in each hand, and the long ends should face away from you. You can buy these L-rods at a store specializing in dowsing tools or online. You can even make these L-rods by bending wire coat hangers. When you use these rods, you have to think clearly about the object or person you are looking for. Keep walking as you do this and allow the rods to point slightly downward. Observe the movement of the rods. If they point in the same direction, then you should move that way too. The rods will point in opposite directions when they want to indicate a no. The L-rods will cross when you find the location of your lost object.

Bobbers

These are rods or wires that are long and flexible. Bobbers often have a coiled spring at their ends for the user to hold. There might also be a weight on the other end. The length of these rods and the spring allows the rod to move while walking without the user exerting influence over their movement. These rods are the bobbers. The direction in which the bobber moves will give you your answer.

Pendulums

These are probably the best dowsing devices that you could use. Most dowsers favor pendulums over other dowsing tools. They are easy to use, portable, and very reactive if used properly. A pendulum consists of a weighted object hanging on one end of a wire, chain, or string. The swinging motion of the pendulum is what indicates the answer it wants to give. The only downside is that pendulums can be a little difficult to use when you are walking or moving around, but you can use them to find things with the help of charts or maps. Pendulums can be used effectively for finding all kinds of things.

Uses for Pendulums

Pendulums can be used in many ways:

1. Tarot reading.

2. Answering yes or no questions.

3. Checking polarity.

4. While using charts.

5. Detecting the presence of negative or unwanted energies.

6. Selecting crystals for healing and chakra balancing.

7. Fortune telling.

8. Finding lost objects or people.

9. Discovering spirit guides.

10. Making decisions.

11. Understanding synchronistic events.

12. Identifying resonant colors.

13. Checking the validity of information or advice.

14. Checking the state of chakras in your body or someone else's.

15. Finding a source of water.

16. Selecting locations for rituals, traveling, or building something.

17. Determining trustworthiness.

18. Healing the mind, body, and spirit.

19. Enhancing intuition.

20. Cleansing a space or a deck of divination cards.

Chapter 2: How to Choose a Pendulum

A lot of people are unsure about how to pick the right pendulum. Since there are many styles and types of pendulums, this is an understandably confusing decision.

Selecting your pendulum will be a fun experience, but it will also be a bit of a guessing game. Are there any specific rules you should be following while choosing a pendulum? Well, the answer is not really, since it is such a subjective and personal experience.

The first thing that you need to make sure of is that you are attracted to the pendulum. When you feel a sort of attraction to a particular pendulum, it is the one you should pick. This experience will be different for everyone, so it is impossible to determine a specific pendulum as the right one in general. There is a bit of information that will help you make your decision.

One of the best pendulums to start using is the basic triangle or teardrop. These are nicely weighted pendulums that are moderate in size and rotate easily. Another advantage is that they will not cost you much money, but this may not be the right pendulum for you. You need to try it out and see how it feels. It is important that a pendulum feels right for you for it to be effective.

Factors to Consider When You Choose a Pendulum

Pendulum Shape

There are a lot of different shapes of pendulums. Some are angular, while others are round. Some pendulums are a mix of these shapes. When your pendulum is round, it has more feminine energy. This applies to all round shapes in nature. For instance, round fruit like pomegranates are considered feminine. When the pendulum is angular and in shapes like square or rectangular, it has more masculine energy. For instance, a tall skyscraper has masculine energy compared to the cathedral's domed ceiling, but no pendulum is completely masculine or feminine.

Many people choose their pendulum based on its aesthetic appeal. When you choose based on shape, it is more about what you find intuitively attractive. It is also important to know that the movement of the pendulum will be affected by its shape. Your pendulum will move according to the position of your hand during dowsing. It is usually better for the pendulum to move in perfect circles during dowsing, so you need to choose a shape and hold your hand up accordingly. Many pendulums are created for specific purposes, but in general you can use any pendulum for any purpose. You just need to focus on finding a pendulum that you feel an attraction to, and that has consistent movement.

Pendulum Weight

Another determining factor when choosing a pendulum is the weight. When the pendulum is heavy, you will need more energy to move it. These heavy pendulums also give stronger feedback. It is much easier to move a lighter pendulum, and their response time is less in comparison. A medium-weighted pendulum might be a good choice in between. Their movement is not too slow or fast, and they move along the axis at the right speed. If the pendulum is too light, it isn't heavy enough for you to feel a connection while dowsing. The problem with a heavy pendulum is that you need a lot more energy and have to pay attention to maintain control over it. It can often fall out of your hands while you are meditating with it, but this will depend on your personal experience.

Pendulum Material

Pendulums can be made of different materials, so which one is the best one for you? Usually, they are either made of wood, crystal, or brass. You can try to experiment with each to figure out which one works well for you.

Wood

A wood pendulum is one of the options you can choose from. These tend to be bigger than crystal or brass pendulums, but their weight is usually lighter. The energy of a wood pendulum will be neutral. They are easy to read and responsive as well. Since wood is a long-lasting material, this pendulum will be durable. You don't have to cleanse a wood pendulum, and you will see that they are versatile.

Brass

A brass pendulum is long-lasting and durable. These pendulums have neutral energy and are also of an appropriate weight. Their movement tends to be good as well. Since brass pendulums don't absorb and store emotional energy from the wearer or the surroundings, they don't need to be cleared.

Crystal

A crystal pendulum is fragile and lighter when compared to a brass pendulum. If you drop it or bang it against a hard surface, you are likely to cause cracks or break the tip, but on the plus side, these pendulums tend to be more responsive and faster. Every crystal pendulum will have its own type of energy. Depending on the type of crystal you choose, the pendulum will have a unique signature. For instance, rose quartz pendulums are good for relationships, since they are linked to the heart chakra. The attributes of the specific crystal that your pendulum is made from will determine its effects. Crystal pendulums also tend to work similarly to charms when worn like a personal item. You will often find crystal pendulum users wearing it around their neck or just carrying it around with them. When choosing a crystal pendulum, it is important to choose one that is harmonious with your personality. Some crystals will not be suitable for you, but they may be the right fit for another person. There is no specific pendulum that works perfectly for everyone. Crystals can be dormant, active, or dead. When you pick up a crystal, you have to pay attention to see if you feel a connection with it. If not, you should put it down and try others. Unlike brass pendulums, crystals have to be cleared or cleansed, since they accumulate energy from their wearer or the environment.

Using More Than One Pendulum

As a dowser, you can own more than one pendulum if you want. Many dowsers have multiple pendulums. Depending on what you want to accomplish from dowsing, you will find certain pendulums more suited to a specific task than others. It is similar to an artist using different brushes while painting. Each brush serves its purpose. It will be beneficial for you to own a few different pendulums for the dowsing tasks you want to carry out.

Since you will usually carry the pendulums around together, you also have to see if they work well together. When you already have one pendulum, test out a few pendulums to see if they work well for you. Just carry the new one in your pouch with the old one for a while. If the results are not to your satisfaction, switch the new one for another. You have to figure out what will be a suitable addition to your pendulum collection. Don't hesitate to change your pendulum if you feel like it isn't working the way you want or expect it to.

For beginners, good pendulums include the basic triangle, basic teardrop, or conical beechwood pendulum. The more you practice using your pendulum, the more your ability grows. As this happens, you will naturally feel the urge to try a few different pendulums after the first one. With experience, you will also see that certain dowsing tasks are better performed with certain pendulums. There are no strict rules that you have to follow here. Listen to your intuition and learn from experience.

Choosing Pendulums for Their Uses

Pendulums are very versatile and aid in the expansion of consciousness and personal growth. It is easy to carry them around with you wherever you go, and they can be used for different purposes at any time you need. These pendulums may be made from various materials like wood, metals, or gemstones. The material of the pendulum gives it unique properties that will affect the task you perform with the pendulum. This is why it is important to consider your primary goals before choosing a pendulum. Learning about the properties of the different materials will help you choose the best one for your needs.

Energy Healing

When you want a pendulum for energy healing practices, choose stones that are linked to the chakras. Different crystals tend to be linked to different chakras, and they help to align them or to clear out any blockages accordingly. Copper is also a good material for energy healing pendulums, since it can amplify, conduct and balance healing energy.

Divination

A pendulum for divination has to be able to conduct higher spiritual energies and elevate them. Ideally, it should also protect the wearer against any negative energies or vibrations. A clear quartz crystal is one of the better options for divination pendulums. It can transform, conduct, and amplify energy.

Another powerful option for those who want to work with spiritual energy is a Merkabah pendulum. These will help to connect with spirit guides and help the wearer connect with their higher self. It is a multidimensional vessel that can act as a link between dimensions and which also protects the wearer when they are in an altered state of consciousness. The Merkabah is also known to connect both halves of the brain. This allows the person to become more creative and well-rounded, while their ability to solve problems is also enhanced.

Indian Rosewood or Sheesham is linked to the divine feminine. It is associated with compassion and the heart chakra. A Sheesham pendulum is an excellent choice when meditating to develop the higher self or while struggling with obstacles. This material is used for making prayer beads for Buddhist Monks since it has healing qualities.

No matter what your purpose or need may be, there is a pendulum that will be suitable for you. All you have to do is give it a try and find the best one for you.

Bond with Your Pendulum

Once you choose a pendulum, you have to develop a relationship with it. Like any divination tool, your pendulum will work best and give you better predictions or readings when you bond with it. There are different ways in which you can bond with different pendulums.

For instance, you can carry the pendulum around everywhere you go. This is one of the easiest ways to create a bond with the pendulum. You can get a special pouch for this purpose, and this bag will help protect the pendulum from any negative energy. Carrying it around means it will come in proximity with other people and the environment, and certain pendulums tend to absorb all kinds of energy from around them. To protect the sanctity of your pendulum, you need to protect it from such energy.

Another way in which you can build a relationship with your pendulum is by letting it guide you. When you do this, it gives you time with the pendulum, and it also displays a high level of trust in the chosen tool. It shows your pendulum that you trust it to guide you to a place or toward anything you seek.

Meditating with your pendulum is one of the best ways to connect with it. Focus on the pendulum and its ability to act as a guide and as a vessel to heal or help you in any way you need it to. It is recommended that you meditate with your pendulum before carrying out a divination session or any long readings.

The stronger you bond with your pendulum, the more effective it will be.

Chapter 3: Preparing for Pendulum Use

Divination allows you to gain insight into things. When you use a pendulum for divination, it can help you in several ways. You can use it for getting answers to certain questions, or you could use it to help you make decisions that you have difficulty making on your own. Rather than accurate fortune-telling, you can rely on pendulums to see potential outcomes for your decisions or choices. It is much better to approach divination with the intention of gaining mental clarity and guidance from the higher powers.

A dowsing pendulum will help you gain material and spiritual insight. In older times, these dowsing pendulums were used to find hidden things below the ground, like water or minerals. You can use your pendulum to do a lot more.

But before you start using a pendulum, you need to prepare it in a certain way. It's not just about picking up a pendulum, asking it a question, and waiting for it to give you all of life's answers. If only it was that easy.

Here are tips that will help you get started with pendulum divination:

Finding the Right Pendulum

There is no specific pendulum that works perfectly for everyone. Think about the kind of pendulum you want for yourself. As you learn more about the different types of pendulums and properties of crystals in later chapters, you can use the knowledge to help you choose a suitable pendulum. There may be a particular stone that you resonate with. If you walk into a store to buy a pendulum, take the opportunity to try each pendulum in your hand. Pick out the pendulum that attracts you or catches your eye. Then hold it in your palm and see if you feel a connection to it. You will be able to tell when a stone interacts with you. When you don't feel anything, just pick up another and keep doing this until you find your preferred pendulum. Start with the purchase of one pendulum for general use and practice with it. You can later acquire a few more pendulums depending on what you want to do with them. If you don't have the option of buying a pendulum, you can make a DIY one to use for a while. Just tie a moderately weighted object to the end of a string, and before you know it, you have a pendulum.

Once you get a pendulum, you have to cleanse it. Don't start using a pendulum right after you get it. Getting rid of any residual energy is important. Stones tend to pick up energy from all the people who hold them or from their surroundings. Only use the pendulum once you are sure it is clear of any residual energy from others. Cleanse your pendulum in one of the ways mentioned in this section and then recharge it with positive energy before you use it.

Work on building a relationship with your pendulum. It is easy to build a relationship with your pendulum and this is something that you should pursue if you want the pendulum to work better for you. The more time you take to do this, the easier it will be for you to understand your pendulum's message during use.

Here is one way in which you can learn the language of your pendulum and get attuned to it:

1. Hold the pendulum with your dominant hand and let the stone hover a few inches above the palm of your other hand.

2. Now, take a few grounding breaths. Allow yourself to feel centered.

3. Speak out to the higher powers to guide and support you.

4. Now, begin asking the pendulum questions so you can learn how it will speak to you in the future. Ask your pendulum to show you a yes movement. Now just wait and observe how the pendulum swings. Note it down. Then ask the pendulum to show you a no movement and take note. You now know how the pendulum will move when you ask it a question that requires a yes or no answer. Then ask the pendulum to show you a maybe movement and observe this response as well. Thank the pendulum and proceed with the next step.

5. You can also ask the pendulum a few questions to which you already know the answer. For instance, if you have brown eyes, ask the pendulum if your eyes are brown. This will help you to observe how the pendulum moves to indicate a yes. Similarly, you can ask another question to indicate a no. If you use this method, just ask clear and objective questions.

6. Now, you can begin asking your pendulum other questions. Sit in a comfortable position in a calm state of mind and begin trying it out. Since you have to hold the pendulum from a string, support the elbow of the hand used so that there is no extra movement. This will give you more stability and help you to hold the pendulum so it can move of its own free will. Ask the pendulum questions that you can receive clear responses to. Reframe your questions in a simple way for this. It can be about anything from relationships to financial issues to more profound spiritual subjects.

7. Remember to use your pendulum wisely. Divination tools should not be misused. Use the pendulum cautiously for the right reasons. When you are in a mentally imbalanced state or very emotional, don't use the pendulum. You can simply ask the pendulum to tell you if you are in the right state of mind to proceed with dowsing. Trust in your pendulum and follow its guidance.

8. Pendulums should not be used as an alternative to actual medicine. If you are ill or need medical assistance for some reason, pendulums or any divination tools cannot replace it. You can only use pendulums as an additional tool to benefit you. Don't endanger your health or wellbeing by depending completely on pendulums or other forms of divination.

9. When you are dowsing, do it for yourself. Don't do dowsing for someone else unless you have their permission or they ask you to do it. It is also important to consider if you have enough experience to do this for someone else. Gain more practice by yourself first, and then you can offer to help or heal someone else with dowsing.

10. Keep your mind open and unbiased when you are about to use a pendulum. If you ask a question assuming that you already know the answer, you are likely to influence the answers that the pendulum gives you.

Although pendulum dowsing is helpful, you should not rely on it too much. You shouldn't rely on your pendulum to make all of your decisions. It will prevent you from taking responsibility for your choices and affect your ability to make decisions. You cannot use the excuse of pendulum dowsing to shirk off responsibility for what you decide to do. While the pendulum will answer your questions, it is only a guide, and the ultimate decisions will always be in your hands.

Meditate to Calm Your Body and Mind

It is important to start using your pendulum with a clear and calm mind. Don't begin a session when you are in an emotional state. This will impact the process and the outcome. Instead, you can use meditation to achieve this calm state. When you can stay detached, calm, and unemotional while using the pendulum, you are a lot more likely to get accurate results or the desired outcome from your pendulum. Here we will explain how to meditate to achieve the ideal state of mind and body before using pendulums.

If you just take a minute to stop and take a few deep breaths during your day, you will notice that it helps you to feel lighter and calmer. These few seconds of breathing intentionally are a type of meditation. Take time in between other things in your day to just sit up straight and take a few deep breaths in and down into your stomach. Do it slowly for a minute and notice how you instantly feel a little less stressed. This kind of mini-meditation exercise is quite useful.

Many people shy away from meditation because they think it will take too much time or find it boring. They imagine a formal meditation session where they will probably have to sit still for about 30-40 minutes while meditating, but this is not the only way to meditate. What you have to start practicing is mindfulness meditation, and it does not involve the kind of long and intense session that you dread.

Mindfulness meditation allows you to let any emotions or thoughts pass through your mind instead of focusing on them and thinking too much about them. Instead, you keep bringing your attention back to your breath. This practice teaches you to be more present instead of worrying about the past or even the immediate future. In recent years, mindfulness meditation has become even more popular, although the concept is quite old. A lot of evidence shows how beneficial this practice is. This is why we recommend that you start practicing mindfulness meditation too. It will help you to improve your state of mental and physical wellbeing. According to several studies, it will help boost your immune system, improve heart health, reduce stress levels, and lower blood pressure. Mindfulness meditation will help you to relax and feel rejuvenated in the same manner that vacation makes you feel.

You should try your best to establish a regular meditation practice to see all these benefits manifest in a more long-term way. You don't have to do a long meditation session if you don't want to. Just put in as much time as you think you can. A few minutes of mindfulness meditation in the morning, before going to sleep, or just before your pendulum dowsing sessions will make a big difference. It is quite easy to fit such mini-meditation sessions into your day. The more you practice meditation, the easier it is to continue doing it every day, and the longer the benefits will last.

No matter how long you decide to spend meditating, it is important to learn how to be mindful first. You need to be more present and non-judgmental. Your attitude toward your inner experience should be one of compassion.

How to Practice Mindfulness Meditation

Deep Breathing

Take one deep breath in, pause and let the air out. Do this a couple of times. This is an easy mini-meditation exercise that can be done anywhere. You may be at work, in your bedroom, or even on a flight. When you take a few deep breaths, your body is not in the state of fight or flight anymore. Instead, it will turn to the resting mode and calm down again. Deep breathing will slow down your heart rate, lower blood pressure, and make you less anxious. It will help you get back a sense of control in any situation. Deliberate deep breathing is helpful no matter what kind of mini-meditation session you decide to practice.

The Way Your Body Reacts

Recognize the way your body acts when you are stressed. Do you feel like your heart rate has quickened rapidly? Are a lot of thoughts racing through your mind? Have you clenched your fists? When you notice any of these things, it means that you are stressed, and your body is responding to it. Even if all you do is just take note of these signs and acknowledge that you are stressed, you will feel a little better because you come to realize that you can do something about how you are feeling. The simplest thing to do would be a mini-meditation session like deep breathing for a couple of minutes.

Label Your Emotions

Pay attention to how you are feeling and give these feelings a name. Are you feeling anxious? Is it anger? Are you stressed? When you can put a label on your emotions, it seems to have a calming effect. It prompts activity in the part of your brain responsible for thinking instead of straining your brain.

Open Eye Meditation

You don't have to close your eyes for every meditation session. Do a mini-meditation with your eyes open. This kind of meditation is not usually done with the intention of helping you sleep or to achieve a higher state of consciousness. Instead, it will promote wakefulness within you. Opening your eyes as you meditate will help you to feel more present. You are more open to what is happening right then. This particular method is useful when you want to meditate without letting anyone else know that you are meditating quietly. Choose a point of reference and concentrate the eyes on it while you breathe.

Practice Mindful Self-Compassion

It is common for most of us to suddenly start imagining situations that make us feel anxious or stressed out. When you notice yourself doing this, pull yourself back to the present and speak kindly to yourself. Reassure yourself so you feel calm and soothed again. Self-compassion helps your agitated spirit to feel better.

Do Activities with Mindfulness

You can choose to practice mindfulness during any activity. It could be while you are out for a walk or even while you are talking to a friend. Compel yourself to focus on that present moment. Focusing complete attention on the present is something that most people fail to do.

Let Your Thoughts Pass By

When a thought pops into your mind, you will usually start thinking more about it and delve deeper than necessary. This is usually not going to benefit you in any way. It is better to just observe your thoughts and let them pass by. When you pay attention to your thoughts in a more detached way, you will learn a lot about yourself and your life. You will notice the things that worry you, what you value, and what you need. You will also notice that some things preoccupy your mind a lot more frequently than others.

Another point to note is that you will see that your thoughts and emotions change or evolve with time. It is not necessary for you to delve into all the thoughts that pass through your head. It is enough to acknowledge them and look at them through the eyes of an observer. If you keep indulging in overthinking, it will do more harm than good. It will also prevent you from focusing on the present and any task that you are currently doing. This exercise will help you to keep your mind on the process of dowsing instead of thinking about other things. It will also help you to avoid manipulating the outcome with your subconscious thinking.

Smile

Consciously make an effort to smile a little at any time. Have you noticed the statues of Buddha meditating? You will see that he always seems to have a half-smile on his face. When you smile, your mind seems to automatically relax a little. You can benefit your mind and body by smiling a little more every day. In fact, some people use laughing meditation to relax themselves.

Recite a Mantra or a Prayer

Words have immense power over your mind and body. You can use a mantra, motto, or prayer to meditate. It could be a phrase that has deep meaning for you. It could be a prayer to the higher powers you believe in. It might be a mantra you have learned. When you repeat it to yourself a few times, you will feel calmer and a little better in any situation. These words will reassure you.

Practice Gratitude

Instead of focusing on everything that is going wrong or might go wrong in your life, focus on the good. Take a few seconds to just think of what you should be grateful for in your life. It could be anything from the food on the table to a goal you might have accomplished last year. Practicing gratitude is a great way to bring stability and happiness into your mind.

All the methods mentioned above are simple ways to meditate, even if they may not seem like it. Try to include any of these practices into your daily life and notice the impact they have on your mental wellbeing in particular. These mini-meditations are also a great way for you to calm your mind before using a pendulum. The more you practice these, the easier it will be for you to be mindful of everything you do in life. Regular meditation will clear your mind of any negative or unnecessary thoughts and instead allow you to find balance.

So, before you start a session with your pendulum for any purpose, take a minute or more to just meditate a little.

Cleanse Your Pendulum and Stones

One crucial part of using pendulums is cleansing. You need to periodically cleanse the pendulum, stones, or any divination tools that you use. They tend to accumulate energy from the wearer or user; their surroundings; and those nearby. Cleansing any such negative energy from the pendulum and other tools will make sure that they function optimally and have no negative effect on the user.

If you have been using pendulums for a while or have just begun, you will notice that sometimes the pendulum acts erratically, or its movements are sluggish. One of the possible reasons for this kind of behavior from the pendulum is that it needs to be cleansed.

Pendulums can be made of stone, crystals, and other gemstones. All these materials will absorb any energy that is near them. As they absorb energy, they also retain it. Until you cleanse the crystal or stone, the absorbed energy will remain within it. To get the best outcomes from the pendulum, you have to make sure that it is only working with your own energy or any other energy that you intend it to work with. You don't have to keep cleansing the pendulums you work with, but it is important that you do a cleansing when you first acquire them. They may have passed through the hands of many people and absorbed their energy. When you claim a pendulum as your own, cleanse it of such energy, and only then can you begin to work with it.

Crystals and natural stones usually pick up most of the energies they come across and they store them within. It could be positive energy and negative energy. While a lot of the energy within a pendulum will come to your aid, too much negative energy will not be useful. This kind of buildup of negative energy will prevent the pendulum from working to its full potential. The periodic cleansing of any crystals, healing stones, or pendulums you have is highly recommended.

There are a lot of different ways in which you can cleanse the energy from these divination tools. We will only mention some tried and tested cleansing methods that will be safe for most types of stones and even for sterling silver. When you look up information on energy cleansing, you will see that many sources recommend using sea salts and liquids. Using these can corrode sterling silver and a few particular kinds of stones. Instead, you can opt for one of the following safer methods that we recommend for energy cleansing.

Smudging

You can buy smudge sticks that are easily available online or in stores that sell tools for divination. Choose a smudge stick made of herbs like white sage or cedar. Light up the smudge stick and then blow out the flame. Now hold your pendulum or other stones above the smoke that is emitted by the smudge stick. Keep passing the pendulum through the fragrant smoke a few times. This is one simple way of cleansing energy.

Energy Cleansing Kit

You can buy a kit made specifically for energy cleansing. These usually come with full instructions and provide you with a cleansing stone or another tool to help you accomplish your purpose.

Brown Rice

Take a small bowl and fill it with dry brown rice grains. It is better to use round grains instead of long grains. Now submerge your stone or pendulum inside the rice. Let it rest there for a day or two. The rice will absorb the unwanted energies from the pendulum and cleanse the stone. You should then throw out the rice after taking the pendulum out. Do not consume the rice since it now contains negative energy that will otherwise be absorbed inside your body.

Other Crystals

Certain crystals can cleanse other crystals. Some powerful cleansing crystals are citrine, selenite, amethyst, and carnelian. Take your pendulum or crystal and place it inside a pouch with citrine crystals. Keep this pouch closed and let it sit undisturbed for a day. You can do this with any of the cleansing crystals, and they will absorb the negative energies from your pendulum.

Sunlight

Sunlight is another cleansing element that you can utilize. While moonlight is a great cleansing medium, so is the sun. The powerful energy of sunlight will charge your crystals to their full potential. Solar energy is more masculine as compared to the feminine energy of the moon. This is why it is more appropriate for programming than cleansing, but you can still place your crystals under direct sunlight to cleanse and program them. When you want to use your crystals for a bigger purpose, having the sun's energy will help bring momentum to your endeavors. Around morning or in the later hours of the afternoon, simply place your crystal or pendulum out to bask under the sunlight. About 3-4 hours is enough for the cleansing to be done. Crystals like amethyst and fluorite lose their color under direct sunlight and should be cleansed with another method. Also, avoid placing your pendulum out if the weather's too hot or around noontime.

Moonlight

One of the purest ways to cleanse crystals is with the help of moonlight. The energy from the moon is powerfully purifying and can clear your crystals of any unwanted energies. The energy from the moon will also charge the crystals with extra vitality after cleansing them. You should place the crystals in a position where they will get light directly from the moon and keep them there overnight. Doing this during a new moon or full moon is most effective. On these particular nights, the moonlight will have very potent frequencies that will benefit your crystals. The feminine energy of the moon will also help when using these crystals during emotional and spiritual healing. Just like sunlight, you can use moonlight for cleansing your crystal, but moonlight is suitable for all crystals and has no restrictions like sunlight. Wait for the full moon and place your pendulum or crystals in a bowl near a window where the moonlight can reach. Leave it undisturbed overnight, and you can start using it in the morning again.

Crystal Clusters

If you have a crystal cluster of citrine, carnelian, amethyst, or any such cleansing crystals, you can place your pendulum in their center and leave it for a few hours. The cluster will help to cleanse the pendulum during that time and is more powerful than just using a single crystal.

Visualization

You can also cleanse your pendulum by visualizing a cleansing light. Keep the pendulum in front of you or in your hands when you perform this cleansing. Now imagine a beautiful white light surrounding it and going through it as it cleanses it. Visualize this healing light washing all through the stone.

Earth

This element is another great way to clear residual energies from your crystals. Just bury your crystal under some earth and allow it to clear out the old energies within the crystal. Trust your intuition to tell you how long you should keep the crystal buried. It might be three days or even eleven.

Water

Water has powerful energy and can be used for all sorts of rituals. The energies from water and crystals are amicable. You can hold your crystal underwater as you purify it. It is ideal to do it in the ocean or under a pure spring. As you hold the crystal underwater, visualize the crystal returning to its natural state as the water washes away any disruptions. You can rub sea salt over the stone with water and cleanse it as well, but it is important to consider that certain crystals will not withstand water. Selenite, for instance, will dissolve if you use water for cleansing.

Sound Vibrations

You can also use gongs, singing bowls, drums, or chimes to cleanse your crystals. Sound vibrations are a powerful cleansing tool. You can either put your crystal in the center of your singing bowl, or you can hold the crystal near as you create waves of sound. The vibrations will clear the unwanted energies from the crystals. All crystals can be cleansed using this method, and you can even do it for a group of crystals at once.

After you use any of these cleansing methods, you can charge the pendulum or crystals with pure positive energy. When you recharge the crystal, you get the chance to put beneficial energy back inside it. Recharging can be done using light, affirmations, sound, or just your physical touch. If you know how to perform reiki, you can use it to recharge your crystal or pendulum. Once you recharge the pendulum, it becomes a lot more responsive and nimble.

Avoid using salts for cleaning, even if you hear others recommend it. Salts can cause corrosion and will damage silver. Certain stones also react negatively when they come into contact with salt. It would be safer to avoid salts altogether instead of trying to remember which stones can be cleansed with salts and which can't. Water is another element that has to be used cautiously, if at all. If you bring silver into contact with water, the natural process of oxidation is hastened. Crystal selenite becomes cloudy when you immerse it in water. This cloudiness may be retained in the crystal forever.

Chapter 4: Activating Your Pendulum

You can consult your pendulum whenever you feel like you need to, but it should not be something that you constantly rely on to make all your big decisions for you. You cannot help yourself if you shirk off responsibility in your decisions and come to rely on such things. Your pendulum will be useful in most situations and can act as a guide. You can use it whenever you feel like you need clarity about something or need help to resolve a dilemma. You have to remember that your pendulum will connect to your energy, so you have to be conscious of it. You will sometimes see that your pendulum gives you different answers for the same question on different days. This is because it is affected by your own energy.

To start using pendulums, first you have to pick out the right one that speaks to you. There is no right or wrong in choosing a pendulum. Trust your instincts and use the one that seems right. Focus on how you feel when you pick up and hold a pendulum. If you trust your intuition, you will be able to choose the right pendulum. It could be any type of pendulum made of any material; it should just feel like it is meant for you.

How to Use Your Pendulum

Once you have picked out your pendulum, you can start consulting it for guidance. Here is how you can start using your pendulum:

Cleanse

As we mentioned before, you have to cleanse your pendulum before you begin using it. Just like crystals, pendulums have to be cleansed of residual energies. You can use methods like smudging to do this. Only after your pendulum has been cleansed of old energies and recharged with positive energy should you start using it. If you use a pendulum that is not cleansed, the residual energy may affect your own energy system. It will also affect the accuracy or efficacy of the pendulum.

Get in Position

It is best to sit up straight with your feet on the ground when you use a pendulum. With your dominant hand, grasp the chain or string of the pendulum using your thumb and forefinger. You can hold the pendulum chain at any point, but there should be enough space between the stone of the pendulum and your fingers to allow free movement. You should then arch your wrist a little as you keep your forearm steady. Resting your elbow or forearm on the arm of a chair or the edge of a table can be helpful. The pendulum should be dangling freely. Hold it firmly so it doesn't fall but is still able to move. Your hand might still shake a little, but it is no cause for worry. This will not affect the outcome.

Understand the Movements of the Pendulum

It is crucial to know what every movement of the pendulum means. You cannot get answers to your questions if you don't know what the pendulum is trying to say. You need to prepare your energy and mind before you use the pendulum. Find a quiet place to sit and meditate first. Once you are grounded, hold the pendulum in your hand and ask the pendulum questions to help you understand its motions. You can simply ask the pendulum questions like: "How do you show me a yes?" You can also ask the pendulum questions that you already know the answer to. You also need to know that the pendulum has many movements, and you can slowly figure out what each means. The most important motions you need to understand are when it wants to answer you with a yes or a no.

Program the Pendulum

While you can ask the pendulum to show you what its movements mean, you can also program the pendulum to move in the way you want it. For instance, you can ask the pendulum to move in a clockwise circle when it means yes. Programming the pendulum for yes, no, and maybe answers should be your first priority. You can then think of any other possible answers that your pendulum might give and program it for those movements. You can then verify the programmed signals by asking the pendulum questions with answers you already know. After you do this, you can ask the pendulum questions.

Program or Verify the Source

Before you ask the pendulum questions, you may also want to establish what the source of the answers is. You can program the pendulum to connect with your higher self and answer your questions in the most truthful way. It is essential for those practicing witchcraft to determine the source of the answer, since negative entities can manipulate the pendulum, and you should avoid that. By programming the source you want, you can make sure that you are getting answers from the right place.

Begin with the Familiar

Begin using the pendulum by asking simple questions. Think of things that you already know the answer to. Ask the pendulum these questions to familiarize yourself with its movements. It will help you to connect with the pendulum, and it will also tell you if your pendulum needs additional cleansing.

Prepare Questions in Advance

Before you begin a session with your pendulum, have a few questions ready. You should think carefully about all the questions that will help you clarify a situation. Make sure to frame these questions so the pendulum can give you accurate yes or no answers. Another thing to remember is that your pendulum may sometimes not answer you at all. It might just stop moving if it doesn't want to answer a question, or it may choose a motion to show you that it is the wrong time to be asking that question.

Be Patient

You need to wait for the answers. While your pendulum may reply very quickly at times, it usually takes more time to give answers. You should completely focus on the question you are asking and wait for an answer from the pendulum. If you think about what you want the answer to be or what you think it will be, the outcome will be affected. You will only get accurate answers if you concentrate and remain detached. You will soon see the pendulum give you an answer in one way or another. Don't rush the pendulum even if you don't get an immediate answer. It may be because you asked the wrong question or framed it the wrong way. Try asking the pendulum differently in a calm way and wait for the answer again. When your pendulum moves with great force, it is a loud answer. If the pendulum moves with a light force, the pendulum is probably giving you a less committed answer.

Be Open

If you want your pendulum to help you, you need to be open to receiving guidance from it. You should be at ease and allow your pendulum to freely communicate with you. If you have a mental block, it will affect the pendulum too. The pendulum will be able to communicate more easily if you are open. Trust in yourself and the pendulum. Enjoy the experience and remember that it is only a tool that is meant to help you. You don't have to rely on it completely, and you should always trust your intuition.

Clear the Pendulum

After you ask a question and receive the answer, you should clear the pendulum. This can be done by touching the stone in the palm of the free hand. This will show the pendulum that you have received your answer and want to move on to another question.

When you are not using your pendulum, keep it safe. You can wear it on your neck at all times and protect it with your energy. You can also carry it in a pouch with you. If you don't want to carry the pendulums you have, you may keep them in a keepsake box, away from anything that might affect their energy.

Ask Permission

A lot of dowsers choose to ask their pendulum for permission before they use it for anything. You can ask for permission in three ways:

- "Can I?"
- "May I?"
- "Should I?"

When you ask the pendulum a question that starts with "Can I?" you are essentially asking the pendulum if you can dowse, heal, or do what you intend to do with the pendulum. For instance, if you want to use the pendulum to search for a lost book in your home, you should ask the pendulum something like, "Can I use dowsing to find my book?" If the pendulum indicates a "no" with its movement, you should probably not use it for dowsing. This happens when you don't have enough experience to successfully use dowsing, but it does not mean that you can never use your pendulum for dowsing. It simply means that you should practice using the pendulum more to connect with it better before using it for dowsing or other activities.

When you ask the pendulum a question that starts with "May I?" you are asking permission from the higher powers to use the pendulum for your purpose. If the pendulum indicates an affirmative answer, you have the go-ahead and can begin using the pendulum. If it gives you a "no" answer, you should not proceed. This often happens when you intend to use the pendulum to ask questions that you are not ready to know the answers to or have no right to ask.

When you ask the pendulum a question that starts with "Should I?" you are asking if it is a good idea to carry out what you want to do with the pendulum. For instance, you might want to use the pendulum for healing someone. But when you ask the pendulum if you should do this, pay heed to the answer you get. If the pendulum says no, it might mean that the healing activity could harm you or the person you want to heal. If you ask the pendulum if you should look for something and it says no, it might mean that you were meant to lose it or that finding it will affect you negatively in some way.

Don't question the answers you get from your pendulum. Go into it with faith and trust in your pendulum. This is the only way that you will be able to truly connect with the pendulum. When you get a no answer, move on. If it says yes, go ahead.

Understand the Movements of Your Pendulum

Pendulums respond to the personality of the user and interpret their movements as well. This means that each person can have a personal code for interpreting the movements of their pendulums. It is not to be expected that a pendulum will communicate in the same way with everyone. Pendulums can be found in many models, but it is best to work with the simplest ones.

Someone with experience can probably use any type of pendulum accurately, so a beginner should avoid getting a heavy one. Your pendulum will be on a string or wire and has to be held from the end of that string/wire. Use your index finger and thumb to hold it and observe the pendulum's different movements in your hand.

The movement of a pendulum that goes clockwise is right-handed and is usually interpreted as a yes. When the pendulum moves anti-clockwise, it is usually interpreted as a no, but left-handed people usually translate the interpretations in the opposite way. This means that a person whose right hand is dominant will interpret the pendulum's clockwise movement as a yes, while a left-handed person will interpret the anti-clockwise movement of their pendulum as a yes.

The Main Movements of Pendulums

While each person should interpret the movements of their pendulums themselves, it is okay to set these general interpretations for beginners. This will help you to understand your pendulum more easily before connecting to it on a deeper subconscious level.

The material your pendulum is made of is not usually important for successful use of the pendulum, but every person has a different response to different pendulums. While someone may respond better to a particular crystal pendulum, another person might connect to a wooden one. Whichever pendulum stimulates a response or connection with you is the one that will be most effective for you.

The following are ways in which your pendulum may move:

- Swinging on a horizontal or vertical axis.
- Turning clockwise or anti-clockwise.
- Swinging along any 360-degree axis.
- Moving in a disorderly or chaotic manner.

- Moving in a straight line.
- Drawing wide or narrow ellipses.
- Drawing narrow or wide circles.
- Standing still.
- Acting gently or vigorously.
- Moving in a spiral.
- Shaking.
- Moving quickly or slowly.

These are all the general ways in which your pendulum may freely move. What you interpret from these movements will be up to you. The simplest way to use pendulums is to decipher your own code to understand when it indicates a yes or no answer. While beginners will mostly use the pendulum for asking questions and only need these yes or no movement interpretations, advanced use of pendulums requires you to have a code for all these movements.

Pendulums can communicate a lot more than just a yes or a no to their bearer and what you need to do is associate responses for each movement. For instance, if the pendulum moves in a vertical straight line, you might interpret it as a "maybe."

If you interpret a horizontal straight-line movement as a "conflict or block" answer, you can ask the pendulum a few more questions that can be answered with a yes or no. For instance, you can ask the pendulum if you are afraid of handling the truth. Or you could ask if the answer would hurt you.

While you associate the movements with answers, you also have to observe the intensity of how the pendulum moves. The intensity of movement might help you to understand the degree of truth or the strength of the pendulum's answer. For instance, if your pendulum moves with force in anti-clockwise movements, it probably means a strong no. Similarly, if the pendulum makes small clockwise movements, it might mean a yes but not a significant one.

The Meaning of Pendulum Shaking

If you notice your pendulum shaking, it might be because it is trying to tell you something, so you are not yet ready to interpret its answer. The shaking of your pendulum could mean that you are asking the wrong question and should reconsider. It could also mean that you are not focused properly on the task at hand.

Your pendulum might also shake erratically if you are in an emotional state while asking it questions. As you will learn from this book, remember to calm and ground yourself before you use the pendulum. Your emotions and thoughts will affect the movements of the pendulum. Any negative feelings or emotions might cause your pendulum to shake. If you feel like this is the reason behind your pendulum shaking, you should stop for a moment to meditate. As you meditate and relax, you can establish a better connection with the pendulum, and it will start moving normally again.

Your pendulum may still be shaking even after you use it in a calm state. This might mean that your pendulum needs cleansing. Doing a pendulum cleanse on a full moon is a beneficial practice. Just choose the method that you prefer and proceed with a cleansing ritual. You can then try using the pendulum again and see if it still shakes.

Chapter 5: Communicating with Your Pendulum

Pendulums can be used for asking all kinds of questions. You might have questions about your career, relationships, or anything that matters in your life. There is no limit on how many questions you can ask your pendulum or how often you can use it. All you should focus on is asking questions that are specific and remaining emotionally neutral so that the pendulum gives you answers as close to the truth as possible.

When you gain more experience and expertise, you can do more advanced pendulum work. You can ask for answers in a different way or use pendulums in other ways. But to start with, ask precise questions that your pendulum can easily give you yes or no responses to.

You might be wondering what the right choice of career is for you. There might be two options that you are torn between. In this case, you can look toward your pendulum for guidance, so you should be asking specific questions, even on this subject. You can ask the pendulum to help you choose between different fields of work. But you can also use it to help you get more insights into your goals. If you are interested in painting, you should ask the pendulum if you would be better at portraits or landscapes. These kinds of specific questions will give you better guidance. You can then use these answers to focus your energy on something more definite, rather than being lost in another dilemma. You can explore a lot more options when you are using pendulums for making such decisions.

If you have a question that doesn't seem to have a definitive answer, just think of how it can be rephrased. Instead of asking a broad question, narrow it down, and it will help you to get a more definitive answer.

Questions for Relationships

Here is how you can ask your pendulum questions about relationships.

First, think carefully about the kind of questions you want to ask. The more specific you are, the more clarity you will get from the answers.

Questions you might want to ask are:

- "Will my love life be a happy one this year?"
- "Will I meet my soulmate soon?"
- "Does the person I love have the same feelings for me?"
- "Am I in the right relationship?"
- "Will I get back together with the person from my past?"

The questions you have will be subjective to your life and what you want to know about your relationships. These are just some common questions that people tend to ask their pendulums.

Now that you know what questions you want to ask, you can begin. First, you have to magnetize your pendulum. For this, hold your pendulum in your hand and let it hover over the palm of the other hand. The palm of this other hand should be turned toward the sky while your pendulum tip faces the palm. The pendulum should be about 5 cm above the palm. Now move the pendulum in a back-and-forth motion. It will start moving in circular motions.

The pendulum will move in one direction first and then in the opposite direction. For instance, it may first move clockwise and then anti-clockwise. It will then stop, and your pendulum is now charged with the energy from your mind and body.

If you are unsure about your pendulum's answer to any of your questions, you can ask other clearer questions for clarification. Ask the pendulum if it is sure or if it is telling you the truth. Then observe how the pendulum moves. It is better not to go into this with doubt. Believing in any divination tool is important for it to work well for you. Trust the pendulum and allow it to express itself. It will give you useful information about any of the relationship queries you might have.

Questions for Careers

If you are confused about things related to your career, you can ask questions like the following:

- "Is now a good time to change my job?"
- "Would this be a good alternative career for me?"
- "Will I be able to move further up the ladder if I take on this role?"
- "Should I take this course to improve my job prospects?"
- "Is it profitable to turn this hobby into a business venture?"
- "Should I ask for a pay hike now?"
- "Do I have enough experience to lead a team?"
- "Is this company going to help me do well in my career?"

These are important questions that most people think about over the course of their careers. Now you can use the pendulum to help you get more clarity while making decisions related to your career. You can use your instincts to ask any question you want, and it will depend entirely on you to trust the answers given by the pendulum.

Questions Related to Fear and Anxiety

Everyone experiences some sort of anxiety or fear about certain things in life. You can use your pendulum to help you with this as well.

You can ask questions like:

- "Is this a trigger for my anxiety?"

- "Is my anxiety caused by the bottled-up emotions inside of me?"

- "Will I be able to reduce my anxiety if I talk to someone?"

- "Can I do this to get over my fear?"

- "Is this crystal going to be effective in helping reduce my anxiety?"

- "Will this crystal help me get over my fear of ...?"

It is better to ask questions about outcomes or decisions you have to make, rather than asking about how you will feel. When you ask a question about someone else, ask it in a way so that the question is related to you. This will give the pendulum a better chance of giving you a good answer. The pendulum is connected to you and not the other person. It will give you answers pertaining to you.

Questions Related to Time

When you want to ask time-related questions, you can frame them similar to these questions:

- "Is this the right time to take on new projects?"

- "Is it the right time to put my money in this business?"

- "Is it a good time to expand my business?"

- "Is next month a good time to move to a new city?"

Tips to Use Your Pendulum Successfully

The following tips will help you to use your pendulum more efficiently so you can get more accurate results. These are tips that a lot of other dowsing practitioners suggest and that they have acquired from experience.

Choose the Right Pendulum

Often, your results will depend on whether you have chosen the right pendulum. You have to pick out a pendulum that you can connect with. When there is no connection between a pendulum and its user, the dowsing or any other practice is unlikely to work. You should take your time while selecting your first pendulum. Use a pendulum that speaks to you. Even if you are simply drawn to the pendulum for its color, just go with it. You can test out a few different pendulums to find the right fit. This will determine the success of your practice to a great extent.

Use Your Dominant Hand

If you are right-handed, use that hand to hold your pendulum or use the pendulum with your left hand if it is your dominant hand. It seems like an obvious course of action, but many people don't think about this. Hold the string or chain of the pendulum comfortably so that it can move freely and give you the right answers.

Do a Cleansing

Cleansing the energy within you and around you is important. One simple way to do this is by using visualization. Visualize white light wrapping itself around you and going through you. Imagine it to be positive energy from the higher powers.

Set a Code for the Movements of Your Pendulum

You can't begin dowsing if you don't know what the meaning of each movement is. You may ask your pendulum a question but if it swings toward the right, for example, what does this movement mean to you? The answer is useless if you don't understand it. So set a code before you use your pendulum. Note down the meaning of every motion the pendulum makes. You can simply ask your pendulum to show you how it moves when it means yes or no.

Begin with Basic Questions

Don't be in a hurry to do heavy pendulum work or to ask deep questions when you just begin. Instead, begin with simple questions that you already know the answer to. This will familiarize you with the way the pendulum gives you answers. It will also help you to connect with the pendulum better before you use it for a heavy purpose.

Before you ask questions, specify the source. When you don't specify the source that you want answers from, your pendulum will give you answers from your subconscious. The answers you get from the higher powers are different from what your subconscious will tell you. You might have some preconceived notions about something or just think of something that is not the right answer to your question. If you don't specify the source, the pendulum will just tell you what you already think. This is why you should begin every dowsing session by reaching out to the higher powers. You can say something similar to, "I call upon the higher powers for guidance and to answer my questions. I seek the absolute truth that is aligned with a higher purpose." Saying something to this effect will help your pendulum to receive the right answers.

Breathe and Be Calm

You can center yourself and calm any anxiety by practicing slow and steady breathing. Just take a few deep breaths in and out before you begin.

Calm your mind. This is important before you begin a dowsing session and also after you end a session. You can do meditation to achieve a calm mind. Just sit quietly and visualize a happy place without any distractions. It could be anything, like the beach or a forest in your mind's eye. Imagine yourself sitting or lying there peacefully. When you visualize this kind of peaceful setting, it helps to calm your mind. It will also set a peaceful tone for your dowsing session. Your conscious mind will be at rest when you do this.

Be Grounded

Before working with your pendulum, spend a few minutes grounding yourself. Find a quiet place where you can sit comfortably in silence. Turn your phone off and make sure no one will disturb you. Meditation is one of the simplest ways to center and ground yourself. No matter what method you use for grounding, just make sure it is part of your dowsing practice. A grounding exercise is always important and will work in your favor. You can do this by visualizing your body being connected to the earth like a tree with roots. Think of these roots going deep into the earth's mantle as they wrap around something like large quartz crystals. This will help you feel like you are centered and connected to the earth.

Be More Objective

Neutrality will be helpful. A lot of people influence the answers of the pendulum with their conscious minds. This happens because they do not seek the truth; they just want the pendulum to make them feel like they are right. But influencing the pendulum will not give you an outcome that is of any use. This is why you have to work on being as objective as you can, and be open to receiving any answer that the pendulum gives you.

Be More Present

Your mind needs to be focused on the present and the task at hand. Don't think about something else when you are using the pendulum. Clear your mind and don't wonder about the past or the future. Just put your mind into the dowsing exercise. Multi-tasking will have a negative effect on the results.

Take Time

Don't be in a rush when you are using the pendulum. Give it time as it gives you answers. It needs a while to swing in the right motions.

Don't Be Emotional

If you use the pendulum when you are in an emotional state, it will impact the outcome. The results from dowsing in an emotional state are unreliable. You should also be more objective while asking questions, instead of asking ones that are emotionally charged. Doing so will prevent you from remaining grounded and from getting accurate answers. Setting your emotions aside will be helpful.

Be Loud and Clear

When you want your answers to be clearer, you should be loud and clear while asking the questions. This will help you to get stronger responses from the pendulum. Use your hand to focus the energy of the pendulum. If your cup one palm below the pendulum, it will help to focus the energy.

Practice as often as possible. The more time you spend working with the pendulum, the better you will get at it.

Tips to Frame Your Questions Well

The quality of the answers you get from the pendulum will also depend on the quality of the questions you ask. The better you frame your question, the easier it will be to get proper answers from the pendulum. It is all in the language.

Be specific when you ask a question—use specific names, places, and times to help narrow down the scope of the question, which will be useful. For instance, if you want to ask about a relationship, you may ask if your crush likes you back, but it would be more specific if you use the name of that person.

Avoid using terms like "supposed to" or "should" in your questions.

Make sure that the question is framed so that it can be answered with a simple yes or no. If you think about it, any question can be reframed to suit this.

How to Tell if the Pendulum Is Telling the Truth

Pendulums can be moved with your consciousness and subconsciousness. For instance, you can tell the pendulum to move in a certain way, like in a clockwise manner. Or when you want the pendulum to give you a yes or no answer, you can tell it how it should move to indicate either of the answers. The pendulum will then move according to the way you tell it to. When you do this, you are using conscious control over the pendulum.

You can trust in the answer given by the pendulum if you don't try to control the exact answer that it gives.

It can be difficult to remain neutral when you are asking certain types of questions to the pendulum. If you ask the pendulum whether you will win the lottery, it will probably give you an affirmative answer because that is what you want. When you ask it a question that has emotional significance for you, you will be affecting the answer most of the time. But if you can achieve a state of neutrality and detach yourself from the outcome, the pendulum will probably give you a much more truthful answer.

You should be calm and ask the pendulum clear questions that will give you clear answers. Asking the questions in the right way will allow you to clarify the binary response that the pendulum gives. You may have a complex issue that you are concerned about. But you need to ask the pendulum about this issue by dividing it into some simple questions. This way, you will find it easier to understand how the higher powers are trying to guide you. The yes or no system will not work when you ask the pendulum something too complex to be answered in that way.

Another alternative way to get answers from a pendulum is to draw a chart with different answers. For instance, you can make a pie chart with different sections starting with different outcomes. It could be divided into sections like yes, no, maybe, change the question, et cetera. The pendulum can then be held over the diagram to tell you what the answer is. If it moves toward "change question," you should rephrase your question in another way. Just make sure that you let the pendulum move of its own free will and don't manipulate its movement with your conscious or subconscious mind.

Pendulums and Affirmations

Positive affirmations help you to live better and attract all that you want in your life, so not everyone sees tangible results from their affirmation practice. The reason behind this failure is usually because the person doesn't believe in those affirmations. If you don't repeat your positive affirmations to yourself regularly and don't believe that it will all work out, you won't see success. Saying "I will become a millionaire" and believing in it is different. You have to believe your affirmations on a conscious and subconscious level for them to work.

Positive affirmations are statements that help you to overcome any negative thinking and believe in your ability to achieve everything you want.

They can help you in many ways:

- To quit smoking.
- To earn more money.
- To find love.
- To lose weight.
- To succeed in your career.
- To build good habits.
- To improve your personality.
- To travel to any destination you want.
- To get rid of bad habits.
- To achieve anything else that you want.

The affirmations you need in your life will depend on you. And they have the power to bring about the change that you need in yourself or your life, so there is no use in speaking out these positive affirmations if you don't believe in them. It is important that you remove any negative vibrations before you work on tapping into positive ones. Any residual negativity will get in the way of these positive affirmations and prevent them from working.

Pendulums are a great way of testing your beliefs and improving the impact that your subconscious has on your positive affirmations. There are many other uses for pendulums in your life, but one of the simplest yet most useful ways is to test if you believe in your affirmations. The answers your pendulum gives you will help you to realize what your subconscious believes.

The subconscious mind does not lie, and this means that your pendulum will not lie. This is because the answers given by a pendulum are a reflection of the subconscious mind. To test any affirmation, hold onto your pendulum with your dominant hand and say the affirmation out loud. For instance, you could say, "I am getting promoted at work." Now watch how your pendulum moves. Does it give you a yes, no, or maybe answer? If it moves in the motion to indicate a yes, you believe you will get a promotion. You subconsciously believe in this affirmation and are good to go. But if you get a no from the pendulum, it means you don't believe in it. If you get a maybe, it means that you want to believe in it but still doubt the possibility. When you don't get a yes, it means that you don't believe in your affirmation and the desired outcome. Testing this out with a pendulum is something that you need to use to your advantage. It will help you to learn more about your subconscious beliefs and allow you to work on them.

Before you check your affirmations with a pendulum, you have to check to see if the pendulum is working accurately. You can ask it basic questions that you know the answer to already. If the pendulum answers them correctly, you can get started. If your pendulum indicates that you do not believe in an affirmation, you can use it to make your subconscious trust in the affirmation. To do this, hold your pendulum and keep repeating the affirmation. Repeat the affirmation out loud till you see the pendulum give you a yes. The more you say it out loud and the better you convince yourself, the stronger the yes will be.

The reason that a pendulum changes its answer is that it is a reflection of your subconscious. When your subconscious beliefs change, so do the answers from the pendulum. You need to repeat your affirmations with the pendulum till it instantly gives you a yes, every time you repeat them. You may have a relapse and question yourself at times. When this happens, you can just practice this exercise with your pendulum again. It will help you to reaffirm and continue on.

Chapter 6: Finding Lost Objects with a Pendulum

One common use of pendulums is finding objects. Are you someone who constantly misplaces your reading glasses or keys? If so, you can depend on your pendulum to help you find them fast.

Pendulums can be used for locating objects in two ways:

1. Directional swing.

2. Asking yes or no questions.

You have to program your pendulum for the yes or no answering method, or if you are using directional swings. You need to confirm how you will be getting answers from your pendulum before you begin using it.

Now let's assume that you lost your reading glasses.

1. To begin, you have to confirm how you will be getting answers from your pendulum.

2. Now, imagine what your reading glasses look like. Keep the image of these glasses in your mind and focus on it. Keep imagining the glasses as you start searching for them.

3. First, ask the pendulum if it is the right time for you to be searching for the reading glasses. You can even ask if your reading glasses want to be found at that moment. Your pendulum will give you a yes or no answer. If you see a "no" movement, the glasses were probably lost for a reason. You should consider it from this perspective and put off the search for a while.

4. If you get a "yes" movement from the pendulum, you can continue looking for the glasses.

5. Now, ask the pendulum if your reading glasses are inside your house or anywhere else that you think you left them. If you get a yes, you can continue looking for them in your house or another location. If you get a no, you need to ask more questions to determine where the glasses have been misplaced.

6. Assuming you lost the glasses in your house or your office, you need to be more specific about the questions now. Ask the pendulum which room you lost them in. For instance, you could ask the pendulum if the glasses are in your bedroom. If you get a yes, then look for them in the bedroom. If you get a no, you have to ask the pendulum the same question while mentioning other rooms in your home.

7. If the pendulum says your glasses are in your bedroom, you should go to the bedroom. Stand at the door of your bedroom and ask the pendulum to show you the direction in which you should look. At this point, the pendulum should move in straight motions towards the direction of the glasses. If your reading glasses are on the right side of the room, the pendulum should move in a straight line toward the right.

8. You now have to move toward the direction in which your pendulum was swinging. As you move around the space, you can keep asking the pendulum questions to clarify where your glasses are. For instance, if you are standing near your bed, you can ask the pendulum if your glasses are below the

pillows or if they are under the bed. In this way, you can easily find the object you misplaced.

One thing to note is that any energetic barrier or obstruction between the object and you could cause trouble in locating the object. When you are looking for the object, the pendulum might move in circular motions instead of giving you accurate directional swings. This will indicate an energy obstruction or barrier. If so, you can move away from that space and to another corner and ask again. If the pendulum's movements remain confusing, you might be in the wrong space. The object you are looking for is probably somewhere else. In this case, you can repeat the process from the beginning and try to figure out what your pendulum is telling you.

If you are not in the space where you lost the object, you can draw a map to help you. Draw a map to scale and use the pendulum over the map. If you think you lost the object in your office, you can draw a rough plan of the office layout. Then use the pendulum in a similar way to look for the object.

Reasons why dowsing for lost objects may not work:

1. You are attached to an outcome. If you are unable to detach yourself from the outcome you are expecting, the dowsing will not be effective. You should not have a predisposed notion of where you want the pendulum to be pointing.

2. Thought-forms. If you have strong thoughts or beliefs about the object or a place, you create a thought-form. You think you already know where the object is, even when you don't. These thoughts in your mind prevent the pendulum from giving you the right location of the object. Instead, it will be inclined to point at the place where you think it is.

3. Someone else's energy of intention. If the object is hidden or your search is cursed by someone else, it will be difficult for you to find it. This is why you might find it very hard to use a pendulum to locate someone else's objects or treasures.

4. The free will of the person or item you seek. If you want to use pendulum dowsing to look for someone, you have to consider whether they want to be found in the first place. If that person or even if your pet doesn't want to be found, your effort may be fruitless.

5. Destiny. Sometimes you won't be able to find certain things because you are not meant to find them. You might have lost something because you were destined to lose it.

It is not easy for everyone to look for objects using dowsing. These factors may play into the process and prevent you from achieving the results you want. If you are always able to locate what you search for, you are indeed a lucky person.

Using a pendulum for finding things is helpful, but it is also a great way to bond with the pendulum. You get to practice using the pendulum, and you also build a stronger connection with it. This will make your future activities with the pendulum more effective and accurate. Your pendulum will be able to resonate with you a lot better.

Chapter 7: Pendulums for Divination and Magic

Divination is a way to gain insight from higher powers. When you use divination tools like pendulums, you can focus better and truly listen to the guidance provided by the spirits or divinity you are seeking answers from.

Your pendulum will act as a receiver and transmitter. It works in the same way that radios pick up unseen radio waves. When you ask your pendulum a question, your subconscious mind will respond and influence the pendulum's movements in your hand. Your outer body uses the pendulum to express what your innermost being already knows. It doesn't matter if you can't understand how pendulums and divination work. What matters is that you believe in it. Anyone can work with a pendulum. Albert Einstein was one of many famous people who used dowsing tools like pendulums. His explanation for it was more scientific and related to electromagnetism. Some other advocates of dowsing through history include Leonardo da Vinci, Robert Boyle, and General Patton.

Pendulums can be used for divination in different ways. You might be surprised by just how much you can learn from the yes or no answers of a pendulum. What is more important is being able to ask your questions in the right way.

Pendulums for Divination and Magic

To Find Lost Items

Pendulums are like dowsing rods that can point you in the direction of the item you have lost. They may even help you to find a person who is missing. In remote dowsing, you can use the pendulum over the map of an area or space. The pendulum will then help you to find your target.

With a Divination Board

A lot of people use pendulums in tandem with divination boards. The pendulum guides the user by pointing toward letters on the board and relays its message. The divination board can have numbers, alphabets, and words like yes, no, or maybe.

With Tarot Cards

If you practice the art of tarot reading, your pendulum can be used for picking out the right card. It can also be used for cleansing or charging the deck.

Finding Magical Sites

People believe that pendulums can be used for locating magical sites. These sites are used for practicing rituals or for carrying out other magical activities. The pendulum can act as a guide to direct the user toward or away from the wrong location.

Pendulums and Tarot

If you love using your pendulums, you are probably wondering if you can use them with other divination tools. Pendulums can easily be incorporated into the practice of tarot readings.

Tarot cards and pendulums are both conduits for your energy. When you conduct a tarot reading, your mind receives a message, and this message is revealed by the symbols that show up in your cards. This is how the universe delivers messages to you with tarot cards. Your pendulum will also work to unscramble this message and help you to understand the message's real meaning. With pendulums, the message is delivered by movements and not simply by the use of symbols. The symbols of every tarot card are known and understood by anyone who uses it. The meaning of the cards does not change. The movements of the pendulum mean different things for different people. You need to understand the motions of your pendulum before you use it during a tarot reading or any other activity. Every movement of your pendulum will give you a specific answer. This is why most witches say that it is important to program pendulums before using them. This means that you teach your pendulum to move a certain way for certain answers, so you could also communicate with the pendulum to learn how it moves by itself. This means that you ask the pendulum how it will move when it means to answer you in a certain way.

Pendulums to Enhance Tarot Readings

If tarot cards are your preferred divination tool, you can also benefit from the use of pendulums. Diving into the imagery of tarot to decipher all the different archetypes and symbols is a wonderful experience. You can dive deep and explore every revelation from the readings.

There is no harm in getting another confirmation on what you read from the tarot cards. If you doubt your neutrality or are just reading for yourself, there is no harm in adding pendulums to your divinatory tools.

Pendulums are a complementary tool with tarot cards. When you can't get a specific answer from the cards, or just want a clear-cut yes or no, it would be a lot more helpful to try adding a pendulum into the mix.

Using the Pendulum with Tarot

Here are ways that usually tend to work best when working with both these divination tools:

Pick a Deck to Work with on a Special Occasion or a Particular Day

First, take out all the decks you have available to you and lay them out on the table or any surface you prefer. Now take your pendulum and ask, "Can I use this deck to work with today?" Hold your pendulum over every deck as you ask this, and note whether the pendulum says yes or no. If you are not sure, you can ask more questions for clarity. When you are shopping for new decks, you can carry your pendulum with you to the shop. Just repeat the same process as you walk around exploring the different decks. Ask the pendulum if you should purchase a particular deck.

Picking Cards During a Tarot Reading

During a tarot reading, you can use a pendulum for picking out cards. Just shuffle your deck like you usually do and then spread them out. Now hold your pendulum up above the cards and start from one end of the spread. You can draw out a card when your pendulum swings toward a yes. To avoid confusion about which card is being indicated, make sure that the cards are spread out well. You can use the pendulum for confirmation as well when you need clarification. While picking out cards in this way, you should either predetermine the number you want to pick out, or you can continue using the pendulum till you reach the end of the spread. You can then lay out the cards picked by the pendulum and carry on with your tarot reading.

Using the Pendulum for Confirming a Tarot Reading

Once you finish a tarot reading, you can make a summary of all the insight that the cards gave you. You can then use a pendulum to confirm this message that you believe you have received from the cards. It will tell you if you understood what the cards were telling you or if you need to give it some more thought. If the pendulum swings toward a no, you should look at the cards from a different perspective.

Determine Which Cards Are More Significant in a Reading and Which Aren't

You can consult your pendulum when you feel stuck during a reading. It could be one for yourself or someone else, and you might be feeling like you can't read enough from the cards to get a clear answer. In this case, you can hold your pendulum over each card you picked and use it as a guide. Ask the pendulum any questions you need and pick out the ones that will give you more clarity during the reading.

Pick Out the Best Questions to Ask the Cards Before You Begin a Tarot Reading

Sometimes you may not be sure about what you want to ask the cards on a particular day. You might be trying to decide what the best question or the most useful one would be. In such cases, your pendulum could guide you. You can say your questions out loud one by one and ask the pendulum which one you should be asking the cards. You can also write each question down on some paper and hold the pendulum over the slips. If you still feel like you aren't getting the answer you need, you can ask the pendulum if you need to consider some other questions. If the pendulum's movement indicates a strong, positive answer, you should probably rethink the questions that you want to ask the tarot cards.

Using a pendulum with tarot cards is an effective way of connecting with your spirit guides, higher self, and even helps you to work on your intuitive abilities. A pendulum will give you some answers, but you need to trust your intuition to determine when you need to use it. One of the most important aspects of working with divination is that you keep an open mind. Go into it with the right mindset, and you will be amazed at the results.

Best Crystals for Tarot or Oracle Readings

1. Amethyst. This crystal is linked to spiritual development and psychic abilities. Most tarot readers keep this stone near while reading cards. It will help you to tap into your intuition. It will also help you to decipher the messages that come through your tarot readings.

2. Angelite. This stone will help you to invite any angels or spirits to your reading.

3. Selenite. This crystal is good for reading cards and for cleansing them. It will allow you to keep your space free from any psychic debris. Placing the selenite crystal over or underneath your deck of cards will help you cleanse them.

4. Black Tourmaline. This protective stone will keep you safe from any outside energies as you are at the peak of your psychic energy.

5. Rainbow Fluorite. This stone will bring mental clarity and help you remain focused on what you are doing. It will prevent your mind from wandering when you are doing a reading.

6. Clear Quartz. This is the purest quartz stone and can amplify the intention of receiving guidance during your tarot reading. Having this crystal near during tarot journaling allows clear thoughts and communication with the cards.

7. Smoky Quartz. It helps to keep you grounded and will allow you to connect to the earth's energy.

8. Rose Quartz. This crystal will remind you to be compassionate and heart-centered as you read your cards. It is a great crystal to use during love readings. This crystal can channel positive energy into a reading.

9. Citrine. Citrine will allow you to identify any blockage caused by fear or other negative feelings. It is difficult to do a successful reading when such blockages are present. This stone enhances self-confidence and will help you to embrace courage. It also promotes successful outcomes from readings.

10. Labradorite. This stone has the power to enhance your intuitive ability during a tarot reading.

11. Jade. This stone will allow unity between the tarot cards and the tarot card reader. It is the stone of love and inner truth.

12. Obsidian. This stone is important for empaths as it can keep them grounded and help them repel the energetic junk from others, so it is important to pay attention to the reaction this stone has with you to see if it suits you or is too grounding.

Tarot Cards and Their Related Gemstones

Every tarot card in your deck can be linked to a gemstone. Using these during your tarot reading session will allow a better reading.

- **The Fool.** The meaning behind this card is innocence, honesty, hope, or a need for a fresh start. The related gemstone is agate.

- **The Magician.** The meaning behind this card is skillful, confident, straightforward, and resourceful. The related gemstone is fire opal.

- **The High Priestess.** The meaning behind this card is intuitive, frank, and spiritually aware. The related gemstone is moonstone.

- **The Empress.** The meaning behind this card is feminine energy, nurturer, and fertility. The related gemstone is peridot.

- **The Emperor.** The meaning behind this card is organized leadership, authority, and virility. The related gemstone is ruby.

- **The Hierophant.** The meaning behind this card is tradition, a strong foundation, authority, and community. The related gemstone is topaz.

- **The Lovers.** The meaning behind this card is equality, intimacy, and the release of yin and yang. The related gemstone is rose quartz.

- **The Chariot.** The meaning behind this card is goal-oriented, willpower, and achieving goals. The related gemstone is carnelian.

- **Strength.** The meaning behind this card is desire, fierceness, power, and courage. The related gemstone is tiger's eye.

- **The Hermit.** The meaning behind this card is seclusion, meditation, wisdom, and looking at the bigger picture. The related gemstone is bloodstone.

- **The Wheel of Fortune.** The meaning behind this card is happiness, prosperity, good luck, and triumph. The related gemstone is aventurine.

- **Justice.** The meaning behind this card is integrity, fairness, and honesty. The related gemstone is garnet.

- **The Hanged Man.** The meaning behind this card is patience, pause, temporary halt, and adaptation. The related gemstone is aquamarine.

- **Death.** The meaning behind this card is change, second chances, endings, and transition. The related gemstone is obsidian.

- **Temperance.** The meaning behind this card is tranquility, development, moderation, and balance. The related gemstone is amethyst.

- **The Devil.** The meaning behind this card is obstacles, traps, oppression, and addiction. The related gemstone is hematite.

- **The Tower.** The meaning behind this card is instability, life-changing events, and conflict. The related gemstone is kyanite.

- **The Star.** The meaning behind this card is simplicity, inspiration, support, and expectations. The related gemstone is sugilite.

- **The Moon.** The meaning behind this card is secrets, intuition, instinct, and self-examination. The related gemstone is pearl.

- **The Sun.** The meaning behind this card is happiness, radiance, accomplishments, and vitality. The related gemstone is sunstone.

- **Judgement.** The meaning behind this card is balance, forgiveness, perception, and re-evaluation. The related gemstone is malachite.

- **The World.** The meaning behind this card is successful outcomes, conclusions, and accomplished goals. The related gemstone is fluorite.

Pendulums and Witchcraft

Traditionally, witchcraft was the act of invocation of supernatural powers to control events or people. The practice of witchcraft usually involved magic or sorcery of some kind. Even though witchcraft is defined differently in various cultures and through different centuries, it has been practiced since ancient times. Wicca is more of a modern pagan religion and is called pagan witchcraft. Its origins exist in pre-Christian religions. The practices involved in both witchcraft and Wicca vary for different places and people. One common factor is that both traditional witches and Wiccans often use pendulums for their practices.

Pendulums are used in many ways in witchcraft and Wicca. Here are some ways that witches use pendulums:

To Unveil the Future

One of the most common uses of pendulums is asking about the future. You can ask the pendulum some simple questions that allow it to give you some yes or no answers. If the pendulum gives you the answers in the predetermined motions that you know and are aware of, then you know that there is someone answering your questions. You should also try to figure out whom you are talking to because it is possible that it might be a deceptive entity like a demon or larvae. There might be some spirits that pretend to be someone else. After you finish a session, you have to say thank you.

With Ouija Boards

You can use your pendulum with a Ouija board as well. Just place the board on some flat surface and hold your pendulum in your dominant hand. Extend your hand so that the pendulum is hovering a few inches above the Ouija board. Now ask your pendulum questions and watch where it points its swings. When the pendulum is moving vertically, it will hover over the number or letter it wants to indicate. You can also use the pendulum to ask questions in a similar way while holding it over some object or photo. Mediums and dowsers use pendulums to check if there are any negative energies or presences in a place too. You can also use the pendulum to find a good place for setting up an altar. You have to remember to respect the entity that answers you and not tire them out or act too persistently. Having an angry entity in your space will only cause harm.

For Health Diagnosis

A pendulum can also be used for checking the body for illness or negative energy. You can simply hold the pendulum over your body or someone else's and ask it where the problem lies. The pendulum then directs its motion to tell you where you need healing.

To Find a Place Appropriate for a Ritual

When witches want to perform a ritual outside, they often turn to the pendulum for guidance. It helps them to find the right spot to perform any ritual. While searching for a place, the pendulum might start moving erratically. If so, it might mean that the spot has spirits or dead bodies, and it is not suitable. You should try sensing the energy around a place and see if you feel comfortable there. If you feel any sensation that makes you uncomfortable, you should leave and look for another place.

To Look for Someone or Something

Witches also use pendulums to look for things or people. You can physically use the pendulum in a space to look for a lost object. It can also be used over a map to determine where the lost or hidden person or object is.

For Guidance During Spells

When a witch is not sure about the ingredients to use during a spell, they may use a pendulum for guidance. Using a pendulum over a calendar or watch can also help to figure out the best time for casting a spell as well.

Enhance Your Intuition with a Pendulum

Every time you practice using your pendulum, you enhance your intuition a little more. You widen your path—in a manner of speaking. Imagine yourself walking through a beautiful garden as you think about some important things. While you wander through the garden, you create a path. The more you wander in the garden, the wider the path gets. It becomes a lot simpler for you to traverse the garden, and you have easier access to the fruits growing there.

With your pendulum, you widen the path that leads you to your higher self. This path is similar to a beautiful garden that is filled with greenery and fruit-laden trees. To access these fruits in the garden, you need to pay attention and find your way in. Similarly, when you want to access your higher self, you have to work on it.

You should practice using your pendulum often and hone your intuitive abilities.

The more you ignore this practice, the harder it is for you to achieve what you seek. Every time you practice with your pendulum and connect to your higher self, the deeper you go inside the path. This is something that holds true for any spiritual or intuitive practice. As you keep using your pendulum, you get better at other intuitive activities like tarot reading, meditation, psychic vision, et cetera.

Find Your Resonant Color with Your Pendulum

Color is electromagnetic energy, and every color you see has different wavelengths. Colors can affect your mental focus, emotional state, physical health, and inner balance. For many decades, research has been conducted to understand the intentional use of color for various applications.

Chromotherapy or color therapy is another kind of energy healing that you may have heard of. The principles behind chromotherapy state that each person has one color that their true self resonates with. This color is their resonant color, and it may differ from one person to another. Yet another use of pendulums is discovering the resonant color of a person. Once you begin using pendulums, you can use yours to determine your resonant color too.

To do this, you need some pens in eight different colors and a white piece of paper. You also need your pendulum. This pendulum should be programmed to give you yes or no answers.

Before you start, state the source of answers from your pendulum. It is also better to use a pendulum of a neutral color for this exercise. You can choose stones like hematite, black onyx, clear quartz, or black obsidian. Relax your mind and body by meditating for a while before you start.

Now take that white piece of paper and write your name once with each of the different colored pens. As you move on to the next color, leave a little space before writing your name again. If you don't want to write your name on the paper with pens, you can also print it out from your computer. Just choose the primary colors to write your name eight times in eight different colors. Once you have this paper, place it on a flat surface in front of you. Hold your pendulum in your dominant hand and let it hover an inch or two above each color. Over each color, ask the pendulum if that is your resonant color. Patiently wait for the pendulum to give you answers. Note down the reactions of the pendulum over each color. The color that produces the most intense yes movement from your pendulum is your resonant color.

You might find that your resonant color is not the color that you usually claim as your favorite. You can still like wearing clothes of your favorite color, but knowing your resonant color has its own use. You can use this resonant color to enhance your vibrational energy. The more you surround yourself with this resonant color, the better it is for you. You could paint your walls in that color or wear more clothes in that shade. It doesn't mean that you have to close off any other colors from your life. Each color has its own impact on a person's life. But the resonant color is the one that is most positively impactful. You can even use your pendulum to determine what colors are lacking in your life and that you need to include more of. When your pendulum gives you an answer for all these questions, you can ask further questions to determine the answer's accuracy.

Use Your Pendulum for Understanding Synchronistic Events

On certain days, you may feel like some random things happen one after the other and that they mean something. While these synchronistic events may truly be random and a coincidence at times, they may also have a deeper significance. The universe works in many ways to send us messages in our life. These events are a way in which the universe sends you protective or healing messages. When you decode these messages, you can gain insight into some important things.

The universe can use anything as a sign, from a song to a penny on the pavement. When you notice something out of the ordinary, and it grabs your attention, try to think about it a little more as it may mean something. It could be a part of a puzzle and have more meaning than you would otherwise give it credit for. You can use your pendulum to contemplate the meaning of such events in your life.

Program your pendulum and ask some questions that will give you clarity, such as:

1. "Are the events that happened today connected?"

2. "Am I supposed to look deeper into the significance of these events?"

3. "Is the universe trying to communicate with me?"

4. "Do these events mean ...?"

5. "Are these events supposed to enlighten me about something?"

As you ask these questions, you can try to get answers from the pendulum to figure out what the synchronized events mean.

Chapter 8: Crystal Pendulum Properties

Pendulums can be used for doing a great number of things. These pendulums can be made of different materials, and crystals are among the most common ones that people like using. You need to understand that each crystal has its own use and will be better suited to different purposes.

Alternative and complementary medicine has picked up popularity in recent years. This includes yoga, acupuncture, and crystal healing. Before you begin using crystal pendulums for healing, it will help you to learn a little more about crystal healing.

Crystals have always held an attraction because of their beautiful colors and forms. But you will also be drawn to them because of their properties. Each crystal is different, and you will get to know their uses, to help heal the body, mind, and soul. They can be used for promoting positive energy flow through the body and getting rid of any energy that could harm you.

Crystal healing is an ancient practice that borrows philosophies from Buddhism and Hinduism. Although there is no scientific evidence to support crystal healing, it continues to be practiced in present times. People are naturally drawn to crystals for their beauty, but the possible benefits of using them for healing hold another attraction.

Reflection, mindfulness, and acceptance play a key role in crystal healing. A lot of research has shown that the mind has healing power. While using crystal pendulums, you will be using this power from your mind as well. Even if you aren't sure about the benefits of crystals, keep an open mind. Trying it out will allow you to explore beyond what you know.

Learning about the properties of each crystal will help you to choose one that is best suited to your purposes. When you select the right crystal pendulum, you will be able to make the most of it, and its powers are magnified. As you hold up the right pendulum, you will feel a connection to it in the form of a sign like a tingling sensation. Once you surrender to your pendulum, it will guide you to the best of its ability. There are endless possibilities with pendulums. If you are ready to pick the right pendulum, learning about the properties of different crystals will help you to invest in one that aligns with your purpose.

Clear Crystal Pendulum

This crystal is linked to the crown chakra and all the elements. It is a colorless or white crystal that is associated with the Sun. It is called the master healer and can amplify your energy and thoughts. Clear crystal also has the ability to amplify the properties of any other crystal you use. It can get rid of all kinds of negative energy and neutralize background radiation like electromagnetic smog. A clear quartz pendulum will balance and revitalize mental, physical, spiritual, and emotional planes. It works as a cleanser for the soul and your physical body. You can use it to connect your mind with the physical dimension. It can also cleanse and enhance your organs. More importantly, you can use a clear quartz pendulum to enhance your psychic abilities. It can unlock memory and improve your ability to concentrate. It also stimulates your immune system and will bring balance back to your body. If you want to restore balance in all your chakras, you can choose a clear quartz crystal.

Amethyst Crystal Pendulum

Amethyst is also called nature's tranquilizer. A pendulum made of this crystal will be an extremely effective healer. It can heal your mind, body, and soul. It is often used for addressing issues like stress, insomnia, and fibromyalgia. The stone is said to bring courage and strength to the wearer. The soothing property of amethyst helps release creativity. Amethyst also promotes tranquility, and this is helpful for those suffering from mood disorders or addictions.

Aqua Aura Crystal Pendulum

If you want to use a crystal for meditation and raise the frequency of your energy, an aqua aura crystal pendulum would be appropriate. This crystal also activates the energy of other crystals and minerals. It is used for addressing issues like anxiety, depression, and promotes overall well-being.

Bloodstone Crystal Pendulum

This crystal has detoxifying and purifying properties. You can use it to boost the immune system and to protect your body from illness. It is also great for treating ailments related to the kidneys, liver, and bladder. If you suffer from anemia, this is the best crystal for healing.

Aventurine Crystal Pendulum

If you have struggled with weight loss, you can use aventurine to stimulate your metabolism. It will help to lower cholesterol levels and balance blood pressure. This crystal can also be used for treating migraines, skin breakouts, and allergies.

Citrine Crystal Pendulum

This crystal is called the "success stone" and is said to help to manifest everything you want in life. It is also used for increasing energy levels. You can use it for treating ailments of the thyroid. It is also good for dealing with chronic fatigue syndrome.

Labradorite Crystal Pendulum

Labradorite is used for purifying energy. It can help to clear any negative energy and open up all blocked chakras. You can use it for filtering your thoughts and calming your mind when it is overactive. It also helps to heal ailments related to the lungs, such as respiratory issues or the common cold.

Lapis Lazuli Crystal Pendulum

This crystal will help you meditate with more depth. It can enhance your insight and is a cleansing stone. Lapis lazuli is also great for people who have rage or anger issues. It can boost your immune system and lower blood pressure. It is also good for alleviating insomnia and migraine issues.

Pyrite Crystal Pendulum

Pyrite is a powerful protective crystal. It is also called "fool's gold." You can use it for protection from negative energy and also from any pollutants in the environment. It is useful in treating lung ailments or infective diseases.

Rose Quartz Crystal Pendulum

It is a pink crystal that is linked to love. This crystal has a very gentle and soothing energy that can calm you when you are agitated. Wearing this pendulum around your neck and keeping it close to your heart makes it even more effective. It will promote self-love and help you heal from any emotional wounds. This crystal will also attract positive relationships in your life. If you are struggling with inner peace or loneliness, this might be the right pendulum for you.

Turquoise Crystal Pendulum

Turquoise is a beautiful blue stone that is considered a good luck charm that balances emotions and allows spiritual grounding. This stone can heal the body, mind, and soul. While dealing with ailments of the immune, respiratory or skeletal system, turquoise pendulums would be the right choice.

Jasper Crystal Pendulum

Jasper is also called the supreme nurturer. It will absorb any negative vibes and protect the wearer. It promotes confidence and courage while allowing quick thinking. This, in turn, will allow the wearer to deal much better when faced with challenging issues. This empowering stone alleviates stress and helps the wearer deal with stressful situations instead of avoiding them.

Obsidian Crystal Pendulum

Obsidian is one of the most protective stones to choose for your pendulum. It acts as a shield against any negativity, emotional or physical. Wearing this stone will help to remove any emotional blockage and promote more compassion and clarity. Obsidian is generally used for detoxification of the body and aids in digestion. It may also help alleviate pain like that from cramps.

Tiger's Eye Crystal Pendulum

A tiger's eye is a golden stone that gives the wearer a boost of power and motivation. It helps to remove any self-doubt from the mind and alleviates feelings of anxiety or fear. This stone can help the wearer achieve balance and harmony, so they can make better decisions. It is also helpful while dealing with matters of the heart.

Moonstone Crystal Pendulum

Moonstones are usually clear, white, or rainbow-colored. This beautiful stone helps to achieve balance and is suitable for females. In ancient times, moonstone was carried as a protective talisman by travelers. Wearing a moonstone pendulum can alleviate depression and anxiety. It is also a good stone for those who suffer from insomnia. According to some, moonstone can be used for healing ailments that are prone during childhood or old age.

Sapphire Crystal Pendulum

Sapphire is a blue stone that is associated with royalty and wisdom. It attracts happiness, prosperity, and peace. It is also said to promote better intuitive abilities. When it comes to physical health, a sapphire will help to heal ailments related to the blood, cells, and eyes. It is also good for treating insomnia and depression.

Ruby Crystal Pendulum

Ruby is an attractive red stone that restores energy and vitality in the wearer. It is linked to higher intellect and better sensuality. This stone can promote self-awareness. There are records of this stone being used to detoxify the blood and improve circulatory health dating back to ancient times.

Garnet Crystal Pendulum

The red hues of garnet are considered to be energizing. The energizing property aids in healing faster. By wearing a garnet pendulum, the entire body is revitalized, and it boosts the immune system. Both emotional and physical well-being are promoted. Garnet is also believed to be a protective stone that can protect a person from bad karma and evil. It is optimal to wear this pendulum around the neck so it can stay near the heart.

Amber Crystal Pendulum

Amber crystals are usually yellow, red, or brown in color. A pendulum of this crystal will aid in alleviating stress and headaches. It also promotes self-expression in the wearer. Amber is a purification stone used for cleansing and helps remove illnesses from within the body. Wearing this stone alleviates pain, and promotes healing in the person.

Citrine Crystal Pendulum

Citrine is considered a manifestation stone and is also a staple for promoting creativity. The stone is a vibrant yellow and should have good clarity. It is linked to the sacral chakra in the body. A citrine pendulum will infuse positive energy in the wearer and increase emotional well-being. It is also good for managing inflammation and pain. Citrine is believed to help heal digestive ailments and liver problems.

Aquamarine Crystal Pendulum

Aquamarine is the color of the ocean and is probably one of the more beautiful crystals you can choose for your pendulum. This stone has a lot of traditional beliefs associated with it. Sailors carried it with them at sea for luck. A lot of people still use this stone for protection. It is also believed that aquamarine can help the wearer cope better during a time of grieving. The stone promotes healing and can bring happiness. It is also used for meditation. Aquamarine pendulums will help to target ailments of the eyes, digestive system, and teeth.

Benefits of Crystal Pendulums

If you choose to use crystal pendulums, you will be able to tap into various benefits associated with them. Crystals have been used for healing the mind, body, and spirit for centuries. Since they are taken from the earth, they are connected to its healing energy. When you use or carry a crystal pendulum, you will be able to tap into its energy and properties. Many benefits are associated with crystal pendulums.

Energy Boost

Everyone feels tired or fatigued at some point. Anytime you feel like you are running low on energy, you can turn toward a particular crystal for a boost. For instance, bloodstone is great for energizing and for increasing your drive. This crystal will help you overcome lethargy, get rid of any negative thoughts, and feel enthusiastic about your tasks. This particular stone was used in amulets in ancient times. It was believed that bloodstone could promote blood circulation by purifying blood. Other red stones like ruby also have a similar energizing effect.

Enhanced Creativity

Have you ever felt like you have a creative block? This is when you feel uninspired or are experiencing burnout. At this point, your creative channels are likely blocked. Crystals can help to unblock these channels and enhance your creative abilities again. The vibrant orange carnelian crystal is one of the most effective stones for this purpose. It will make you more enthusiastic and help you work towards achieving your goals. This stone promotes vitality and will make you more active.

Mental Clarity and Optimal Health

Silica forms the quartz crystals that you obtain from the earth. When you come in contact with silica, it brings energy together. Crystals improve your health and encourage healing when you are ill. You can use your crystals to balance your mind and body. They raise your vibrations and bring more mental clarity. They also help you to express yourself and release any emotional buildup.

Relief from Stress or Anxiety

Stress and anxiety are a part of all our lives. Most people suffer from some kind of anxiety disorder these days. This is another area where crystals will help you. Various crystals have a stress-relieving effect and bring peace to the minds of the users. Amethyst and Celestite are some crystals that are good for battling anxiety. Once you begin using these, you will realize how much easier it is to get a good night's sleep or work without feeling stressed out.

Bring Abundance and Prosperity

Certain crystals are effective in attracting abundance and prosperity. Citrine, for instance, will help you control your spending and manage your finances better. Many people believe that this stone helps to ensure that there is always more money coming into your wallet than going out of it. Malachite is another crystal that brings luck when the carrier is making business deals or handling any financial matters. A stone-like green Peridot will help you take advantage of any financial opportunity that comes your way.

Better Career

You can also use crystals for improving career prospects. Crystal pendulums can help you choose the right career path. They can also guide you while making decisions during the course of your career. Bloodstone will help you work through projects that might be stuck. Obsidian may help to run things smoothly. Serpentine will help you adjust to any new transitions.

Cultivate Love

Rose quartz is one of the most commonly used crystals in the world and is used for cultivating love. Crystals like this one will help to open the heart and make the person more open to receiving and giving love. You can use them to guide you while making decisions related to your relationships. They will also help you recover from emotional wounds.

How to Care for Your Crystals

Cleansing

Cleansing the crystal allows you to purify it and honor its significance. When you cleanse your crystals, you acknowledge the path they took before coming into your hands.

The purpose of cleansing crystals is to bring them back to their purest and clearest state. When they pass through different hands or are carried through different places, they absorb the energy that comes into contact with them, which is why it's important to cleanse them. If you use a crystal without cleansing it, you will be subjecting yourself to these energies as well. Think of it as picking up the dirt all around it and needing a wash.

Every impurity or negative energy that your crystal comes in contact with will be felt when you hold or use it without cleansing. It is important to have a clear mind during the process of purification. Your intentions and mind need to have clarity. You can use bells or sage to clear the room where you will be cleansing the crystal. Saying a mantra will be helpful as well. The process of cleansing is a ritual, so you need to go about it in a peaceful and vigilant manner. The various methods of cleansing have been explained in detail in a previous section of this book. You can use anything from moonlight bathing to smudging for cleansing your crystals.

When to Clear

Every crystal should be cleared off old energies as soon as you acquire them. Crystals also keep absorbing energy as you use them. You need to clear and recharge your crystals from time to time in between uses. At times, you will notice that your crystal feels dull or heavy. This usually means that your crystal needs a cleansing and recharging session.

When you use your crystal for some intense work like healing an illness, you should remember to cleanse it. Clearing the crystal before using it again will allow it to work more effectively. The more often you work with crystals, the deeper your connection gets with them. You have to acknowledge your crystals as a blessing and honor them in the way they deserve. If you take care of your crystals, they will work even better for you. At some point, you may even feel like a crystal has served its purpose for you and has to be gifted to someone else who will benefit from it. Listen to your intuition and the messages your crystals send you.

How to Store Your Crystals

When you carry or store your crystals, you have to be mindful about keeping them in a way that will prevent any damage. Rough stones should be kept separated from any tumbled stones. You have to store your crystals in a way that they don't get scratched or chipped.

You should also keep hard stones separately from soft stones. The hard stones may damage the softer ones. Minerals like mica and talc are on the soft end of the Mohs Hardness Scale. These are so weak that it is difficult to even store them together. Selenite, alabaster, and desert rose are all on soft stones. These should be kept dry and can disintegrate easily if scratched with hard stones. You can use a soft cloth to rub these crystals clean. Hard stones on the other end of the scale can even scratch glass. You can use an eyeglass cloth to clean these. Any dust or debris can be cleared by bathing such stones in saltwater.

If you use large crystals, keep them on a shelf or anywhere they won't be in contact with anything that can damage them. The biggest threat to most of your crystals is another crystal. For the smaller ones that you carry, use a silk or satin pouch. Treating your crystals with care will allow them to stay pure and effective. When you travel with more than one crystal, wrap each one individually. The roughly finished ones should not come in contact with each other as the sharpness may damage that which is touched by it. You can use anything like tissue paper to wrap the crystals.

Things to remember:

- Certain crystals will fade when kept under direct sunlight. This includes citrine, amethyst, opal, fluorite, topaz, aquamarine, and kunzite. Moonlight cleansing is better for such stones.

- Take time to do some research before using any crystal. It is easy to look up information on anything on the Internet or in a book. You should use the right crystals for the right purpose and cleanse and charge them in the most suitable way.

- Mistakes happen. You might end up damaging or breaking a crystal even if you are careful, but it is not something to fret too much about. You might still be able to use it. It might also be a sign that you should not be using that crystal.

Chapter 9: Using Pendulums for Physical Healing

Pendulums can be a handy tool when you conduct a physical healing session. This is something that a lot of holistic healers do and recommend as well. While a pendulum will not treat an ailment, it will help to diagnose and is useful in similar ways. They can be used in quite a few ways when it comes to physical healing. Pendulums are a complementary form of holistic healing. Even if you aren't a practicing healer, you can take some steps toward becoming one after learning more about this.

As you know, a pendulum is a powerful tool. This can be used to find things, predict something, and diagnose illnesses. A pendulum can be used to detect an illness in the body and can even heal to a certain extent, depending on the properties of the crystal being used. How you can do this will be explained next.

First, you have to understand that pendulums have to be used in the right way for you to get accurate results. Different crystal pendulums will be useful in detecting different ailments. If you read the section on crystal properties earlier in the book, you will get a better idea about the illnesses each specific crystal is linked to. Depending on the region of the body the crystal is linked with, you will be able to detect and heal using dowsing. Some pendulums that are better for multiples purposes include rock crystal, bloodstone, and moss agate. You can use a universal pendulum like these and use specific pendulums depending on the illness you think you have.

Detect Illness Using a Pendulum

1. Are you using the pendulum for yourself or someone else? Accordingly, hold the pendulum over the body and then ask it any question you have. For instance, if you feel like there is a tumor in the body, you can use a Shungite pendulum and ask it to help you detect the tumor's location. Or you could just ask it if you have a tumor at all. Similarly, you need to use the crystal associated with the illness you wish to diagnose or heal. You can use the pendulum for getting answers to anything that you have in mind. Remember, this is not a replacement for conventional medicine, see a doctor if you are worried you may have a tumor.

2. Now, once you have asked the question, start moving the pendulum over the body. Slowly let it wander over every possible region in the body. It is important to take your time while doing this because the pendulum will need time to react when it detects any ailment.

3. When the pendulum is held over an area that needs to be healed, it will usually start vibrating. The pendulum's vibration may indicate an illness that has already manifested itself, or it may be telling you that there is an energy block that could lead to a problem. You have to pay attention to the subtle movements of the pendulum to tell when it is reacting.

4. You will notice that the pendulum normally moves in a swinging motion when it is over parts of the body that have no issues. If there is an illness in a particular part, the pendulum will start moving in circles instead of continuing the back-and-forth motion.

5. If you notice this change of movement over any part of the body, focus on that spot. Move the pendulum over that part thoroughly to understand where the illness might have spread. It is important to be slow while doing this. Repeatedly ask the pendulum if there is an illness present and confirm whether you are guessing the right illness.

6. When you do this a few times, you will get an answer to your question. After detecting the problematic region with your pendulum, you can start taking steps for healing. While some pendulums are just used for detection, others will help you to heal illness as well.

Now you know how to detect an illness with a pendulum. What do you do when you have diagnosed a problem? The next step is to heal, and this is another way you can use a pendulum, but it is important to know that a pendulum cannot be the sole instrument of healing. It is usually only one aspect of treatment, and you need to take any necessary steps to make sure that the illness has been removed from your body or that of the person you are healing.

Healing with a Pendulum

1. If you follow the steps mentioned above, you can use your pendulum to detect the region in the body with an illness. Once you detect this issue, you have to work on healing.

2. Use the appropriate pendulum and ask it to help you heal the illness. Hold the pendulum over the problematic region and ask the pendulum to eliminate any negative energy that may have accumulated there. There might be a blockage, and you should ask it to release that blockage so there can be a free flow of healthy energy. Ask the pendulum to send healing energy into that problematic part of the body. As you do this, use the power of visualization to imagine the pendulum healing that area.

3. Hold the pendulum over that place and slowly keep moving it around the area that the illness was detected. Keep your focus on visualizing how the illness can be eradicated from the body.

4. Take at least ten minutes to hold the pendulum over that ailing area. You could also keep moving the pendulum over the entire body if you think it will help. Stop after ten minutes and then repeat the process. Keep doing this and using your strength for it until you think you have done as much as you can as far as healing that area is concerned.

5. The pendulum should be used over the problematic region even during the remission period. Keep repeating this healing process until you think that the body is completely healed.

When the pendulum starts vibrating over the problematic region, the vibrations can enter the field of that person's aura, and the pendulum can share healing energy to the ailing region. Your pendulum will help you to heal on an energy level. It can help you give the body a lot of healing energy to heal itself faster. The positive energy from the pendulum is absorbed by the ailing region and is used for healing.

When you want to heal a physical ailment in the body, you should also be taking other steps like eating a healthy diet and following the directions given by your doctor. Other alternative treatments that can be used with pendulum healing include aromatherapy.

Pendulums for Healing

Some other uses for pendulums include:

1. Grounding.

2. Aura cleansing.

3. Chakra healing.

4. Picking crystals for healing.

5. Chakra balancing.

Grounding

Before you carry out other forms of therapy, you have to make sure that you or the person you are healing is grounded. If you are not grounded, there can be some unpleasant symptoms that manifest in the body.

• First, you should ask the person to lie down on their back on a flat surface. Make sure they are comfortable before you begin.

• Now, ask the light for the highest guidance for yourself and the person you are healing.

• Connect to the heart of the person you want to heal. For this, you have to hold a pendulum over the heart area. Keep a firm grasp over the pendulum and remain calm as you do this. As you hover over the heart region with the pendulum, ask it to help you link to the heart. You will see that the pendulum continues swinging as it links you to the heart and suddenly stops once the link has been built. If it doesn't stop, it may just move in a yes motion that signifies that the task is complete.

• Now move toward the person's feet and slowly move about 5 inches past their feet. Remain in line with their body. Now ask the pendulum if the person is grounded. The pendulum will move in a yes or no motion. If it swings in a no motion, you need to work more on the grounding process. If you get a positive answer, then you can move on with the next steps to treat the illness.

- If the pendulum indicates that the person is not grounded, then you need to work on grounding a little longer. Stand a few inches away from the feet, as mentioned before, and hold the pendulum. Now request your pendulum to ground the person. Keep doing this till the pendulum gives you an indication that the person is grounded. It will either move in a circular motion or a movement that means yes.

- When the pendulum indicates that the client is grounded, you should ask the pendulum again to confirm that the grounding is complete. If you still don't get a yes response, you will have to repeat the whole process again. If you get an affirmative answer, you should thank the pendulum and move on with the healing session.

Aura Cleansing

Each person has an energy field surrounding them, and this is known as their aura. This auric energy field is affected by everything that happens in a person's life. It might be some big event, or it might be something small. Arguing with someone will affect your mental wellbeing, and so will bumping into someone you don't like. All these events in your life leave a dent in the auric field. There is an even bigger impact from events that leave you significantly traumatized.

If you suffer damage or there is an imbalance in the layers of your aura, it may make you susceptible to illness or psychic attacks. It will also make your auric field easily absorb negative energy from around you. This is why it is important for your aura to be balanced and free from any damage.

For this, you can use your pendulum and your hands.

- Similar to how you work on chakras, you will be holding the pendulum in your dominant hand and move the free hand over your body.

- First, you have to place your hands a few inches above your body or that of the person whose aura you want to cleanse.

- Now, slowly move your hand over their body. First, go over the front of their body and then down their sides. As you do this, come back to the head first, and move downwards toward their feet.

- You will be sensing the energy of their aura while doing this aura scan. You will be able to feel certain changes in the energy field as you move your hands around.

- While you move your free hand over the body, you must keep following it with the hand holding the pendulum. When you can sense an energy change with your hands, you should also see some change in your pendulum's movement. This will confirm what your aura scan is telling your hand.

- If there is no dent in your aura and everything is in balance, you will get a springy sensation. But if there is an imbalance, you might be able to feel a dip in the aura. This dip might feel different in different places. You may experience a tingly sensation in your palm or maybe some heat or cold. There can be other ways in which you experience these dips in the auric field. Just trust your intuition and take note of the places where you feel the dips.

- After you have gone through this process, you can keep your pendulum aside. Now call to the light and ask for its assistance. Place both your hands hovering over the top of your head and slowly move downwards toward the feet. Do this in a stroking or pulling motion. Keep repeating this about ten times.

- After this, you should move your hands over the regions where you felt a dip in the aura. Try feeling those dips again. At this point, you should not be able to differentiate the energy in these areas from that in others. If you still feel the dips, you should repeat the previous steps. At the very least, you should be able to notice a positive change in a few parts. When the trauma is severe, or the dent in your aura is too deep, it might take a little extra work to bring balance back.

- Once you have finished the process of cleansing the aura, you should express gratitude to the light again. After the process is complete, you should check again to see if the person is grounded.

- Most people don't notice when their aura is affected in any way, but they should feel a little better or different after an aura cleanse.

In this way, you can use pendulums for healing the aura.

Unblock the Chakras

- The person has to be lying down in a comfortable position in the same way as mentioned in the grounding process.

- Now, take your pendulum and hold it a little above the body. Slowly move it across all the chakra points in the body. As you pass each point, ask the pendulum if that particular chakra is blocked. Take time to observe the response from the pendulum. Does the pendulum say yes or no? Repeat this process over every chakra point individually. Keep noting down the responses from the pendulum.

- When you move the pendulums over the chakra points, start from the top and go sequentially to the lowest chakra. Start at the crown chakra and move down until you reach the root chakra. Going in this order is important so that you do not cause any disruption in the energy flow. Chakras are present in the front and the back, so you need to ask the pendulum about each one. The root and crown chakras are the only ones not present in the back. While going over the back chakras, you can ask the person to turn over and lie on their stomach. But if they are not comfortable doing so, you can continue in the same position. Sometimes, asking the person to move can be disruptive to the process.

• After you have checked through all the chakras, you will know if there is an energy blockage in any. After identifying the chakra blockages, you can start working on chakra balancing. As you do this, you have to keep ensuring that the person is grounded.

Balance the Chakras

• While the subject is lying down comfortably, hold the pendulum of your choice in your dominant hand. Use your free hand to hover a few inches over the crown chakra. At this point, you don't need to make any requests to your pendulum. The pendulum should be swinging in circular motions by itself. Notice if the pendulum is moving in a clockwise or anti-clockwise direction. Keep your free palm hovering over the crown chakra for a couple of minutes as you observe the swing of the pendulum.

• If you see that the pendulum is not swinging, you can ask for help from the light. Ask it to start the swinging motion of your pendulum. You will soon see that your request is granted.

• Once your pendulum has started swinging over the crown chakra, you can move forward to the chakra below it. The pendulum should now start moving in the opposite direction. If it was swinging clockwise over the crown chakra, it should be swinging anti-clockwise over the third eye chakra. Similarly, the pendulum movements have to be alternating as they move over every chakra one by one.

- If you see that the pendulum is moving in the same direction as it was moving over the previous chakra or if there is any other restriction in its movement, it indicates an imbalance or blockage in that chakra.

- Move over every chakra to observe the movements of the pendulum. After you have reached the root chakra, use the pendulum to check if the person is grounded. Then thank the light or higher powers for helping you through the process.

- Once the person sits back up after the session, you should offer them some water. Give them the chance to talk about their experience with you. Any imbalance or blockage in the chakras would have resonated with the client. They will be able to link certain situations in their life with these blockages. Taking this time to connect with the person after using the pendulum is also important.

Pendulum Healing with Charts

When you use pendulums for healing, they move in a way that allows you to identify areas in your body that need attention. A pendulum can detect the differences in energy in different parts of your body. It can also detect energies that are strong or weak in the environment around you.

Dowsing for health is not just for detecting illness in the body. The environment around you affects your health just as much as what is within you. The food you eat, the weather, and many other factors affect your health. Your body and mind are constantly subjected to these things. You can use your pendulum when you are buying fruit and vegetables to check if they are fresh. You can also use it to see if the foods you eat will benefit you or have a negative impact on your body. Pendulums can also be used to detect areas in your home or office that resonate better with your frequency.

Using a pendulum to ask questions that yield yes or no answers is the simplest way to go. Your pendulum will move in one way to say yes and in another to say no. Asking objective questions will help you get easy answers. For instance, you can ask if a certain food will make you gain weight. It is better than asking if that food will make you gain weight or lose weight. The latter is not a simple yes or no question, so you will not get clear answers.

You can also use your pendulum for fan chart readings. A fan chart is one that has a full circle or a half-circle that is divided into some equilateral angles. These allow room for different answers when you ask the pendulum a question. You can use a fan chart for deciding what foods you should eat on a particular day. You can write down some different fruits and vegetables or even the names of some dishes on the chart. You can then hold the pendulum over the fan chart and ask what you should eat on that day. Wait for the pendulum's movement, and it will swing toward the foods that you should be eating that day. Note down the answer the pendulum gives you. You can then ask it again if there are any additional foods from the chart that you should eat. You can keep asking these questions till your pendulum stops answering or gives you a no.

You can also use your pendulum with a body chart. A body chart contains the outline of your body. These charts may have drawings of your organs, or you can even draw the chakras in. The pendulum can then be used over the chart to indicate any part of the body that is ailing or any chakra that is blocked. Body charts are often used by healers doing a remote reading. But this is something that those with more experience are better at. In a remote reading, you don't have to be in the same room as the healer or the person you want to heal. The remote reading session with a body chart can be used to diagnose an illness and send healing energy to the person even though they are elsewhere. Their physical presence is not required.

While using a pendulum for healing, it is important to be focused and relaxed. You need to concentrate on the question you are asking the pendulum. You also have to keep your mind open and receptive to get the right answer from your pendulum. Dowsing with a clear and focused mind will allow effective healing, but it is important to remember that pendulum healing cannot replace allopathic medicine. It is more of a complementary practice and will help the person heal faster as they also get allopathic treatment.

Chapter 10: Using Pendulums for Energy Healing

If you take meditation or yoga classes, you will often hear the instructors talk about chakras and their role in your body and life. The importance of keeping these chakras balanced and allowing a free flow of energy through them is always emphasized. This is because the state of your chakras has a deep impact on your mental, physical and spiritual health. When there is some blockage or imbalance in the chakras, it will manifest itself negatively. Chakra healing can be done in many different ways, and this includes the use of pendulums. Here you will learn more about what chakras are, how they affect you, and how you can heal the chakra system using your pendulum.

What are Chakras?

The term chakra has Sanskrit origins and means wheel or disk. A chakra is an energy center in your body. Since there is a constant flow of energy through these chakras, they are visualized as wheels of energy, which gives it its name. Every chakra in your body corresponds to the major organs and nerve bundles. They impact the function of the various systems in your body and your overall wellbeing. The chakras need to be open and balanced for them to function optimally. When there is some imbalance or blockage, you will experience emotional or physical symptoms according to the affected chakra.

Every person has seven main chakras in their body. These run from the top of the head to the lower body along the spine. The lowest one is present at the base of the spine, while the topmost chakra is at the crown of the head, but these seven chakras are only the main ones. There are more than 100 chakras in your body. But it is more important to focus on these seven and ensure that energy is constantly flowing through them in a free manner.

The Seven Chakras

The chakra system has seven main energy systems at different locations along the spine. Each chakra has its own significance and should be studied individually.

Root Chakra

Muladhara is the lowest chakra and is present at the base of a person's spine. This chakra gives you a foundation for life. It helps a person feel grounded and helps them overcome any challenges they face in life. If your root chakra is stable, it will give you a sense of stability and security.

When this chakra is blocked, you will experience the following symptoms:

- Pain in your legs and feet.
- A feeling of insecurity and instability.
- Chaotic life at home.
- A feeling of inadequateness or that you are not good enough.
- Stressed due to outside circumstances.
- Sluggish and stuck in a rut.

Sacral Chakra

Svadhisthana is present above the root chakra. It is located a little below the belly button. The sacral chakra is linked to a person's creative and sexual energy. This chakra is responsible for how you relate to your emotions and also how you react to the emotions of others around you.

When this chakra is blocked, you will experience the following symptoms:

- Mobility issues in the hip and lower back.
- Emotionally overwhelmed.
- Closed off from emotions.
- Lack of creativity and imagination.
- Struggling with self-image issues.
- Difficulty in sexual and emotional intimacy.

Solar Plexus Chakra

Manipura is the chakra present in the stomach region. This chakra is linked to self-esteem and confidence. If it is balanced, it gives you a sense of control over your life.

When this chakra is blocked, you will experience the following symptoms:

- A feeling of powerlessness.
- Pain in the abdomen.
- Digestive problems.
- Acting subdued in relationships.
- Lack of self-esteem.
- Commitment issues.
- Overinflated ego.
- Inability to stick to plans or goals.

Heart Chakra

Anahata is the chakra present near your heart. It is located at the center of the chest. This chakra is linked to compassion and love. When it has free energy flow, you are better able to express these emotions to others.

When this chakra is blocked, you will experience the following symptoms:

- Tendency to hold grudges.
- Pain in the chest and upper back.
- Having no self-compassion.
- Difficulty in connecting with others emotionally.
- Allergies or asthma.
- Feeling like you are hard to love.

Throat Chakra

Vishuddha is the chakra present in your throat. It helps you communicate freely and express yourself.

When this chakra is blocked, you will experience the following symptoms:

- Difficulty in expressing yourself or speaking up even when you want to.
- Feeling of a blocked throat.
- Stiffness or pain in the neck.
- Tendency to continue talking nervously.
- Struggling in standing up for yourself or your opinions.

Third Eye Chakra

Ajna is a chakra that lies between the eyes. When this chakra is healthy, your gut instinct will be strong. It is linked to intuition and imagination.

When this chakra is blocked, you will experience the following symptoms:

- Lack of inspiration.
- Tension in the brow region.
- Headaches.
- Difficulty in decision making.
- Brain fog.
- Overactive imagination.

Crown Chakra

Sahasrara is the topmost chakra in the body. It is present at the top of the head. It is linked to your spiritual connection with the universe, yourself, and others. This chakra impacts the purpose of your life.

When this chakra is blocked, you will experience the following symptoms:

- Excessive attachment to materialistic things.
- Migraines.
- Inability to see things from others perspective.
- Difficulty in establishing a spiritual connection.

When you notice any of the symptoms mentioned above, you can tell if there is some blockage in your chakras. If there is, it is imperative to work on unblocking the chakras. Stress is one of the most common reasons why energy flow in the chakras is disturbed. When you are stressed or anxious, it impacts you physically and in your energetic dimension as well. The more this stress builds up, the bigger the negative manifestation in your mind and body. If you want to live in a happy and healthy manner, you have to unblock these chakras. And this can be done with the assistance of pendulums.

When you hold a pendulum over any chakra, there will be some movement. The movement of the pendulum will tell you about the energy being emitted from the chakra. The level of energy will be indicative of the energy block, imbalance or balance within that chakra. The pendulum will help you diagnose and heal the chakras so you can improve the state of your physical, emotional, and spiritual being.

Crystal Pendulums for Each Chakra

Root Chakra

• **Garnet.** It will help to balance energy and re-energize the chakra.

• **Hematite.** It will block any negative energy, improve blood circulation and provide groundedness. It promotes better relationships.

• **Red Jasper.** It will absorb any negative energy and will aid in feeling grounded.

Sacral Chakra

• **Carnelian.** It will provide motivation and restore vitality. It will also give courage and promote positivity.

• **Amber.** It can help to relieve pain. It is a re-energizing stone and will also help to bring serenity.

Solar Plexus Chakra

• **Citrine.** It promotes imagination and manifestation.

• **Agate.** It will strengthen intellect and provide protection. It brings luck and increases creativity.

• **Yellow Jade.** It makes you more confident and helps in better control over your life.

• **Tiger's Eye.** It will provide mental clarity, confidence, and improve intuitive abilities.

Heart Chakra

- **Rose Quartz.** It will help you to feel calm and compassionate.

- **Aventurine.** It promotes optimism and brings prosperity.

- **Amazonite.** It helps you speak your mind.

Throat Chakra

- **Turquoise.** It acts as a protective stone and will promote mental relaxation and better communication.

- **Blue Apatite.** It will help with better communication and promote creativity.

- **Celestite.** It is a stone of good communication.

Third Eye Chakra

- **Sapphire.** It brings happiness and more insight. It aids in fulfilling goals and resolving problems.

- **Lapis Lazuli.** It will promote intuition and bring wisdom.

- **Sodalite.** It increases the ability to focus and think clearly.

Crown Chakra

- **Clear Quartz.** It will magnify the power of any other stone you use and help to bring enlightenment.

- **Amethyst.** It will heal your aura and aid in spiritual connections.

- **Moonstone.** It makes you open to receiving love.

How to Check the Energy Flow in Your Chakras with a Pendulum

Using a pendulum is one of the best ways to sense the state of energy flow in the chakras. The pendulum will act as an amplifier for the energy that is flowing through each chakra. As you observe the manifestation of this energy flow in your pendulum's swing, you can learn a lot about your chakra system.

You have to remember that your chakras are always opening and closing as they undergo different phases. It is good for your chakras to be open, but it is not always bad for some chakras to be closed either. The energy system in your body will constantly adjust the energy flowing through all your chakras. This means that sometimes a chakra is closed to promote better health in a person's body. This usually happens in relation to some issues in your body that are related to that chakra.

There is no special pendulum that you have to use for working with your chakras. Use any pendulum that you can connect better to.

Here are some ways in which you can check the state of energy flow in your chakras:

Ask Someone for Help

This method requires you to take help from another person. You just need a pendulum and someone you trust, like a friend. Before you start the exercise, you have to connect with your pendulum and state the source of the answers it will give you. It is also important that you are both calm and are not expecting any particular outcome from the reading.

Find a comfortable place to lie down and ask your friend to stand near you as they hold the pendulum over your body. The pendulum should be a few inches above the chakra that it is held over. They should then notice the pendulum's movement over each chakra and note the direction and the intensity of the movement. Once they do this over the chakras on the front of your body, turn over and allow them to do the same on your back. Ask them to note down the readings from your back as well. You should then compare these readings and pay attention to any differences. Compare the intensity of the movements, the swing's size, and the direction for each chakra. When the pendulum gives a large swing, it usually means that there is more energy moving through that chakra. When the swing is small, there is less energy propelling it. In ideal conditions, the swing will mostly be the same throughout, and all the chakras will be open, but it is far more likely for there to be differences and some blockages. When you can identify the differences, you can identify the blockage or imbalance.

Here are some common interpretations of the pendulum movements:

- When it moves clockwise, the chakra is open, and the energy is flowing freely and is balanced.

- When it moves counterclockwise, the chakra is closed, and there is a restriction in the movement of energy through that chakra. It is either blocked or out of balance.

- When the pendulum moves in a straight line, the chakra is partially closed. This means that there is partial blockage or some imbalance in the energy flow.

- If the pendulum moves in an elliptical way, there may be an imbalance in the chakra's left or right-hand side. There is energy flowing through the chakra, but it is blocked or out of balance on one side.

- If there is no movement from the pendulum, the chakra is blocked. This means that there is no energy going through the chakra, and it is completely blocked.

Use a Proxy

Another way to check your chakras is by using a proxy. For this, you need a printout of the symbols depicting the seven major chakras in color and your pendulum. State the source of the answers before you begin using the pendulum. The chakra printout is what acts as a proxy for your body or the person whose chakras you want to analyze. Take a few moments to meditate so you can calm your mind first. Then hold your pendulum over the topmost chakra and begin there. Visualize the chakra in your body as you do this and observe the movements of the pendulum. Note these down as you move from one chakra symbol to another. Avoid thinking about how you think the pendulum should be moving. Just let the movements flow by themselves and keep recording them. You can then interpret the movements the same way that you usually do.

Use Charts

You can also do a pendulum reading with a chakra pendulum chart. The chart will have every chakra marked on it. You need to lay it flat on some surface and then hold your pendulum over it. Ask the pendulum questions to help you determine the energy flow or state of each pendulum. You can ask questions like, "Which chakra is out of balance today?" You can also be more specific about the questions you ask and use questions like "Which chakra is causing me anxiety today?" Just make sure that you frame all the questions so that the pendulum can give you clear answers.

How to Use a Pendulum to Balance the Chakras

If you want to heal your chakras, pendulums will be a great way to begin.

- First, hold the pendulum of your choice over the location of the chakra. For instance, if you noticed a blockage in the third eye chakra, hold the pendulum over the middle of your forehead.

- Now hold still and wait till the pendulum begins moving by itself. This movement will show you the direction of the energy in this chakra.

- You can focus on a particular chakra, or you can go through each chakra individually. If you want to work on all the chakras, start from the crown chakra or the root chakra and go in order.

- If your pendulum moves erratically over any chakra, there is an imbalance in energy there.

- If the pendulum does not move at all, it usually indicates a blockage.

- After you go through all the chakras, use the pendulum to ask for harmony in your chakra system.

- You just have to ask the body and the higher powers to restore balance within your chakras.

- When you are doing this pendulum healing exercise on someone else, you should ask them to ask for this harmony. Communicate with them about the chakras and their functions. Empower them with knowledge so they can do their own bit to heal their chakras.

- The pendulum itself will not be doing the healing but is a useful tool in the process. You have to ask the body to heal itself and realign the chakras.

- Use the pendulum to check if the movements indicate a healthy energy flow through every chakra at the end of the exercise.

Pendulums are an accessible tool for chakra balancing. They are not expensive, and you don't have to put in too much effort to use them either. Your intent and patience are more important in the process.

It is important to clean the pendulum of any negative energy after you use it for healing. This needs to be done so you can use it properly for any other purpose later. A pendulum that has accumulated a lot of negative energy and is not cleansed will not function properly.

Conclusion

Thank you for reading *Pendulums: The Ultimate Guide to the Magic of Pendulums and How to Use Them for Divination, Dowsing, Tarot Reading, Healing, and Balancing Chakras.* By now, you know a lot more about pendulums than many experts claim to. You should be able to find a suitable pendulum for yourself and begin practicing with it successfully. Your pendulum has the potential to improve your life in many ways. Trusting in it and being open to its guidance will make all the difference. Use the tips given in this book to try using pendulums for anything from tarot reading to chakra balancing. With practice, you will be able to use pendulums with even more accuracy than you may expect. So, get your pendulum and start dowsing!

Here's another book by Mari Silva that you might like

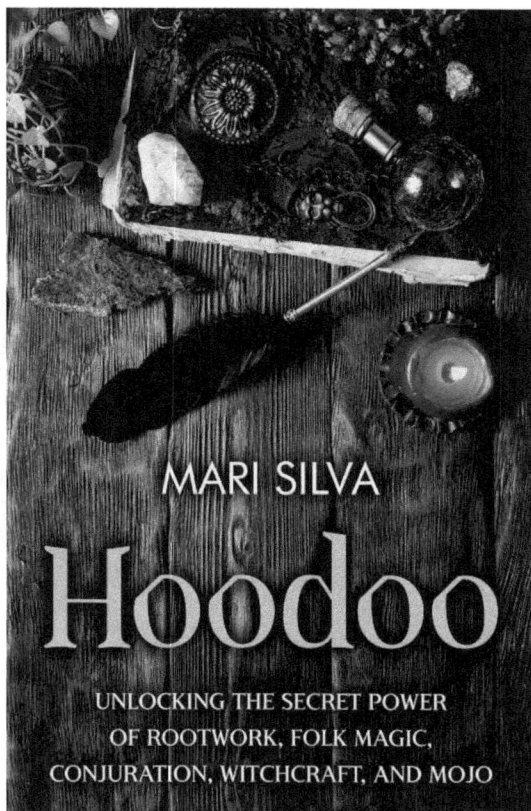

MARI SILVA

Hoodoo

UNLOCKING THE SECRET POWER
OF ROOTWORK, FOLK MAGIC,
CONJURATION, WITCHCRAFT, AND MOJO

Your Free Gift (only available for a limited time)

Thanks for getting this book! If you want to learn more about various spirituality topics, then join Mari Silva's community and get a free guided meditation MP3 for awakening your third eye. This guided meditation mp3 is designed to open and strengthen ones third eye so you can experience a higher state of consciousness. Simply visit the link below the image to get started.

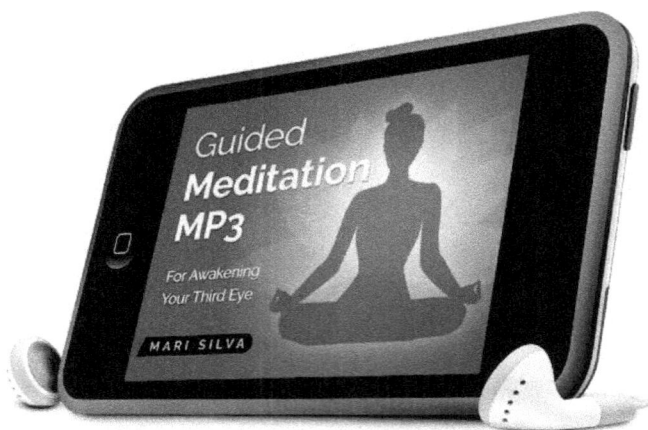

https://spiritualityspot.com/meditation

References

Ana. (2020, September 13). How to Use a Pendulum, Asking Questions About Love, Future, and More. Https://Buddhatooth.com/. https://buddhatooth.com/how-to-use-a-pendulum/

Asttaria, B. (2019, August 1). Selecting a Pendulum: Understanding the Differences. Adermark.com.

https://www.adermark.com/selecting-a-pendulum/

Caro, T. (2020, August 23). Here's How to Ask Pendulum Questions About Relationships. Magickal Spot.

https://magickalspot.com/asking-pendulum-about-relationships/

Caro, T. (2020, May 28). Why Does my Pendulum Shakes? [Meaning Explained]. Magickal Spot.

https://magickalspot.com/pendulum-shake-meaning/

Different Pendulums and Their Uses. (2015, August 17). Instant Karma Asheville.

https://instantkarmaasheville.com/different-pendulums-and-their-uses/

Five Ways You Can Use a Pendulum to Enhance Your Tarot Readings | Inner Goddess Tarot. (2018, August 12). Inner

Goddess Tarot. https://innergoddesstarot.com/2018/08/five-ways-you-can-use-a-pendulum-to-enhance-your-tarot-readings/

How to Cleanse Pendulum and Stone Energies. (n.d.). Ask Your Pendulum.

https://askyourpendulum.com/pages/how-to-cleanse-pendulum-and-stone-energies

How to Use a Pendulum. (n.d.). Ask Your Pendulum. https://askyourpendulum.com/pages/how-to-use-a-pendulum

How to Use Your Pendulum to Find Lost Objects. (n.d.). Ask Your Pendulum.

https://askyourpendulum.com/pages/how-to-use-your-pendulum-to-find-lost-objects

How to Use a Pendulum to Find Anything. (2013, April 2). Hibiscus Moon Crystal Academy.

https://hibiscusmooncrystalacademy.com/how-to-use-pendulum/

Kahn, N. (2018, November 29). What Is Crystal Pendulum Dowsing? This Practice Can Help Answer Your Biggest

Questions. Bustle. https://www.bustle.com/p/what-is-crystal-pendulum-dowsing-this-practice-can-help-answer-your-biggest-questions-13207938

Luna, A. (2017, December 18). How to Use a Dowsing Pendulum For Divination - Beginner's Guide ★ LonerWolf.

LonerWolf. https://lonerwolf.com/dowsing-pendulum/

Pendulum Dowsing History | Timeline (Updated 2020) - Journey To Ascension. (2020).

Https://Journeytoascension.com. https://journeytoascension.com/pendulum-dowsing-history/

Pendulums for Beginners: 6 Helpful Tips for Successful Dowsing. (2013, June 6). Love & Light School of Crystal

Therapy. https://loveandlightschool.com/pendulum-dowsing-for-beginners-some-helpful-tips-for-successful-dowsing-by-kelly-small/

Rekstis, E. (2018, June 21). Healing Crystals 101: Finding the Right One for You. Healthline.

https://www.healthline.com/health/mental-health/guide-to-healing-crystals#Different-types-of-healing-crystals

Sara. (2016, August 3). Pendulum And Tarot | The Sisters Enchanted. The Sisters Enchanted.

https://thesistersenchanted.com/pendulum-and-tarot/

Selig, M. (2017, March 1). 12 Quick Mini-Meditations to Calm Your Mind and Body. Psychology Today.

https://www.psychologytoday.com/us/blog/changepower/201703/12-quick-mini-meditations-calm-your-mind-and-body

Questions to ask a pendulum. (n.d.). https://www.circa1890.com/home.html.

pendulum.html

Clairvoyance | psychology. (n.d.). Encyclopedia Britannica. https://www.britannica.com/topic/clairvoyance

Doors To Other Worlds by Buckland, Raymond. (n.d.). Www.biblio.com. https://www.biblio.com/doors-to-other-worlds-by-buckland-raymond/work/991425

Medium | occultism. (n.d.). Encyclopedia Britannica. https://www.britannica.com/topic/medium-occultism

Mediumship Quotes (14 quotes). (n.d.). Www.goodreads.com. https://www.goodreads.com/quotes/tag/mediumship

ThriftBooks. (n.d.). Reunions: Visionary Encounters with... book by Raymond A. Moody Jr. ThriftBooks. https://www.thriftbooks.com/w/reunions-visionary-encounters-with-departed-loved-ones_raymond-a-moody-jr/292870/#edition=2269514&idiq=1005995

Arnold, Kim. "10 Fascinating Facts about Tarot: Ten Tantalising Tidbits of Tarot Trivia!"

Hay House, Inc. November 30, 2018.

https://www.healyourlife.com/10-fascinating-facts-about-tarot

Cafe Astrology.com "The Elements in Astrology."

https://cafeastrology.com/natal/elements-astrology.html

Café Astrology. "What is Astrology?"
https://cafeastrology.com/whatisastrology.html

The Cut. "A Beginner's Guide to Tarot Cards." April 27, 2020.

https://www.thecut.com/article/tarot-cards.html

The Cut. "What Is Your Life-Path Number?" May 14, 2020.

https://www.thecut.com/article/life-path-number.html

Decoz, Hans. "Numerology's Master Numbers 11 – 22 – 33."
Hans Decoz and World Numerology LLC.
https://www.worldnumerology.com/numerology-master-numbers.htm

Divination Foundation. "A Short History of Divination." May 16, 2007.

https://divination.com/a-short-history-of-divination/

Garis, Mary Grace. "How to Read a Natal Chart—Planets, Symbols, and All." Well+Good

 LLC. March 31, 2020.

https://www.wellandgood.com/how-to-read-natal-chart/

Gilbert, Robert Andrew. "Divination: religion." Encyclopedia Britannica. February 16, 2001.
https://www.britannica.com/topic/divination

Hurst, Katherine. "Numerology: What is Numerology? And How Does it Work?" The Law

Of Attraction by Greater Minds. December 18, 2017.

https://www.thelawofattraction.com/what-is-numerology/

Israelsen, James. "55 Celestial Facts about the Zodiac | Fact Retriever LLC. September 11,

2020. https://www.factretriever.com/zodiac-facts

Kahn, Nina. "Your Guide To The Planets In Astrology & How They Affect You." Bustle.

July 24, 2020.

https://www.bustle.com/life/how-each-planets-astrology-directly-affects-every-zodiac-sign-13098560

Mastering the Zodiac. "How to Read a Birth Chart.. in Minutes!" February 19, 2016.

https://masteringthezodiac.com/how-to-read-a-birth-chart/

Linder, Jean. "Tarot Spreads You Need Right Now." Kelleemaize.

https://www.kelleemaize.com/post/tarot-spreads-you-need-right-now

Lovejoy, Bess. "10 Historical Divination Methods for Predicting the Future." Mental Floss. June 12, 2019

 https://www.mentalfloss.com/article/585258/historical-divination-methods-predict-future

Newcombe, Rachel. "Rune Guide - An Introduction to using the Runes." Holistic Shop.

https://www.holisticshop.co.uk/articles/guide-runes

Psychic Library, LLC. "Astrological Tarot Spread."

https://psychiclibrary.com/astrological-tarot-spread/

The Rune Site. "Casting layouts and spreads."
http://www.therunesite.com/casting-layouts-and-spreads/

Sons of Vikings. "Viking Runes Guide | Runic Alphabet Meanings | Norse / Nordic

Letters." February 28, 2017.

https://sonsofvikings.com/blogs/history/viking-runes-guide-runic-alphabet-meanings-nordic-celtic-letters

Tarot.com Staff. "The Major Arcana Tarot Card Meanings." Tarot.com. March 3, 2021.

https://www.tarot.com/tarot/cards/major-arcana

Tarot.com Staff. "The Minor Arcana: Meanings Behind the Number Cards." February 3,

2021. https://www.tarot.com/tarot/meaning-of-numbers-in-minor-arcana

Time Nomads. "Elder Futhark Runes Cheat Sheet." January 11, 2020. https://www.timenomads.com/elder-futhark-alphabet-cheat-sheet/

Tracey, Ashley. "What Does Your Sun, Moon, and Rising Sign Really Mean?" Mindbody,

Inc. April 15, 201

https://explore.mindbodyonline.com/blog/wellness/what-does-your-sun-moon-and-rising-sign-really-mean

Wigington, Patti. "What Is Rune Casting? Origins and Techniques." Learn Religions.

January 31, 2020.

 https://www.learnreligions.com/rune-casting-4783609

Wille. "11 Popular Tarot Spreads for Beginners and Advanced readers." A LITTLE

SPARK OF JOY. December 23, 2020.

https://www.alittlesparkofjoy.com/easy-tarot-spreads/

yourchineseastrology.com. "Chinese Palmistry."

https://www.yourchineseastrology.com/palmistry/

Mediumship - New World Encyclopedia. (n.d.). Www.Newworldencyclopedia.org.

https://www.newworldencyclopedia.org/entry/Mediumship

(PDF) Telepathy: Evidence and New Physics. (n.d.). ResearchGate.

https://www.researchgate.net/publication/323811942_Telepathy_Evidence_and_New_Physics

Psychic Readings | Tarot Reading | Psychics.com. (n.d.). Www.Psychics.com.

The Editors of Encyclopedia Britannica. (n.d.). Clairvoyance | psychology. Encyclopedia Britannica. https://www.britannica.com/topic/clairvoyance

www.ingramcontent.com/pod-product-compliance
Lightning Source LLC
Chambersburg PA
CBHW071854090426
42811CB00004B/609